THE LONDON BOROUGH
www.bromley.gov.uk

Renewals
01159 293388
www.bromley.gov.uk/libraries

Please return/renew this item
by the last date shown.
Books may also be renewed by
phone and Internet.

The Power of Being Thankful

365 Devotions for Discovering the Strength of Gratitude

JOYCE MEYER

HODDER &
STOUGHTON

First published in Great Britain in 2014 by Hodder & Stoughton
An Hachette UK company

First published in paperback in 2015

Published in association with FaithWords
Hachette Book Group
237 Park Avenue
New York, NY 10017

1

A CIP catalogue record for this title is available from the British Library

ISBN 978 1 473 625402
eBook ISBN 978 1 444 797978

Printed and bound in Great Britain by Clays Ltd, St Ives plc

Hodder & Stoughton policy is to use papers that are natural, renewable and recyclable products and
made from wood grown in sustainable forests. The logging and manufacturing processes are
expected to conform to the environmental regulations of the country of origin.

Hodder & Stoughton Ltd
Carmelite House
50 Victoria Embankment
London EC4Y 0DZ

www.hodderfaith.com

Introduction

I believe one of the most important things we can do is be thankful for our lives and all that God gives us and does for us. Too often, we focus on what we don't have or what we wish was different in our lives, and this focus causes us to go through life feeling dissatisfied and defeated. But when we stop and take the time to focus on what we already have and all the ways God has already blessed us, it gives us a new perspective—our mind is renewed, our attitude is affected, and our joy overflows.

That is why I'm excited about *The Power of Being Thankful*. This devotional is one year's worth of thankful thoughts compiled from some of my most popular books that will help you develop and maintain a heart of thanksgiving. Regardless of where you are in your journey with the Lord, I believe *The Power of Being Thankful* is going to help you begin enjoying your life with Him in a whole new way.

I pray that you will set aside the next year to pursue God with a thankful heart. Don't go through your life frustrated, miserable, and unhappy; God has something much better in store for you.

Live each day with a thankful heart, grateful for every good thing—no matter how big or how small—that God has done in your life. As you begin to remember the good things God has done in your past and realize the blessings you have in the present, you can't help getting excited about what He is going to do in your future.

Be thankful and be ready...God has something amazing in store for your life!

Joyce Meyer

Thank [God] in everything [no matter what the circumstances may be, be thankful and give thanks], for this is the will of God for you [who are] in Christ Jesus [the Revealer and Mediator of that will].   1 THESSALONIANS 5:18

The Power
of Being
Thankful

The Best Way to Begin in Prayer

They are also to stand every morning to thank and praise the Lord, and likewise at evening. 1 CHRONICLES 23:30

No matter what we pray for, thanksgiving can always go with it. A good habit to develop is starting all of our prayers with thanksgiving. An example of this would be: "Thank You, Father, for all You have done in my life; You are awesome and I really love and appreciate You."

I encourage you to examine your life, to pay attention to your thoughts and your words, and to see how much thanksgiving you express. Do you murmur and complain about things or are you thankful?

If you want a challenge, just try to get through an entire day without uttering one word of complaint. Develop an attitude of thanksgiving in every situation. In fact, just become outrageously thankful—and watch as your intimacy with God increases and as He pours out greater blessings than ever before.

Prayer of Thanks

Thank You, Father, for the way You guide me in prayer. Help me to come to You in thanksgiving before I do anything else. Let gratitude be the foundation of my prayer life. I make the decision today to put aside complaining, being thankful in prayer instead.

Living at Peace

Peace I leave with you; My [own] peace I now give and bequeath
to you. Not as the world gives do I give to you. Do not let your
hearts be troubled, neither let them be afraid.   JOHN 14:27

Peace is one of the most important elements to enjoying your life.

A life of frustration and struggle, a life without peace, is the result of focusing on things you can't do anything about. When you worry about things beyond your control, stress and anxiety begin to creep into your life.

The apostle Paul said, "Be anxious for nothing, but in everything by prayer and supplication, with thanksgiving, let your requests be made known to God; and the peace of God, which surpasses all understanding, will guard your hearts and minds through Christ Jesus" (Philippians 4:6–7 NKJV).

Once we realize we are struggling with something and feel upset, we need to start praying and immediately turn the situation over to God, thankful He will provide according to His will and offer us peace. You and I are not called to a life of frustration and struggle. Jesus came so we could have righteousness, joy, and peace!

Prayer of Thanks

Father, I am grateful for peace. It is a wonderful gift that You
have given me, and I ask for Your help to always be peaceful
in every situation.

Let Your Light Shine

You are the light of the world. A city set on a hill cannot be hidden.
                                                            MATTHEW 5:14

As believers in Christ, we can be bubbling over with life. We can be vibrant, alive, active, energized, peaceful, and joy-filled.

It is our approach to God that determines our attitude and countenance. When we approach God with boldness, thankful for His grace and confident that He loves us and He is for us, we can't help but be full of life. However, a legalistic, religious approach to God steals life. It does not nourish it. Remember, Paul said, "The Law kills, but the Spirit makes alive" (2 Corinthians 3:6). When we follow the Spirit, we feel alive.

Each of us should ask ourselves the question, *Would people want what I have by watching my life and looking at my countenance? Is my life reflecting a thankful, expectant heart, excited about what God is going to do each new day?*

We are to be the light of the world. Make sure your light is shining brightly today.

Prayer of Thanks

Father, I am thankful that I don't have to approach You through the law, but I can come boldly to Your throne because of Your amazing grace. Thank You that Your grace and joy brighten my life and allow me to be a light for the world to see.

Expect Something Good

May the God of your hope so fill you with all joy and peace in believing [through the experience of your faith] that by the power of the Holy Spirit you may abound and be overflowing (bubbling over) with hope. ROMANS 15:13

One of the most powerful forces in the universe is hope. And as a child of God, you can have hope in unlimited measure. That's something to be thankful for!

Hope is the happy anticipation that something good is going to happen in your life. It's expecting something good. What are you expecting? Have you even thought about it? If you're expecting nothing, or if you are expecting just a little bit, you are going to get what you expect.

I always say, "I'd rather believe for a whole lot and get half of it than believe for a little bit and get all of it."

God wants you to trust Him and have a happy expectation for something good. If you're in a tough situation today, expect it to change. If you're in a good situation today, expect it to get even better. God is a God of hope.

Prayer of Thanks

Lord, thank You for the power of hope in my life. Thank You that You are going to do something good, and I can trust You and hope for the best.

Practice Seeing the Positive

*A happy heart is good medicine and a cheerful mind works
healing, but a broken spirit dries up the bones.*

PROVERBS 17:22

I encourage you to be a thankful, positive person. If you aren't it's just a matter of forming a new habit.

I was so negative at one time in my life that if I even tried to think two positive thoughts in succession my brain seemed to stop functioning. But now I am very positive and actually don't enjoy being with people who are negative.

If you have not formed the habit of being positive yet, you can begin today! Put reminders around your house or in your car, little signs that say, "Be positive." Ask the Holy Spirit to remind you if you are slipping into negativity. Ask your friends to help also. Set aside time during the day to focus on and be thankful for the good things God has blessed you with.

Positive, thankful thoughts don't happen by accident; you can choose to practice them. And remember, practice makes perfect.

Prayer of Thanks

*Thank You, Father, for helping me think positive thoughts. I am
grateful that I am not a prisoner to negative thinking and that I
can choose to be happy and joy-filled.*

Enjoy the Reward

Men will say, Surely there is a reward for the [uncompromisingly]
righteous; surely there is a God Who judges on the earth.

PSALM 58:11

Taking time to enjoy the fruit of your labor is one of the main
things that will keep you pressing on in difficult times.

God gave many men and women in the Bible difficult tasks to
perform, but He always promised a reward. Looking to the reward
helps us endure the difficulty. The Bible says in Hebrews 12:2 that
Jesus despised the cross, but He endured it for the joy of obtaining
the prize that was set before Him. He is now seated at the right
hand of the Father.

I encourage you not to look merely at the work you do, but look
also at the promise of the reward. Take time to be thankful for and
enjoy the fruit of your labor and then you'll be energized to finish
your course.

Prayer of Thanks
Thank You, Father, that I can always look forward to Your
reward in my life. I am grateful that difficult times never last
forever, but I can learn from them and expect Your goodness
in my life.

The Importance of Right Thinking

For as he thinks in his heart, so is he.   PROVERBS 23:7

The mind is the leader or forerunner of all actions. The steps we take each day are a direct result of the thoughts we allow ourselves to think.

If we have a negative mind, we will have a negative life. On the other hand, if we renew our mind according to God's Word, we will experience "the good and acceptable and perfect will of God" for our lives (Romans 12:2).

So many people's struggles are rooted in wrong thinking patterns. Negative thinking can actually cause them to create the problems they experience in their lives; thankfully, though, we don't have to live captive to those thoughts. We can choose to line our thoughts up with the Word of God.

The mind is a battlefield. Decide to resist destructive, negative thinking and dwell on godly thoughts for your life instead. The more you change your mind for the better, the more your life will also change for the better.

Prayer of Thanks

Father, I'm thankful that I don't have to live as a captive to my thoughts. With Your help, I can change those negative thoughts that are affecting my life. I can win the battle of the mind by spending time in Your Word, meditating on Your promises, and making a conscious effort to think God-honoring thoughts over my life.

Keep On Keeping On

*Let us not become weary in doing good, for at the proper time we
will reap a harvest if we do not give up.*   GALATIANS 6:9 NIV

One of the most important truths you can be grateful for is that
God has promised to never leave you—He is always by your side!

That's why it is important to remember this: No matter how
difficult the circumstances may seem around you, don't give up!
God is for you, and He is bigger than any trouble you may be
facing.

You can regain the territory the devil has stolen from you. If
necessary, regain it one inch at a time, being thankful for and
always leaning on God's grace and not on your own ability to
get the desired results. In Galatians 6:9, the apostle Paul simply
encourages us to keep on keeping on! Don't be a quitter! Have an
"I can do all things through Christ" attitude. God is looking for
people who will go all the way through to the other side with Him.

Prayer of Thanks
*Thank You, Father, that You give me the strength to never quit.
I am grateful that You are always with me and that You fight
my battles.*

Discipline and Self-Control

Like a city whose walls are broken through is a person who lacks
self-control. PROVERBS 25:28 NIV

We can live a disciplined life filled with self-control. It is one of the keys to living a joyful life. The Bible teaches us in many places the importance of living a disciplined life.

If we don't discipline ourselves, our circumstances will eventually become situations we regret, but thankfully, God's Word teaches us to be temperate, which means to be marked by moderation, to hold ourselves within limits (to compromise between two extremes or find the middle ground).

Clearly we are to maintain balance. The area of finances is an example of where discipline is required. It is wrong to overspend, but it is also wrong to underspend. God gives us money not to hoard, but to enjoy. Wisdom means saving some, spending some, and giving some away.

In every area of your life—relationships, finances, exercise, eating, career, thoughts, and words—ask God to help you live with discipline and self-control. Don't be led by emotional, in-the-moment thinking. Use the wisdom of God to live in balance and really enjoy your life!

Prayer of Thanks

Thank You, Father, that You have given me the fruit of self-control, and by Your grace, I can discipline myself. You give me strength and wisdom, and You guide me every step of the way.

Pursuing Peace

I have told you these things, so that in Me you may have [perfect] peace and confidence.   JOHN 16:33

Peace is one of the greatest blessings that God has given us, and we should thank Him for it daily. Simply desiring a life of peace is not enough. You have to pursue peace with God, peace with yourself, and peace with those around you. I have found that the more thankful I am, the more peaceful I am. Gratitude helps me focus on what I have instead of what I don't have, allowing me to stay focused on my blessings instead of worrying.

When walking in peace becomes a priority, you will make the effort needed to see it happen. I spent years praying for God to *give* me peace and finally realized He had *already* provided peace, but I had to choose it. Jesus said in John 14:27, "Peace I leave with you." Jesus has already provided your peace. Make the decision to walk in that peace today!

Prayer of Thanks

Father, thank You that You have provided everything I need to live at peace. Today, I choose to pursue that peace and live at rest, knowing You are greater than any trial or tribulation I may be going through. You are everything I need. You are my peace.

Taking the Time for Gratitude

*At all times and for everything giving thanks in the name of our
Lord Jesus Christ to God the Father.*   EPHESIANS 5:20

Throughout the Bible, we see people celebrating progress and
victory in a variety of ways. One of those ways was to specifically
take the time to give an offering to God and to thank Him. Noah
did it. Abraham did it. And we can do it too.

We would quickly add a lot of celebration time to our lives if we
would take the time to give thanks when God does amazing things
for us. An attitude of gratitude shows a lot about the character of a
person. It keeps God first, knowing that He is the source of every
blessing we receive. Gratitude is never about feeling entitled—it's
an attitude that says, "I know I don't deserve God's goodness, but
I am sure grateful for it."

Prayer of Thanks

*Father, I am thankful that You have blessed me with so many
good things in my life. Today, I take time to meditate on Your
goodness and thank You for Your blessings.*

There Is Always Time for Prayer

And they raised up their voices and called, Jesus, Master, take pity
and have mercy on us!   LUKE 17:13

Whether you are a mother, a schoolteacher, an executive, a
mechanic, or a brain surgeon, you are probably busy! You not only
have the requirements of your job to fulfill, you may also have
caretaking responsibilities with family or extended family. No
matter how busy you are, be encouraged: God hears all prayers—
even short ones—and that is something to be thankful for!

Prayer is something you can do throughout the day no matter how much you have on your to-do list. For example, if you
are an exhausted stay-at-home mom who cleans up the house and
changes diapers all day, then just take one minute to be still and
say, "Oh, Jesus, I love You. Strengthen me right now. God, I need
some energy. I am worn out."

It is okay to talk to God in a very simple way. By praying
throughout the day in this simple, meaningful way, we invite God
into every area of our lives, and that is exactly what He desires.

Prayer of Thanks

I thank You today, Father, that prayer doesn't have to be long
and complicated. You hear even my short, heartfelt prayers.
I am grateful that I can have a continuous conversation with
You all through the day, and that You hear and answer me.

Living Beyond Your Feelings

When I am weak [in human strength], then am I [truly] strong
(able, powerful in divine strength).   2 CORINTHIANS 12:10

On any given day, we may feel good or bad, happy or sad, excited or discouraged, and a thousand other things. Although feelings can be very strong and demanding, we do not have to let them rule our lives.

We can learn to manage our emotions rather than allowing them to manage us. This has been one of the most important biblical truths I have learned in my journey with God. It has also been one that allows me to consistently enjoy my life.

If we have to wait to see how we feel before we know if we can enjoy the day, then we are giving feelings control over us. But thankfully, we have free will and can make decisions that are not based on feelings. If we are willing to make right choices regardless of how we feel, God will always be faithful to give us the strength to do so.

Prayer of Thanks

Father, I thank You that I no longer have to let my feelings
control me. I am so grateful that I don't have to wait to see how
I feel every day before I know how to act. With Your help, I am
going to live beyond my feelings—I'm going to live the joy-filled
life Jesus came to give me!

Waiting Well

But let endurance and steadfastness and patience have full play
and do a thorough work, so that you may be [people] perfectly
and fully developed [with no defects], lacking in nothing.

JAMES 1:4

Patience is extremely important for people who want to glorify God and enjoy their lives. If we are impatient, the situations we encounter in life will certainly cause us to react emotionally.

The next time you have to wait on something or someone, instead of just reacting, try reminding yourself, *Getting upset will not make this go any faster, so I might as well enjoy the wait.* Then perhaps say out loud, "I am developing patience as I wait, so I am thankful in this situation." If you do that, you will be acting on the Word of God rather than reacting to the unpleasant circumstance.

Remember, patience is a fruit of the Spirit that God wants to develop in your life. Don't merely think about how hard and frustrating it is, but think about how blessed you can be as you learn the art of waiting well.

Prayer of Thanks

Father, I am grateful that You have planted patience in
my spirit and that through You, I can react properly to any
situation. Help me today, and every day, to exercise patience
in all things.

Getting Along with Difficult People

If possible, as far as it depends on you, live at peace with
everyone.   ROMANS 12:18

How do you react to people who are rude? Do you respond in love as the Word says we should, or do you join them in their ungodly behavior? I think there are a lot of rude and unpleasant people in the world today largely because of the stressful lives most people live.

We can be very thankful that we know the Word of God and have Him in our lives to help us and comfort us—to keep us from falling into the traps that stress can cause. But we must remember that a lot of people in the world who are difficult to get along with don't have that. Jesus said that we have done nothing special if we treat people well who treat us well, but if we are kind to someone who would qualify as an enemy, then we are doing well (see Luke 6:32–35).

People are everywhere, and not all of them are pleasant. Will you act on the Word of God and love them for His sake?

Prayer of Thanks
Father, when I am in a situation that requires me to deal with
a hard-to-get-along-with person, let me pray for them rather
than react to them emotionally. Thank You for giving me
the grace to be kind to everyone—no matter how they act
toward me.

Believing the Best of Others

Love bears up under anything and everything that comes, is
ever ready to believe the best of every person, its hopes are
fadeless under all circumstances, and it endures everything
[without weakening].   1 CORINTHIANS 13:7

The Bible teaches us to always believe the best of every person.

However, if we merely let our thoughts lead us, they usually tend toward negativity. Sadly, the flesh without the influence of the Holy Spirit is dark and negative. Thankfully, we don't have to walk in the flesh, but we can choose to be led by the Spirit (see Romans 8:5). When we choose to let the Spirit lead us, we will see the best in other people, and we will be filled with life and peace in our souls.

I encourage you to begin seeing other people as children of God rather than as adversaries. Decide to look past their faults and see them as God sees them. Be grateful that the Spirit can help you see the best in every person in your life.

Prayer of Thanks

I thank You today, Father, that You forgive my sins and don't
hold them against me. I ask You for Your strength in doing the
same thing for others.

Trusting God

For You are my hope; O Lord God, You are my trust from my
youth and the source of my confidence.   PSALM 71:5

Trusting God allows us to enter His rest, and rest is a place of peace where we are able to enjoy our lives while being confident God is fighting our battles.

God cares for us; He will solve our problems and meet our needs, and thankfully, we can stop thinking and worrying about them. I realize this is easier said than done, but there is no time like the present to begin learning a new way to live—a way of living that is without worry, anxiety, and fear.

This is the time to begin believing and saying, "I trust God completely; there is no need to worry! I will not give in to fear or anxiety. God is the source of my confidence." The more you think about this truth, the more you will find yourself choosing trust over worry.

Prayer of Thanks

Father, thank You that I don't have to worry! I trust You to take care of me and to always be with me.

Loving Your Life

*The thief comes only in order to steal and kill and destroy. I came
that they may have and enjoy life, and have it in abundance (to the
full, till it overflows).*   JOHN 10:10

Do you believe God wants you to enjoy your life? Well, He does!
In fact, part of God's will is for you to enjoy every moment of it. I
know this is true because His Word says so in many places.

King Solomon, who is considered to have been very wise, wrote
in Ecclesiastes 2:24: "There is nothing better for a man than that
he should eat and drink and make himself enjoy good in his labor.
Even this, I have seen, is from the hand of God."

Solomon said to make yourself enjoy the good of your labor.
We should learn to value enjoyment because it is vital to being a
balanced and healthy person. This does not mean that all of life
becomes a huge party or a vacation, but it does mean that through
the power of God we can learn to be thankful for and enjoy all of
life.

Prayer of Thanks

*Father, I am grateful that Jesus came so that I might have
abundant life. When times are tough and my joy feels low, help
me to remember that You have promised I can enjoy my life.
Thank You for the joy, peace, and security I find in You.*

The Bible Teaches Us to Be Thankful

*I have inclined my heart to perform Your statutes forever, even to
the end.*   PSALM 119:112

Just as the Bible instructs us to praise God and to worship Him, it
also gives us reasons to thank Him and teaches us how to offer our
gratitude to Him, as shown in the Scriptures below:

* *We give praise and thanks to You, O God, we praise and give
  thanks; Your wondrous works declare that Your Name is near
  and they who invoke Your Name rehearse Your wonders.*
  Psalm 75:1
* *It is a good and delightful thing to give thanks to the Lord, to
  sing praises [with musical accompaniment] to Your name, O
  Most High . . .* Psalm 92:1
* *Let us come before His presence with thanksgiving; let us
  make a joyful noise to Him with songs of praise!* Psalm 95:2
* *Enter into His gates with thanksgiving and a thank offering
  and into His courts with praise! Be thankful and say so to
  Him, bless and affectionately praise His name!* Psalm 100:4

Prayer of Thanks

*Father, I am so thankful for the promises and instruction that I
find in Your Word. Today, I choose to live a thankful life simply
because You instruct me to in the Word of God. I will act in
obedience and I believe that Your Word teaches me the best way
to live.*

Jesus Lived a Life of Thanksgiving

At all times and for everything giving thanks in the name of our
Lord Jesus Christ to God the Father.   EPHESIANS 5:20

Part of prayer's power is the power of thanksgiving...because
there is not powerful living apart from a life of thanksgiving. During His earthly ministry, Jesus lived a life of thanksgiving. He gave
thanks to the Father on many occasions and for many things.

For example, He gave thanks to God when He broke the loaves
and fishes and fed the 4,000 people (see Matthew 15:36). He
thanked God that He had heard His prayer concerning the raising
of Lazarus from the dead (John 11:41–42). And He gave thanks to
God when He gave the bread and wine to His disciples at the Last
Supper even though He knew His suffering and death were very
close (see Mark 14:22–23).

If it was important for Jesus to live a life of thanksgiving, it
should certainly be important for us to do the same thing.

Prayer of Thanks

Thank You, Father, for the example of Jesus and the thankful
life He modeled for us. Help me to enter Your gates with
thanksgiving every time I come to You in prayer. You are good
and You are worthy of my thanksgiving and my praise.

A Matter of Focus

Looking unto Jesus, the author and finisher of our faith.

HEBREWS 12:2 NKJV

It is very important to focus on the right things. This is why the Word of God instructs us to look away from all that distracts us and to look to Jesus, who is the Author and Finisher of our faith.

Whatever we focus on becomes magnified in our minds. When we focus on our problems, we continually roll them over and over in our minds, which is like meditating on them. The more we think and talk about our problems, the larger they become. A relatively small matter can grow into a huge issue merely because we focus on it too much.

Instead of meditating on our problems, we would be wise to meditate on God's Word and His promises for our lives and to aggressively thank Him for them. When we do, we will see the faithfulness of God revealed, and our problems won't seem so big after all.

Prayer of Thanks

I am grateful, Father, that You are bigger than my problems, trials, and uncertainties. You are good and my heart is filled with thanksgiving for You and Your love.

Giving and Receiving Love

I give you a new commandment: that you should love one another.
Just as I have loved you, so you too should love one another.

JOHN 13:34

Of all the things that we have to be grateful for in our lives, love is at the top of the list. Loving and being loved bring purpose and meaning to life. The world is looking for love, but they are really looking for God because God *is* love.

People look for fulfillment in life in many ways that may seem good at first but often leave them feeling frustrated, disappointed, and empty. Only by receiving God's love and walking in love (putting love into action by continually reaching out to others and making an effort to show them love through various acts of kindness) can they find the true fulfillment they are so desperately seeking.

Love will change your life! Ask God to help you receive and give love, and be thankful as you watch His love bring a fulfillment to your life you have never known.

Prayer of Thanks

Father, I am so thankful that You love me and that You have given me an ability to love others. Let Your love flow through me today in ways that will be a blessing to others.

Blessed to Be a Blessing

Let each of you esteem and look upon and be concerned for
not [merely] his own interests, but also each for the interests
of others.   PHILIPPIANS 2:4

Everyone needs a blessing. We all need to be encouraged, edified, complimented, and appreciated. And you have the ability to bless others. Be thankful that God not only blesses you, but that He has made you a blessing. We all get weary at times and need other people to let us know that we are valuable and appreciated.

I believe God blesses us so we can be a blessing—not only in a few places but everywhere we go. Look for people who are needy and bless them. Share what you have with those who are less fortunate than you are. And remember, everyone needs a blessing— even the successful people who appear to have everything.

When you live to meet needs and encourage those around you, you will find "joy unspeakable" in the process (see 1 Peter 1:8 KJV).

Prayer of Thanks

Father, I am so grateful for Your blessings in my life, and I am also grateful that You have enabled me to be a blessing. Help me reach out to others every day and focus on adding to their encouragement.

Prayer as the First Option, Not the Last Resort

For everyone who keeps on asking receives; and he who keeps on seeking finds; and to him who keeps on knocking, [the door] will be opened.   MATTHEW 7:8

One day I woke up with a throbbing headache. I walked around with that miserable headache almost all day, telling everybody I met about how terrible I felt—until I finally realized that I had complained most of the day and had never taken the time to simply pray and ask God to take the pain away.

Unfortunately, that response is rather typical for some of us. We complain about our problems and spend a majority of our time trying to figure out what we can do to solve them. We often do everything except the one thing we are told to do in the Word of God: ask, that we may receive and our joy may be full (see John 16:24 KJV).

Thankfully, God wants to provide for our every need. We have the awesome privilege of "asking and receiving," and we should always pray as a first response to every situation.

Prayer of Thanks

I thank You, God, in everything, no matter what the circumstance may be. I desire to be the most thankful person I can be, and I ask You to help me reach my goal.

Agreeing with God

Fight the good fight of the faith; lay hold of the eternal life to which you were summoned and [for which] you confessed the good confession [of faith] before many witnesses.   1 TIMOTHY 6:12

Take a step of faith and no matter how you feel, agree with God that He loves you. You are wonderfully made and have many talents and strengths. You are valuable, and as a believer in Jesus, you are the righteousness of God in Him. You have rightness before God instead of wrongness—be thankful for that amazing gift!

Begin to speak out against feelings of insecurity and say, "I belong to God and He loves me!" (see Ephesians 2:10). We believe more of what we hear ourselves say than what others say, so start saying something good and drown out the other voices that condemn you.

Fight for yourself! Fight the good fight of faith and refuse to live below the level at which Jesus wants you to live. His kingdom is righteousness, peace, and joy (see Romans 14:17). Don't settle for anything less.

Prayer of Thanks

I thank You, Father, that I can boldly declare in faith who I am in Christ. Thank You that You created me as one of a kind and You love me dearly. Today, I choose to believe that I am Your workmanship.

Just Do It

He said, Come! So Peter got out of the boat and walked on the
water, and he came toward Jesus.   MATTHEW 14:29

Indecision wastes a lot of time, and time is too precious to waste. If you'll become a confident, decisive person, you'll accomplish a lot more with less effort.

No one learns how to hear from God without making mistakes. Don't be overly concerned about errors. Don't take yourself too seriously. You are a fallible, imperfect human being, but you can rejoice with thanksgiving because you serve an infallible, perfect God.

Learn from your mistakes, correct the ones you can, and trust God for His guidance and protection. If you feel that God is prompting you to give something away, help someone out, or make a change in your life, do it! Take some action and sow seeds of obedience. When you feel you have guidance from God, move in faith instead of stagnating in doubt and fear.

Prayer of Thanks

Father, I am thankful that I can trust You to help me learn
from my mistakes. I don't have to worry or be afraid that I'll
make the wrong decision, because I know You are with me.
Thank You that You will lead and guide me—even through my
mistakes.

Living Amazed

And they were amazed at His teaching, for His word was with
authority and ability and weight and power.   LUKE 4:32

I think that many times we let what should be extremely special
to us—things we should be extremely grateful for—become too
commonplace. Several years ago, I was "prayer murmuring" to
the Lord (praying but kind of murmuring at the same time), and I
said, "Lord, why don't I have those exciting, special things happen
in my life like I used to when I first started to know You?"

And I'll never forget what the Lord spoke to my heart so clearly.
He said, "Joyce, I still do the same things all the time, it's just that
you've gotten used to it." *Ouch!*

I believe that if we'll stay amazed at the things God is doing in
our lives—even the little things—we'll never be without hope. I
encourage you to realize what you have, be thankful, and decide
to live amazed...jaw-dropping, wide-eyed, "Wow! That was
God!" amazed.

Prayer of Thanks

I am grateful that You are always doing special things in my
life, Lord, and I pray that I will recognize them and be generous
in my praise and gratitude. Help me live amazed.

Shelter in the Storm

He who dwells in the secret place of the Most High shall remain
stable and fixed under the shadow of the Almighty [Whose power
no foe can withstand].   PSALM 91:1

The best way to be safe during a natural storm is to take cover. If
you do not seek shelter, the storm may harm you.

The Word of God gives us instructions on how to take cover
when we face the spiritual storms of life. The first place you need
to run when a storm hits in your life is to the secret place of the
Most High, the presence of God. Meditate on His Word; pray;
worship Him; thank Him and tell Him you trust Him as the winds
of adversity blow. These are the spiritual disciplines no foe can
withstand. When you practice these habits, you actually construct
spiritual walls of protection around yourself. These walls will
provide protection and enable you to stand strong in the midst of
any storm.

Prayer of Thanks

Lord, I thank You that You are my shelter in the storm. When
life's difficulties come my way, I don't have to be afraid because
You are with me. I trust that You will calm the storms in my life
and bring me safely through them. Thank You that You'll never
leave me nor forsake me (see Hebrews 13:5).

Worry or Worship?

Give to the Lord the glory due to His name; worship the Lord in
the beauty of holiness or in holy array.   PSALM 29:2

Worry and worship are polar opposites, and we would be much
happier if we learned to become worshippers instead of worriers.
Worry creates an opportunity for the enemy to torment us, but
worship (reverence and adoration of God) leads us into His presence, where we will always find peace, joy, and hope.

God created us to worship Him. He wants us to develop a deep,
personal relationship with Him and an outrageous love for Him.
This kind of love flows from a grateful heart, appreciative of who
God is and what He has done.

Don't waste another day of your life worrying. Determine what
your responsibility is and what it is not. Don't try to take on God's
responsibility. When we do what we can do, God steps in and
does what we can't. So give yourself and your worries to God, worship Him, and begin enjoying the abundant life He has for you.

Prayer of Thanks

I thank You, Father, that I can choose to worship You rather
than worry about my problems. Help me to see that You are
greater than any obstacle I may face, and I can trust You to do
in my life what I cannot.

Joyful in Every Circumstance

[After all] the kingdom of God is not a matter of [getting the] food
and drink [one likes], but instead it is righteousness (that state
which makes a person acceptable to God) and [heart] peace and
joy in the Holy Spirit.   ROMANS 14:17

A wise person does not allow the moods of other people to alter
theirs.

There is a story of a Quaker man who was walking down the
street with a friend when he stopped at a newsstand to purchase
a newspaper. The storekeeper was very rude and unfriendly. The
Quaker man responded respectfully and was quite kind in his
dealing with him. After paying for his paper and continuing to
walk down the street, his friend asked, "How could you be so cor-
dial to that man considering the terrible way he was treating you?"
The Quaker man replied, "Oh, he is always that way; why should I
let him determine how I am going to act?"

This is one of the amazing traits we see in Jesus—He changed
people, they did not change Him. I encourage you to follow the
example of Jesus. Do what God expects you to do and don't live
under the tyranny of other people's moods and attitudes.

Prayer of Thanks

Father, I thank You that I can be joyful in every circumstance.
Today, I choose not to let other people determine how I am
going to live. With Your help, I am going to live in joy regardless
of the circumstances around me.

No More Complaining

Bless (affectionately, gratefully praise) the Lord, all you His hosts,
you His ministers who do His pleasure.   PSALM 103:21

When we maintain an attitude of thanksgiving, we close the door
to grumbling and complaining—which seem to be ever-present
temptations in our lives. The truth is we don't develop a complaining attitude; we are all born with one. But with God's help, we can
develop and nurture a thankful attitude.

If we practice regularly praising, worshipping, and thanking
God, there will be no room for complaining, faultfinding, and
murmuring. The Bible says in Philippians 2:14: "Do all things
without grumbling and faultfinding and complaining..." Complaining opens the door for the devil to cause us trouble, but
thankfulness opens the door for God to bless us.

***

Prayer of Thanks
I am grateful, Father, that with Your help I can develop a
thankful attitude. I worship You for Your goodness, Your power,
and Your might. I choose to be thankful for Your presence in
my life rather than grumble and complain about things of the
world.

Keep Life Fresh and Exciting

*Delight yourself also in the Lord, and He will give you the desires
and secret petitions of your heart.*   PSALM 37:4

It's good to occasionally (or perhaps frequently) do something
that would be unexpected, something new or "out of the box." Do
something that will surprise people and perhaps stretch you a bit.
It will keep your life interesting, and you'll end up thanking God
for your exciting new challenge or adventure.

We are not created by God to merely do the same thing over
and over until it has no meaning left at all. God is creative. Just
look at the amazing variety in His creation and you will have to
agree that His creativity has no end.

In case you haven't noticed, God frequently changes things up
in our lives. Don't be afraid of change. Go ahead and do some of
the things you would like to do but have kept putting off because
you have never done them before.

Prayer of Thanks

*I am grateful, Father, that You make my life fresh and exciting.
Each day is a new challenge and an adventure. I thank You that
I can be excited about the future ahead of me and I can live a
fresh, bold, creative life in You.*

The Key to Self-Acceptance

When they measure themselves with themselves and compare
themselves with one another, they are without understanding and
behave unwisely.   2 CORINTHIANS 10:12

Advertising is often geared to make people strive to look the best, be the best, and own the most. If you buy "this" car, you will really be number one! If you buy "this" particular brand of clothes, you will be just like "this" famous star and people will really admire you. The world constantly gives us the impression that we need to be something other than what we are.

Confidence begins with self-acceptance—which is made possible through a strong faith in God's love and plan for our lives. I believe it is insulting to God when we compare ourselves with others and desire to be what they are. Make a decision to be grateful for the person God made you to be, and then you will never again compare yourself with someone else. Appreciate others for who they are and enjoy the wonderful person you are.

Prayer of Thanks

Father, help me to love and appreciate the person You created
me to be. I thank You that I don't have to compare myself to
others in order to be accepted. You created me with a unique
and wonderful purpose. I'm thankful that to You, I am special
and beyond compare.

The Warfare of Love

Above all things have intense and unfailing love for one another,
for love covers a multitude of sins [forgives and disregards the
offenses of others].   1 PETER 4:8

One of the most amazing things I've learned, something that still thrills my soul, is that love is actually spiritual warfare. This truth makes spiritual warfare fun, because loving people is very enjoyable.

First Peter 4:8 teaches us to have intense love for one another. The *King James Version* uses the word "fervent." The verb form of the Greek word translated *fervent* means "to be hot, to boil." Our love walk needs to be hot, on fire, boiling over, not cold and barely noticeable.

If we are hot enough with love, Satan won't be able to handle us. We might say we're "too hot to handle." Have you ever microwaved something for too long and couldn't get it out because it was too hot to handle? That's the way we should want to be.

On fire with love—and too much for the devil to handle!

Prayer of Thanks

I am grateful, Father, that You love me. Help me to follow
Your example and love the people around me. Thank You that
regardless of how people act toward me, I can love people with
Your perfect, unconditional love.

Your Shield of Faith

*Lift up over all the [covering] shield of saving faith, upon which
you can quench all the flaming missiles of the wicked [one].*

EPHESIANS 6:16

In years past, soldiers protected themselves with shields, and in
Ephesians 6:16, the Bible speaks of "the shield of faith." Since
shields provide protection, faith must be a way to protect ourselves when the enemy attacks. We can be grateful that God gives
us a defense system. However, just like with an actual shield, His
shield is only effective when it is raised up. It won't help a soldier if
it is on the ground or by his side.

When the devil attacks us with unpleasant circumstances or
thoughts that cause us to feel afraid, we should immediately lift up
the shield of faith. The way we do that is by deciding that we will
trust God instead of trying to figure out our own way to victory.
It is helpful to say out loud, "I trust God in this situation!" Say it
firmly with conviction. Jesus talked back to Satan by saying "It is
written" and quoting Scripture (see Luke 4), and we can do the
same.

Prayer of Thanks

*Father, I thank You that Your Word is a powerful shield, and it
is effective against everything the enemy tries to do in my life.
My faith is based on Your Word and Your promises for my life.*

The Fast Pace of Life

Come to Me, all you who labor and are heavy-laden and
overburdened, and I will cause you to rest. [I will ease and
relieve and refresh your souls.]   MATTHEW 11:28

We really do live in a time-crunched world; just about everything
we do seems to be urgent. We live under incredible pressure and
run from one thing to the next—to the point that we may neglect
the things that are really important in life: family, our health, God,
and building up our spiritual lives.

The truth is we cannot handle life apart from God. We cannot
handle the pressure, the confusion, and the stress without Him.
Our marriages will suffer, we will experience financial pressure,
and our relationships won't thrive if we do not study God's Word
and take time to pray.

But there is good news to be thankful for—God will strengthen
us and enable us to handle life peacefully and wisely if we start
praying about things instead of merely *trying* to get through the
day. God will renew our strength and enable us to handle life and
not be weary (see Isaiah 40:31).

Prayer of Thanks

Father, I am so thankful that You give me peace and rest even
in the midst of a busy life. Help me to lean on You today and
use wisdom in setting my schedule. You are the strength of my
life and I totally depend on You.

Learning to Cope with Criticism

*Rejoice and exult in hope; be steadfast and patient in suffering
and tribulation; be constant in prayer.*   ROMANS 12:12

No matter what we do in life, at some point in time we will all face
a level of criticism. But it is possible to learn how to cope with
criticism and not let it affect your life.

We can be grateful for the example the apostle Paul set for us.
Paul experienced criticism often, but he said that he was not concerned about the judgment of others. He knew he was in God's
hands and that in the end he would stand before God and give
an account of himself and his life. He would not stand before any
man to be judged (see 1 Corinthians 4:3–4).

You may not always do everything right, but God sees your
heart. If you're attempting to live for God and looking for ways to
love others, God is pleased (see Matthew 22:37–40). Don't worry
about the criticism of others; God loves you. His love and approval
are all you need.

Prayer of Thanks

*Father, I thank You that I don't have to listen to the criticism of
others. You see my heart and You know my motives. I thank You
that Your approval is greater than the approval of any person.*

One of the Most Powerful Things You Can Do

By this shall all [men] know that you are My disciples, if you love one another [if you keep on showing love among yourselves].

JOHN 13:35

Purposely forgetting about ourselves and doing something for someone else—even while we are hurting—is one of the most powerful things we can do to overcome evil. And thankfully, God can help us do that.

When Jesus was on the cross in intense suffering, He took time to comfort the thief next to Him (see Luke 23:39–43). When Stephen was being stoned, he prayed for those stoning him, asking God not to lay the sin to their charge (see Acts 7:59–60). When Paul and Silas were in prison, they took time to minister to their jailer (see Acts 16:27–34).

If we will wage war against selfishness and walk in love, the world will begin to take notice. We will not impress the world by being just like them. But how many unsaved friends and relatives might come to know Jesus if we genuinely love them instead of ignoring, judging, or rejecting them? I believe it is time to find out, don't you?

Prayer of Thanks

Father, I pray that You will give me the ability to put the needs of others before my own. Thank You that Your love has the power to change lives. Help me demonstrate that power today.

Attitude of Gratitude

*Do all things without grumbling and faultfinding and complaining
[against God] and questioning and doubting [among yourselves].*
PHILIPPIANS 2:14

You and I have many opportunities to complain on a regular basis.
But complaining doesn't do any good; all complaining does is
open the door for the enemy. It doesn't solve problems; it just creates a breeding ground for greater problems.

Instead of complaining, let's choose to respond to the Lord
each day by developing an attitude of gratitude. This is not just
an occasional expression of thanks, but a continual lifestyle of
thanksgiving. The person who has developed an "attitude of gratitude" is one who is thankful and grateful for every single thing
that God is doing in his or her life day by day.

_____

Prayer of Thanks
*Father, thank You for the way You provide for every area of my
life. Instead of complaining about what I want or about what I
don't have, I choose to be grateful for everything I do have. You
have been good to me—thank You for Your goodness.*

A New Level of Commitment

Commit your way to the Lord [roll and repose each care of your load on Him]; trust (lean on, rely on, and be confident) also in Him and He will bring it to pass.   PSALM 37:5

God wants to take us to a new level of commitment. This is something to be excited about and grateful for because with commitment comes blessing. It's not always easy, but it is worth all it requires. We all fight battles and face the temptation to stop fighting and just give up, but commitment is the thing that enables us to resist that temptation.

When you are fiercely committed to God's purpose for your life, you will begin to experience all that He has for you. God loves you and He wants you to be in a committed relationship with Him—for life. I can't imagine anything more satisfying, more rewarding, or more adventurous. He has more in store for you than you have ever asked or imagined, but in order to see His plans become a reality in your life you will need to be 100 percent committed to Him and His will.

Prayer of Thanks

Father, I choose to commit my life fully to You. I thank You that You are leading me into the destiny You have for me. With Your help, I will focus on You and commit every part of my life to Your plan and purpose for me.

Living a Guilt-Free Life

*Therefore, [there is] now no condemnation (no adjudging guilty
of wrong) for those who are in Christ Jesus, who live [and] walk
not after the dictates of the flesh, but after the dictates of the
Spirit.*   ROMANS 8:1

We are not built for guilt. God never intended His children to be
loaded down with guilt, so our systems don't handle it well at all.
Had God wanted us to feel guilty, He would not have sent Jesus to
redeem us from guilt. He bore, or paid for, our iniquities and the
guilt they cause (see Isaiah 53:6 and 1 Peter 2:24–25).

As believers in Jesus Christ and as sons and daughters of God,
we can be thankful that we have been set free from the power
of sin (see Romans 6:6–10). That doesn't mean that we'll never
sin, but it does mean that when we do, we can admit it, receive
forgiveness, and be free from guilt. Our journey with God toward
right behavior and holiness is progressive, and only when we stop
dragging the guilt from past mistakes along with us will we really
make progress toward true freedom and joy.

Prayer of Thanks

*Father, I thank You that I don't have to carry guilt and shame
around with me as I go through my life. Help me to let go of
my past mistakes and walk in the freedom of Your grace and
forgiveness.*

Facing Fear Head-On

Those who trust in, lean on, and confidently hope in the Lord are like Mount Zion, which cannot be moved but abides and stands fast forever.   PSALM 125:1

One meaning of the word *fear* is "to take flight," so when we use the phrase "fear not," in a very real sense we are saying, "Don't run away from what frightens you." Remember, you don't have to do it in your own strength—God is with you. You can move forward with a grateful assurance in Him.

Whatever the situation is, face it; don't run from it. Don't try to hide from it; just meet it head-on, even when you feel like you'd rather not. Every man or woman who has ever been given the opportunity to do something great has had to face fear. What will you do when you are tempted to be afraid? Will you run, or will you stand firm, thankful God is with you?

Prayer of Thanks

When I am in a situation where I begin to feel fear, help me, Father, to stand firm in Your strength. I am thankful that I do not have to flee. I can stand strong knowing that fear has no control over my life.

Making Each Day Extraordinary

...But David encouraged and strengthened himself in the Lord his
God.   1 SAMUEL 30:6

No day will seem ordinary if we are thankful for the gift God is giving us at the start of each day. An extraordinary attitude can quickly turn an ordinary day into an amazing adventure. Jesus said He came so that we might have and enjoy life (see John 10:10). If we refuse to enjoy it, then it's no one's fault but our own.

I would like to suggest that you take responsibility for your joy and never again give anyone else the job of keeping you happy. You can control what you do, but you cannot control what other people do. So you may be unhappy a lot of the time if you depend on them as your source of joy. The psalmist David said that he encouraged himself in the Lord, and if he can do it, then we can do it too.

Prayer of Thanks

Father, I am grateful for this new day that You have given me.
Regardless of the actions or attitudes of others, I am going to
enjoy this day because You are the source of my joy.

Responding to Encouragement

. . . For out of the fullness (the overflow, the superabundance) of the
heart the mouth speaks.   MATTHEW 12:34

The more we encourage people, the better they respond. In fact, compliments actually help people perform better, while nagging makes them perform worse.

Choose a person who you would like to have a better relationship with and begin to sincerely and aggressively encourage and compliment them. I believe you will be amazed at how much better they respond to you. Your first concern might be, *If I ignore their faults, won't they just take advantage of me?* Of course, that can happen, but it usually doesn't.

What frequently happens is that the person being encouraged is so grateful for the encouragement, they have a change of heart and they work harder to do their part to make the relationship good. They are now doing it because they choose to and not because you are trying to force them.

Prayer of Thanks

Thank You, Father, that You encourage and build me up
through the promises in Your Word. I pray that You will help
me do the same for others. Thank You for showing me ways to
encourage the people in my life today.

Enjoy the Fruit of Your Labor

There is nothing better for a man than that he should eat and drink and make himself enjoy good in his labor. Even this, I have seen, is from the hand of God.   ECCLESIASTES 2:24

It is not in God's plan for His children never to enjoy the fruit of their labor. It is good to work hard, but it is equally good to take time to enjoy life. Thankfully, God is El Shaddai, the God of more than enough. He is Jehovah Jirah, the Lord our Provider. He said that He was able to do exceedingly, abundantly, above and beyond all that we could ever dare to ask, think, or imagine (see Ephesians 3:20).

Certainly God wants and even commands us to serve and give to others generously—but God never intended that we feel guilty if we take time to enjoy the fruit of our labor. Hard work deserves reward, and we must not ever think that it doesn't. God rewards those who diligently seek Him (see Hebrews 11:6), so set aside some time to relax and enjoy the things He has rewarded you with.

Prayer of Thanks

Father, I thank You that I can enjoy the fruit of my labor. Help me find the balance between working hard and enjoying what I have worked for. Help me to enjoy what You have given me the strength to work for.

Grateful for Grace

Now Stephen, a man full of God's grace and power, performed
great wonders and signs among the people.   ACTS 6:8 NIV

Grace can be of benefit to you in your everyday life. For example: When you get into a situation that begins to cause you to
become frustrated, just stop and say, "O Lord, give me grace."
Then believe in faith that God has heard your prayer, and be grateful that He is working out that situation simultaneously as you go
about your daily routine.

Faith is the channel through which you and I receive the grace
of God to meet our needs. The Bible says that grace is the power
of God coming to us through our faith to meet our need. The next
time you begin to feel frustrated, stop and choose to rely on the
grace of God.

Prayer of Thanks

Father, I thank You for the power of Your grace in my life. Help
me to rely on You today and not on my own strength. I thank
You that You are with me and I can put my trust in You.

It's Okay to Be Different

The sun is glorious in one way, the moon is glorious in another
way, and the stars are glorious in their own [distinctive] way;
for one star differs from and surpasses another in its beauty
and brilliance.   1 CORINTHIANS 15:41

We are all different. Like the sun, the moon, and the stars, God
has created us to be different from one another, and He has done it
on purpose. Each of us meets a need, and we are all part of God's
overall plan.

Thankfully, we can be secure people, knowing God loves us
and has a plan for our lives. We don't have to be threatened by the
abilities of others. We can be free to love and accept ourselves and
one another without feeling pressure to compare or compete.

When we struggle to be like others, not only do we lose ourselves, but we also grieve the Holy Spirit. God wants us to fit into
His plan; He doesn't want us feeling pressured to fit into everyone
else's plans. Different is okay; it is all right to be different.

Prayer of Thanks

Father, You have created me to be distinct and unique, and
I thank You for that. With Your help I'm going to avoid the
temptation to compare myself to others. I'm going to be secure
in who You've created me to be today.

Rejoice and Be Glad

Rejoice in the Lord always [delight, gladden yourselves in Him];
again I say, Rejoice! PHILIPPIANS 4:4

Many serious things are going on in this world, and we need to be aware of them and prepared for them. But at the same time, because of the Spirit of God in our lives, we can learn to relax and take things as they come without getting nervous and upset about them.

Thankfully, with God's help, we can learn how to enjoy the good life He has provided for us through the death and resurrection of His Son, Jesus Christ. Twice in Philippians 4:4–7, the apostle Paul tells us to rejoice. He urges us not to fret or have any anxiety about anything but to pray and give thanks to God in everything—not *after* every difficulty is over.

In spite of all the troubling things going on around us in the world, our daily confession can be, "This is the day the Lord has made; I will rejoice and be glad in it."

Prayer of Thanks

Father, no matter what goes on around me today, I thank You
that I can rejoice and be glad. Thank You that my joy is not
found in my circumstances—my joy is found in You.

The Leading of the Holy Spirit

But the Comforter (Counselor, Helper, Intercessor, Advocate,
Strengthener, Standby), the Holy Spirit, Whom the Father
will send in My name [in My place, to represent Me and act
on My behalf], He will teach you all things. And He will cause
you to recall (will remind you of, bring to your remembrance)
everything I have told you.   JOHN 14:26

The Holy Spirit acts somewhat like a traffic policeman inside of us. When we do the right things, we get a "green light" from Him, and when we do wrong things, we get a "red light." If we are about to get ourselves into trouble, but have not fully made a decision to proceed, we get a "caution signal."

The more we stop and ask God for directions, the more sensitive we become to the signals from the Holy Spirit within. Thankfully, He doesn't scream and yell at us; He simply whispers in the still, small voice (see 1 Kings 19:12) and lets us know we are about to make a mistake. Each time we listen and obey, it becomes easier to hear Him the next time. He will always lead us to newness of life and inner peace if we yield to Him.

Prayer of Thanks

Father, when I am in a situation where I'm not sure whether to
proceed or not, help me to hear Your voice. I thank You that You
have a clear direction for my life and that You will lead me and
guide me into Your plan for my future.

Equipped to Meet the Needs of Others

And [God] Who provides seed for the sower and bread for eating will also provide and multiply your [resources for] sowing and increase the fruits of your righteousness [which manifests itself in active goodness, kindness, and charity].   2 CORINTHIANS 9:10

God blesses us so we can bless others. He wants us to have our needs met, and He wants us to be equipped to help people who are in need. This is one reason God promises to provide for us and to do so abundantly.

To help other people, we need strength, good health, and clarity of mind. We need money to help people who are struggling financially. We need clothes to be able to share with people who need them. We need joy to help those who are in despair.

God always provides these things—and more—as seed to a person who is willing to sow (see 2 Corinthians 9:9–10). This means, if you are thankful for what you have and willing to share with others, God will not only meet your needs, He will give you an abundance of supply so you will always be able to give. We can all win the battle against stinginess by simply practicing generosity.

Prayer of Thanks

I thank You, Father, that You bless me so I may bless others. Help me to see the needs around me, and help me to do my part to meet those needs. Thank You that there have been people who have helped me along the way. With Your help, I want to do the same for others.

Hearing, Receiving, and Obeying God's Word

Behold, I long for Your precepts; in Your righteousness give me renewed life ... I will keep your law continually, forever and ever [hearing, receiving, loving, and obeying it]. And I will walk at liberty and at ease, for I have sought and inquired for [and desperately required] Your precepts.   PSALM 119:40, 44–45

Our joy is full when we gratefully receive God's promises for our lives and obey His commands. When we believe the Word and obey whatever Jesus puts in our hearts to do, we overcome the things that try to upset or frustrate us. Believing God's Word delivers us from struggling so that we may rest in the promises of God.

The Word says, "For we who have believed (adhered to and trusted in and relied on God) do enter that rest" (Hebrews 4:3). If your thoughts have become negative and you are full of doubt, it may be because you have stopped hearing, receiving, and obeying God's Word. As soon as you start believing God's Word, your joy will return and you will be "at ease" again. Thankfully, that place of rest in God is where He wants you to be *every day* of your life.

Prayer of Thanks

Father, I am so grateful for Your Word. I know that the promises and instructions You give me are for my benefit. As I hear, receive, and obey the Word of God today, help me to experience the joy-filled, overcoming life Jesus came to give me.

Making a Trust Confession

The Lord is good, a Strength and Stronghold in the day of trouble;
He knows (recognizes, has knowledge of, and understands) those
who take refuge and trust in Him.   NAHUM 1:7

When you choose to confess and meditate on the thought, *I trust
God completely; there is no need to worry*, you will eventually form
a new mind-set that will enable you to put your trust in God with
ease. You will habitually look for what is good and magnify it,
thanking God for each victory along the way. Life is very enjoyable when we decide to pray about everything and worry about
nothing.

Don't be discouraged if forming mind-sets seems difficult in
the beginning. You may have to say that you will trust God and
not worry 1,000 times before you start to feel the effects of doing
it. Just remember that each time you think and say the thing that
agrees with God, you are making progress. Satan will relentlessly
try to get you to give up, but if you will relentlessly decide to trust
God, I guarantee that you will see the result in due time.

Prayer of Thanks

I thank You, Father, that You are trustworthy and I can depend
on You in every area of my life. I trust that You can handle any
and every problem I'm facing. I won't worry; I will trust in You.

Something God Responds To

That I may make the voice of thanksgiving heard and may tell of
all Your wondrous works.   PSALM 26:7

Giving thanks is an important part of prayer because, like praise
and worship, it is something God *responds* to. It's something God
loves, something that warms His heart. Anytime we please God
like that, our intimacy with Him increases—and that makes for a
better prayer life.

Also, when we are thankful, we are in a position to receive
more from the Lord. If we are not thankful for what we have, why
should God give us something else to murmur or complain about?
On the other hand, when God sees that we genuinely appreciate
and are thankful for everything He gives us—the big things and
the little things—He is inclined to bless us even more.

Prayer of Thanks
Father, thank You that I can have a personal relationship with
You. I pray that You are blessed by my thanksgiving. I love You
and I am so grateful for each thing that You have given me, no
matter how big or how small.

Whose Opinion Is Right?

*So shall My word be that goes forth out of My mouth: it shall
not return to Me void [without producing any effect, useless],
but it shall accomplish that which I please and purpose, and it
shall prosper in the thing for which I sent it.*   ISAIAH 55:11

Opinions are very interesting because we all have different ones.
You are entitled to your opinion, but that does not mean you
should always give it to others. Most of the time people don't want
our opinion; and even if they do ask for it, they hope we agree with
the opinion they have already formed. Wisdom knows when to
keep quiet and when to talk.

Not only should we be wise about how freely we give our opinion, we should also resist letting popular opinion become ours just
because it is popular. Thankfully, God has given us His truths that
can shape and form our opinions. If we'll decide to base our mind-
sets and opinions on the unchanging Word of God, it doesn't matter what culture says or what seems popular at the time; God will
reward you because His Word never returns void.

Prayer of Thanks

*I thank You, Father, for the inspired Word of God that gives me
truth to base my thoughts, mind-sets, and opinions on. Help
me to know the difference between what is popular at the time
and what is true and unchanging. Help me develop wise and
encouraging opinions.*

The Power of a Simple Prayer

Ask and keep on asking and you will receive, so that your joy
(gladness, delight) may be full and complete.   JOHN 16:24

I often tell people that one of the things they can do to enjoy their lives is to simplify their lives—that includes their prayer life too. Now when I say "simplify" your prayer life, I don't mean you should not pray often. The Bible says, "Pray without ceasing" (1 Thessalonians 5:17 NKJV). We can and should go to God frequently in prayer.

What I mean is that if you try to sound too eloquent, you can complicate your prayer life to the point of it being unbearable. It is good to know that we don't have to try to impress God with our prayers. Thankfully, we can just talk to Him like a friend; tell Him the way we truly think and feel. With God, you can always be sincere, and you can always be yourself. You don't have to put on religious airs. You can be real with God and simply enjoy spending time with Him.

Prayer of Thanks

Father, I thank You that talking with You is not a complicated process. I am so grateful that I can be myself with You and just pray what is on my heart. Help me to remember that prayer is a conversation and that I can come to you anytime throughout the day.

Waiting for a Breakthrough

Then David said, God has broken my enemies by my hand,
like the bursting forth of waters. Therefore they called the name
of that place Baal-perazim [Lord of breaking through].

1 CHRONICLES 14:11

There are many times when people give up just before a breakthrough—on the very brink of success. But don't give up! You can wait for 10 years and then suddenly, one day you wake up and everything has changed. Your dream has finally been fulfilled, the situation you lived in for so long is finally over, or you finally achieved the accomplishment for which you labored for years.

Be grateful that God has a plan for you and He has heard your prayers—you may not realize how close you are to your breakthrough. Even if you have to wait three, four, or five more years, if you will keep pressing on, thankfully, you will have the victory you need. Whatever you do, do not give up on the brink of your breakthrough. Do not stop hoping, believing, and obeying God. Instead say, "I will never quit; I will never give up."

Prayer of Thanks

Thank You, Father, that my breakthrough is on the way. I am
not without hope and I am not on my own. You are with me,
and You have a good plan for my life. I trust You, Lord, and I
refuse to give up.

The Best Kind of Knowledge

For I resolved to know nothing while I was with you except Jesus
Christ and him crucified.   1 CORINTHIANS 2:2 NIV

The apostle Paul possessed a lot of knowledge. He was a Pharisee
of Pharisees, learned, educated. And before he was converted on
the road to Damascus, he was very proud of what he knew. Isn't it
interesting that sometimes the more people know, the more proud
they become?

In 1 Corinthians 8:1, Paul said that knowledge puffs up. If we
knew everything we think we would like to know, we wouldn't
lean on God because we would be so proud and we'd think we
didn't need Him.

Paul did a 180-degree turn from thinking he knew everything
to saying that he had resolved to know nothing but Jesus Christ
and Him crucified. I think Paul was saying, "All I know is Jesus,
and I don't have to know anything more than that."

Jesus is the most important thing. Think about how much frustration you would save yourself if you gave up worrying and trying
to figure everything out and were resolved to know nothing but
Jesus. Thankfully, you can do exactly that!

Prayer of Thanks

I thank You, Father, that Jesus came to this earth and died for
my sins. I may not have everything figured out, but I know the
most important thing: my hope, peace, and joy are all found in
Your love for me revealed in the sacrifice of Jesus.

Fellowship with the Lord

*Then you will seek Me, inquire for, and require Me [as a vital
necessity] and find Me when you search for Me with all your
heart.*   JEREMIAH 29:13

No matter how many principles and formulas you and I learn, we
will never have lasting victory in our Christian life without spending time in personal, private fellowship with the Lord. The victory
is not in methods; it is in God. If we are to live victoriously, we are
going to have to look beyond ways to eliminate our problems and
find the Lord in the midst of our problems.

The good news is that when we set aside time with God, He
meets with us. We can be grateful, knowing that when we seek
Him, we will find Him. God has a personalized plan for each of
us, a plan that will lead us to victory. That is why principles, formulas, and methods are not the ultimate answer, because they do
not allow for the individual differences in people. As good as all
these things may be as general guidelines, they are not substitutes
for personal fellowship with the Living God.

Prayer of Thanks
*Thank You, Father, that I can meet with You at any time of
the day or night. You're always here for me and You desire to
spend time with me. Your Word says that when I seek You, I
will find You. So help me, Lord, to find You in every part of my
life today.*

Beckenham Library

Customer ID: ************8514**

Items that you have checked out

Title: power of being thankful : 365 life
changing devotions
ID: 30128802229917
Due: 28 September 2021

Total items: 1
Account balance: £0.00
07/09/2021 17:24
Checked out: 1
Overdue: 0
Reservation requests: 0
Ready for collection: 0

Thank you for using Beckenham Library

A Confident Person Avoids Comparison

But by the grace (the unmerited favor and blessing) of God I
am what I am, and His grace toward me was not [found to be]
for nothing.   1 CORINTHIANS 15:10

Confidence is not possible as long as we compare ourselves with other people. No matter how good we look, how talented or smart we are, or how successful we are, there is always someone who is better, and sooner or later we will run into them.

I believe confidence is found in knowing God loves us, realizing the gifts we have and being thankful for them—then we do the best we have with what God has given us to work with. Confidence is never found in comparing ourselves with others and competing with them.

Always struggling to maintain the number one position is hard work. In fact, it's impossible. Our joy should not be found in being better than others, but in being the best we can be for the Lord.

Prayer of Thanks

I thank You, Father, that I don't have to be better than others to
be accepted by You. I am confident and secure because I know
that You love me just as I am. Thank You for the peace that
comes when I refuse to compare myself with others.

A New Nature

Therefore if any person is [ingrafted] in Christ (the Messiah) he
is a new creation (a new creature altogether); the old [previous
moral and spiritual condition] has passed away. Behold, the
fresh and new has come!   2 CORINTHIANS 5:17

God's Word teaches us that when we receive Christ as our Savior
and Lord, He gives us a new nature (see 2 Corinthians 5:17). He
gives us His nature. He also gives us a spirit of discipline and self-
control, which is vital in allowing us to choose the ways of our
new nature. And He gives us a sound mind (see 2 Timothy 1:7).
That means we can think about things properly without being
controlled by emotion.

Every believer can be thankful that the way we once were
passes away, and we have all the equipment we need for a brand-
new way of behaving. With God's help we can choose spirit over
flesh and right over wrong. Our renewed spirits can now control
our souls and bodies or, to say it another way, the inner person
can control the outer person. Then we can live out God's plan for
our lives.

Prayer of Thanks

Father, I thank You that I am a new creation in You. I am so
grateful for a fresh start and the new nature You have given me.
Help me to leave the old ways behind today and live a brand-
new, joy-filled life of victory in You.

Living Free of Regret

*One thing I do [it is my one aspiration]: forgetting what
lies behind and straining forward to what lies ahead.*

PHILIPPIANS 3:13

Without God's help, we have difficulty doing things in moderation. We can eat too much, spend too much money, have too much entertainment, and talk too much. We are excessive in our actions because we behave emotionally. We feel like doing a thing, and so we do it, without any thought to the end result. After the thing is done and cannot be undone, we regret doing it.

But thankfully we do not have to live in regret. God gives us His Spirit to enable us to make right and wise choices. He urges us, guides us, and leads us, but we still have to cast the deciding vote. Forming new habits will require making a decision not to do what you feel like doing unless it agrees with God's will. With the help of the Holy Spirit, you can change your actions and live a life free of regret!

Prayer of Thanks

*I thank You, Father, that I don't have to live stuck in regrets
over my mistakes. You have forgiven me and made a new way
for me. Help me to let go of yesterday's shortcomings and make
better decisions today. Help me to live free of regret over my
past and full of faith for my future.*

Following God's Example

And God saw that the light was good (suitable, pleasant) and
He approved it; and God separated the light from the darkness.

GENESIS 1:4

As believers, you and I have the same quality of life available to us that God has. His life is not filled with fear, stress, worry, anxiety, or depression. And thankfully, ours doesn't have to be either. Instead of worrying, God takes time to enjoy His creation, the works of His hands.

In the account of Creation as recorded in Genesis 1, Scripture frequently says that after God had created a certain portion of the universe in which we live, He saw that it was good (suitable, pleasant, fitting, admirable), and He approved it. (See verses 4, 10, 12, 18, 21, 25, 31.) It seems to me that if God took the time to enjoy each phase of His creation, His work, then you and I can also take time to enjoy our work. We can rejoice with gratitude knowing that God gives us the freedom to enjoy our accomplishments.

Prayer of Thanks

Father, thank You for the example You have set for me and for the life You have made possible for me to live. I don't have to live full of stress, fear, or worry. Help me to leave those things behind and enjoy the life You have given me.

Stepping Out into New Things

The wicked flee when no man pursues them, but the
[uncompromisingly] righteous are bold as a lion.

PROVERBS 28:1

God created you for an exhilarating life that often requires you to take bold steps of faith, and then see Him come through for you. So many people are unsatisfied with their lives simply because they won't step out into the new things they desire to do. They want to stay in "the safe zone," which may feel secure, but is not always where the joy and adventure of life can be found.

We can be thankful that God has a vibrant life in store for us. Don't let fear keep you from enjoying that life and destroying your destiny. As I like to say, "Feel the fear and do it anyway—do it afraid!"

I encourage you to include more variety in your life. Try new things; when you start feeling that life is getting stale and taste-less, add a little spice by doing something different. Start thinking and saying, "I will not live in fear."

Prayer of Thanks

Father, I pray that You will help me break out of ruts and
boring, lifeless routines. I thank You that You have a vibrant,
exhilarating life in store for me. And I thank You that new
adventures are just around the corner. Help me enjoy each and
every new thing that You bring my way.

Praise, Worship, and Thanksgiving

Sing to the Lord, O you saints of His, and give thanks at the
remembrance of His holy name.   PSALM 30:4

Praise, worship, and thanksgiving are some of the simplest ways
we can pray, and yet they are powerful spiritual dynamics. They
are types of prayer because they are expressions of our hearts
toward the Lord. When we praise, worship, or give thanks, we are
talking to God—and that's all prayer really is.

Praise, worship, and thanksgiving enhance and empower our
prayer lives because they keep our hearts focused on the Lord
instead of on ourselves. They allow us to connect with God in
passionate ways and to encounter His presence in our everyday
lives. We do not need to wait for a church service or a corporate
gathering in order to experience or express praise, worship, and
thanksgiving; we can incorporate them into everything we do, all
day long.

Prayer of Thanks

Father, I thank You that I can come to You in praise, worship,
and thanksgiving all through the day. Help me to keep my heart
focused on You instead of the circumstances around me. Thank
You that You hear me and You are pleased with my praise.

Enjoy the Little Things

O give thanks to the Lord, for He is good; for His mercy and
loving-kindness endure forever!   1 CHRONICLES 16:34

All it takes to begin to enjoy life to the fullest is a decision. And that decision affects everything—even the overlooked areas of our lives.

For example, you can decide to enjoy not only your work and your accomplishments, but even the commute to work in the mornings. Don't get so frustrated about traffic and have your mind on what you need to do when you arrive that you fail to enjoy the trip.

We can be grateful in traffic—grateful that we have a car, grateful that the car is running properly, grateful that we have a job, and grateful that we have a few extra minutes to spend time with God while we're stuck in traffic.

I encourage you to enjoy the little things today. Enjoy your home, your friends, your children . . . and yes, even the commute to work. Remember, all it takes is a decision.

Prayer of Thanks

Father, today I am deciding to be grateful for the little things
and the overlooked things in my life. Help me have a heart of
thanksgiving that chooses to see You and Your blessings in every
situation.

Thank God for His Mercy

*But I have trusted, leaned on, and been confident in Your mercy
and loving-kindness; my heart shall rejoice and be in high spirits
in Your salvation.*   PSALM 13:5

God is slow to anger and plenteous in mercy (see Psalm 103:8). It
is impossible to deserve mercy, and that is why it is such a waste
of time to try to pay for our mistakes with good works or guilt. We
don't deserve mercy, but God gives it freely. This free gift is something to be thankful for!

Mercy overrides "the rules." You may have grown up in a home
that had lots of rules, and if you broke any of them, you got into
trouble. Although God does intend for us to keep His commands,
He understands our nature and is ready to extend mercy to anyone who will ask for and receive it.

When we learn to receive mercy, then we will also be able to
give it to others—and mercy is something many people seriously
need.

Prayer of Thanks

*Thank You, Father, for the way You extend mercy to me each
and every day. I desire to please You in everything I do, but I
thank You that when I fall short, You never fail to bless me with
the free gift of Your love and mercy.*

Contagious Generosity

Let all men know and perceive and recognize your unselfishness
(your considerateness, your forbearing spirit). The Lord is near
[He is coming soon].   PHILIPPIANS 4:5

With the help of the Lord, we can be a model of generosity for
all those we come in contact with. If you are a giver rather than a
taker in life, it won't take long before people realize you are quite
different from what they are accustomed to. As they witness your
joy, they will see that a thankful heart and a generous spirit make
a person happier than being selfish.

Jesus encouraged us to let all men see our good and kind deeds
so they would recognize and glorify God (see Matthew 5:16). Jesus
did not mean that we should be show-offs or do things for the purpose of being seen; He was encouraging us to realize how much
we do affect the people around us. Certainly, we can negatively
affect others, but generosity also affects those around us in very
positive ways, and makes us happy people.

Prayer of Thanks

Father, I thank You for the measure of influence You have given
me. With Your help, I am going to use that influence to model
a generous spirit. Help me, Father, to be a light in the darkness
today.

Start Strong, Finish Well

[We pray] that you may be invigorated and strengthened with
all power according to the might of His glory, [to exercise] every
kind of endurance and patience (perseverance and forbearance)
with joy.   COLOSSIANS 1:11

Everything we undertake in life has a beginning and an end. Typically, we are excited at the beginning of an opportunity, a relationship, or a venture; we're also happy when we can celebrate our achievement and have the satisfaction of a fulfilled desire. But between the beginning and the end, every situation has a "middle"—and the middle is where we often face our greatest challenges.

Between our beginnings and our endings we must develop the determination necessary to overcome the difficult circumstances we encounter in the middle. We can be people who finish what we begin. And we can be thankful that we don't have to do it alone— God will help us if we let Him.

You may be in the middle of something right now. Whatever you find yourself in the middle of, ask God for His strength and wisdom, discipline yourself a little while longer, and determine to see it all the way through to the finish.

Prayer of Thanks

I thank You, Father, that I am not alone in the middle of this
situation. You are right here with me, and You are giving me
the strength I need. With Your help, I am determined not to
quit. I'm going to see this through and give You the glory with a
successful finish!

God Loves You and Sees the Good in You

Are not two little sparrows sold for a penny? And yet not one of
them will fall to the ground without your Father's leave (consent)
and notice. But even the very hairs of your head are all numbered.
Fear not, then; you are of more value than many sparrows.

MATTHEW 10:29–31

The Song of Solomon is an allegory of the love story between God
and His people. Look closely at the following Scripture: "[He
exclaimed] O my love, how beautiful you are! There is no flaw in
you!" (Song of Solomon 4:7).

God loves you and sees the good in you. Isn't that wonderful?
That is certainly something to be grateful for! God sees what you
are becoming and will be; He is not overly concerned about your
faults. He knew all of them when He invited you to be in an intimate relationship with Him.

All God wants is your love and a willingness to grow in Him.
Your presence is a present to the world. You are unique and one of
a kind. Do not ever forget, for even a day, how very special you are!

Prayer of Thanks

Father, I thank You that Your Word shows me just how much
You love me. Regardless of what others may say, or even how I
may feel myself, I choose to believe that I am deeply loved and
wonderfully made by my heavenly Father.

Childlike Faith

Whoever will humble himself therefore and become like this little child [trusting, lowly, loving, forgiving] is greatest in the kingdom of heaven.   MATTHEW 18:4

A child's faith is simple. A child doesn't try to figure everything out and make a detailed blueprint of exactly how he will get what he needs. He simply believes because his parents said they would take care of him.

Thankfully, the same can be true for us. As believers, our joy and peace are not based in doing and achieving—trying to figure everything out and fix it ourselves. They come with believing.

Joy and peace come as a result of building our relationship with the Lord. Psalm 16:11 tells us in His presence is fullness of joy. If we have received Jesus as our Savior and Lord, He, the Prince of Peace, lives inside us (see 1 John 4:12–15; John 14:23). We experience peace in the Lord's presence, receiving from Him and acting in response to His direction. Joy and peace come from knowing and believing—trusting in the Lord with a simple, childlike faith.

Prayer of Thanks

I am thankful that my joy and peace are not based on my abilities. Father, it is in You that I find everything I need. Today, I come to You with a childlike faith, trusting that You will take care of any problem in my life. Thank You, Father, that You are in control of my life, and my joy and peace are found in You.

Strength in the Waiting

I am looking and waiting for the Lord more than watchmen for the morning, I say, more than watchmen for the morning.

PSALM 130:6

If you have a problem, don't merely pray for the problem to go away, or that you will get something you need or desire; pray that God will strengthen you during your waiting period. Pray that you will have the grace to wait with a thankful attitude.

The Bible teaches us that when we pray, if we believe we have received and do not doubt, our prayer request will be granted (see Mark 11:22–24). But it does not say we will immediately get what we ask for.

Because God's timing is perfect, we can trust Him in the waiting process. I believe that the attitude we wait with partially determines how long we have to wait. An attitude of gratitude glorifies God and is a good witness of our faith to others.

Prayer of Thanks

Father, help me learn to wait with a thankful attitude. I thank You that You have a good plan and purpose for me, and You know exactly what I need and when I need it. So I trust in You with a grateful heart.

Patience and Wisdom Go Hand in Hand

*For the Lord gives skillful and godly Wisdom; from His mouth
come knowledge and understanding.*   PROVERBS 2:6

God wants us to use wisdom, and wisdom encourages patience.
Wisdom says, "Wait a little while, until the emotions settle down,
before you do or say something; then check to see if you really
believe it's the right thing to do." Wisdom is grateful for what you
already have and patiently moves into what God has for you next.

Emotions urge us toward haste, telling us that we must do
something and do it right now! But godly wisdom tells us to be
patient and wait until we have a clear picture of what we are to do
and when we are to do it. We need to be able to step back from
our situations and see them from God's perspective. Then we can
make decisions based on what we *know* rather than on what we
feel.

Prayer of Thanks

*I thank You, Father, that patience is a fruit of the Spirit I can
demonstrate in my life. With Your help, I am determined to
make decisions today with wisdom and patience. Thank You
for guiding me along the way.*

Thankful and Enjoying Today

This is the day which the Lord has brought about; we will rejoice
and be glad in it.   PSALM 118:24

Often young parents delay enjoying their child until he has reached a certain stage of growth. When he is an infant they say, "I'll be glad when he gets out of diapers (or stops cutting teeth or learns to walk)." Then they say, "I'll be glad when he's in kindergarten." Then it becomes, "I'll be glad when he is in school all day." Later they say, "I'll be glad when he graduates."

On and on it goes until the child is grown and gone, and the parents have never really enjoyed any stage of his life. They were always waiting to be glad *when*. Let me encourage you: Don't postpone being glad until everything is perfect—thank God for every single stage along the way. Learn to rejoice and be glad in the Lord, this day and every day along the way in your life.

Prayer of Thanks

Father, I thank You for the stage of life I am in right now. Even when I face challenges and difficulties, help me remember that You have been good to me, and help me to be grateful for today.

True Prosperity

Beloved, I pray that you may prosper in every way and [that your body] may keep well, even as [I know] your soul keeps well and prospers.

3 JOHN 1:2

A person is never truly prosperous if all he has are things and money; real prosperity requires far more than that. The Bible gives a more complete approach to prosperity, and so should we.

When our bodies prosper, we are strong and physically healthy. Even if we currently have a physical ailment we can pray for and expect God to help us. True prosperity includes peace of mind and contentment. When our souls prosper, we flourish on the inside. We are at peace; we are full of joy; we live with a sense of purpose; we are growing spiritually; and we have strong, loving relationships with others.

Jesus said that He came so we could have and enjoy life in abundance and to the full (see John 10:10). God is a god of abundance, and He wants us to live abundant lives filled with thanksgiving and joy.

Prayer of Thanks
I thank You, Father, that You prosper my body and my soul.
I pray today for the health and the peace that You promise in
Your Word. Thank You that I am made whole in You.

Reach Your Full Potential

We are hard pressed on every side, but not crushed; perplexed, but not in despair.   2 CORINTHIANS 4:8 NIV

I fully believe that reaching your potential is linked to the way you handle adversity. Adversity isn't always bad. Actually, adversity can be something to be thankful for because God can use it to strengthen you. Winston Churchill said: "Difficulties mastered are opportunities won," and I wholeheartedly agree.

If you allow difficulties and challenges to frustrate, intimidate, or discourage you, you will never overcome them. But if you face them head-on and press through the adversities you encounter, refusing to give up in the midst of them and moving forward with a heart of gratitude, you will develop the skills and determination needed to be everything you were created to be and experience everything God intends for you.

Prayer of Thanks

I thank You, Father, that I don't have to give up when I face adversity—I can meet it head-on, knowing that You are always with me. Thank You for the promise that greater is He who is in me, than he who is in the world.

You Are Christ's Ambassador

So we are Christ's ambassadors, God making His appeal as it
were through us. We [as Christ's personal representatives] beg
you for His sake to lay hold of the divine favor [now offered you]
and be reconciled to God.   2 CORINTHIANS 5:20

God has always said to His people and is still saying to us: "You and I are partners. You are My body in the earth today." We are the representation of Who God is. We are His mouth, His hands, His feet, His face. We are the ones who express His heart, demonstrate His love, and reveal His power to those around us. What an awesome privilege to be thankful for!

In humility, we should be moved to pray each day, "Father, thank You that I have the chance to be Your representative to the world today. Thank You for using me." We would be wise to also pray to access the wisdom and the resources of heaven for ourselves and for others. By the grace of God, we can partner with Him so that His purposes will come to pass in our lives and in the lives of those around us.

Prayer of Thanks

I thank You, Father, that You pour out Your treasure
into earthen vessels. Thank You that You are using me to
demonstrate Your love, kindness, power, and grace to the world
around me. Help me to be Your ambassador to the world today.

Resting in God

And the Lord said, My Presence shall go with you, and I will give
you rest.   EXODUS 33:14

We can be thankful that we don't have to worry about things, figure out everything, or carry heavy burdens in our lives. It is actually quite refreshing—and something to be grateful for—to realize
that I don't need to have all the answers to my problems. We need
to get comfortable with saying, "I don't know the answer to this
dilemma, and I'm not going to worry about anything because God
is in control and I trust Him. I'm going to rest in Him!"

When we're overloaded with the cares of life—struggling,
laboring, and worrying—we need a mental and emotional vacation. Our minds need to rest from thinking about how to take
care of problems, and our emotions need to rest from being upset.
Worry isn't restful at all. In fact, it steals rest and the benefits of
rest from us. So next time you feel you are carrying a heavy load
in your mind or you find yourself worried and anxious, remember,
you can put your trust in God and enjoy His rest.

Prayer of Thanks

Father, I am grateful that You give me rest. Thank You that I
don't have to have all the answers all the time—I can trust in
You and live a life of peace, contentment, and rest.

With all Your Heart

But if from there you will seek (inquire for and require as necessity)
the Lord your God, you will find Him if you [truly] seek Him
with all your heart [and mind] and soul and life.

DEUTERONOMY 4:29

When we think about how little time most people actually give God, we can understand why the Bible so strongly encourages us to seek Him. The fact is, we are missing the greatest thing in life if we never really get to know God personally.

The apostle Paul said that his determined purpose was to know God and the power that flowed out from His resurrection (see Philippians 3:10). The word *seek* is a very strong word. In its original language, it means "to crave; to pursue; to go after with all your might."

We can be thankful that our God is a wonderful God worth seeking. He is worth loving! He is worthy of all your passion and devotion. So don't wait until you find yourself in a desperate situation. Determine to seek and love God with all your heart from this moment on.

Prayer of Thanks

I thank You, Father, that I can seek You with all my heart and
live in close relationship with You. Like Paul, I want to make
it my determined purpose to know You. I thank You that You
love me and that You reward me with Your presence when I seek
after You.

Life Is a Journey

... But when the cloud was taken up, they journeyed; whether it was taken up by day or by night, they journeyed.

NUMBERS 9:21

Thankfully, our enjoyment in life is not based on always having enjoyable circumstances. It is an attitude of the heart, a decision to enjoy everything because all things—even little, seemingly insignificant things—have a part in the overall "big picture" of life.

Life is a journey. Everything in it is a process. It has a beginning, a middle, and an end. All aspects of life are always developing. Life is motion. Without movement, advancement, and progression, there is no life. In other words, as long as you and I are alive, we are always going to be going somewhere.

If you have not been enjoying the journey of your life, it is time to start. If you have been enjoying your life, then thank God and look for ways to enjoy it even more.

Prayer of Thanks

I thank You, Father, that my life is a journey. I'm not going to stay stuck in a difficult or trying situation forever—You are taking me through it. Help me to experience Your joy regardless of my surroundings. Help me to enjoy my life today!

Grateful and Aware of God's Love

Praise the Lord! (Hallelujah!) O give thanks to the Lord, for
He is good; for His mercy and loving-kindness endure forever!

PSALM 106:1

God is always good to us, always faithful to us, always working so diligently in our lives. He is always doing something for us and acting in our best interest, so we need to respond by letting Him know we appreciate His abundant goodness.

For example, "Lord, thank You for a good night's sleep," or "God, I thank You that my visit to the dentist didn't hurt as much as I thought it might," or "Father, thank You for helping me make good decisions today," or "Lord, thank You for keeping me encouraged."

We can thank God silently in our hearts, and we can also voice our thankfulness aloud because that helps us stay conscious and aware of God's love, which He demonstrates through His goodness to us.

Prayer of Thanks

I thank You, Father, that You are always faithful to me. Even when I can't see it, You are working on my behalf because You love me and You have a great plan for my life. Thank You for all the ways You demonstrate that love on a daily basis.

Harmony's Sweet Sound

So let us then definitely aim for and eagerly pursue what makes for harmony and for mutual upbuilding (edification and development) of one another.   ROMANS 14:19

While I was ministering in a church, God gave me a great illustration of what it means to live in harmony with each other.

I asked the entire worship team to return to the platform, and then I requested them to sing and play a song of their choice. I knew, of course, that they would all choose a different song because I had given no instructions on what song to sing or play. As they sang and played, the sound was horrible! There was no harmony. Then I asked them to play "Jesus Loves Me." It sounded sweet, soothing, and wonderfully comforting.

Disharmony is noise in God's ears. But when we live in harmony, we produce a sweet sound. When we learn the value of each other, we become thankful for each other and we learn to work together.

Prayer of Thanks

Father, I am grateful for the people You have put in my life. I want to live in harmony, not strife, so that my relationships will be a sweet sound to Your ear. Thank You for giving me the patience and wisdom I need to live in harmony with others.

The Greatest of These Is Love

But earnestly desire and zealously cultivate the greatest and best gifts and graces (the higher gifts and the choicest graces). And yet I will show you a still more excellent way [one that is better by far and the highest of them all—love].   1 CORINTHIANS 12:31

Where does love fit into your list of priorities? Jesus said, "A new commandment I give to you, that you love one another; as I have loved you" (John 13:34 NKJV). It seems to me that Jesus was saying love is the main thing on which we should concentrate. The apostle Paul states that "faith, hope, love abide...but the greatest of these is love" (1 Corinthians 13:13).

One of the greatest things we have to be thankful for is that God is love. So when we choose to walk in His love, we abide in Him. That is why love is the greatest thing in the world. It is the best thing to commit our life to, to seek to excel in.

I encourage you to do yourself a favor and show love to someone today. Love not only blesses others; it also blesses the one doing the loving.

Prayer of Thanks

Father, thank You that You love me and You demonstrate that love every day. Help me to receive Your love, and help me to turn around and share that love with others.

Refuse to Live in Fear

The Lord himself goes before you and will be with you; he will never leave you nor forsake you. Do not be afraid; do not be discouraged.   DEUTERONOMY 31:8 NIV

Fear is a spirit that produces feelings. When God told Joshua to not be afraid, He was not commanding him to not "feel" fear; He was commanding him to not *give in* to the fear he was facing.

I often encourage people to "do it afraid." That basically means when fear attacks you, you need to go ahead and do whatever God is telling you to do anyway. You may do it with your knees shaking or your palms sweating, but do it anyway. That's what it means to "fear not."

We can be thankful we have Scripture to meditate on when we feel afraid. God's promises strengthen us to keep pressing forward, no matter how we feel. The Word of God will give you the faith you need to overcome any feeling of fear.

Prayer of Thanks

Thank You, Father, that I don't have to give in to a feeling of fear. With Your help, I can press forward and do what You have called me to do regardless of my feelings. Thank You, Father, that I can do it afraid.

Letting God Have Control

Many plans are in a man's mind, but it is the Lord's purpose for
him that will stand.   PROVERBS 19:21

If you haven't done a good job of running your own life, why not turn it over to the One who created you and knows more about you than you will ever know about yourself? If you start having trouble with an automobile, you take it back to the people who manufactured it to fix it. A similar principle is true with God. He created you and loves you very much. If your life is not satisfying to you, then take it to Him to fix it.

Your life will not change unless you make that very important decision to turn control of it over to God. And here is the good news: When you ask God to have His way in your life, He says, "Yes." He will repair the damaged areas, give you direction to keep you safe as you travel through life, and give you a joy you've never known. With God in control, you can be grateful that your life has a new direction, purpose, and hope for the future.

Prayer of Thanks

Father, today I ask You to take absolute control of my life. Help
me let go! Thank You that You can run things better than I ever
could. I pray that You would heal, transform, and restore my
life. I am grateful for the exciting new things in You that are in
my future.

Dealing with Unresolved Issues

If possible, as far as it depends on you, live at peace with
everyone.   ROMANS 12:18

We all have days when we feel more emotional than other days. This can happen for many reasons, but sometimes we feel emotional because something upset us the day before and we didn't resolve it.

I remember a night when I was unable to sleep. Finally, around five in the morning, I asked God what was wrong with me. Immediately I recalled a situation from the day before in which I had been rude to someone. Instead of apologizing to them and asking God to forgive me, I rushed on to the next thing in my day. Obviously, my conduct was irritating my spirit. As soon as I asked God to forgive me and made a decision to apologize to the person, I was able to go to sleep.

If you feel unusually sad or as if you are carrying a heavy burden, ask God what is wrong. And when He shows you, be grateful that you have a chance to make the situation right.

Prayer of Thanks

I thank You, Father, that You want me to live in peace. If there
are any unresolved issues that are causing me to feel anxious
or burdened, I ask You to show them to me and give me the
strength and wisdom to resolve them. I thank You that You will
be with me every step of the way.

Invest in Your Healing

*For you have need of steadfast patience and endurance, so
that you may perform and fully accomplish the will of God,
and thus receive and carry away [and enjoy to the full] what
is promised.*   HEBREWS 10:36

What a blessing it is to know that the Holy Spirit helps us overcome our past. Thankfully, with faith and patience, you can
recover from your past pain, from things that have been done to
you, or from mistakes that you have made, but the recovery will
require an investment of time on your part. You can either continue to invest in your misery, or you can begin to invest in your
healing.

One of the ways you can deal with the past is by confessing
God's promises instead of talking about negative, defeated feelings. When you confess God's promises instead of your problems,
you are exercising your faith and investing in your healing. This is
a powerful way to really begin enjoying your life.

Prayer of Thanks

*Father, I'm grateful that I can invest in my own healing by
confessing Your Word over my life. Help me to focus on Your
promises rather than my problems. Thank You that You have
good things in store for my life.*

The Power of Praise and Prayer

Enter into His gates with thanksgiving and a thank offering and into His courts with praise! Be thankful and say so to Him, bless and affectionately praise His name!   PSALM 100:4

The spiritual weapons that God gives us to use in our lives are tremendous blessings that we can be grateful for. One important weapon at our disposal is praise.

Praise defeats the devil, but it must be genuine heartfelt praise, not just lip service or a method being tried to see if it works. Praise and all other forms of prayer involve the Word. We praise God according to His Word and His goodness.

Prayer is born out of relationship with God. It is coming and asking for help, and always remembering to praise Him for all of His goodness. It is talking to God about something that bothers us. It is fellowship, friendship, and an opportunity to express gratitude for all that God is and does. If you want to have an effective prayer life, develop a good personal relationship with the Lord. Trust that He loves you, that He is full of mercy, and that He will help you when you ask.

Prayer of Thanks

Thank You, Father, for the power of praise and prayer in my life. I want to live each day in amazement of all that You have done for me. Help me to incorporate praise and prayer into my daily walk with You.

Staying Power

Looking away [from all that will distract] to Jesus, Who is the Leader and the Source of our faith [giving the first incentive for our belief] and is also its Finisher [bringing it to maturity and perfection].   HEBREWS 12:2

People who finish well in life are the ones with strong character. As believers, we can be grateful that the Holy Spirit is developing the character in us that we need to do what God calls us to do—we have "staying power." Jesus did not quit when His circumstances were rough, and He is our example. The Bible says we are to look away from all that distracts and look to Jesus instead.

I think most of us want to do and be everything God intends for us, and to enjoy it along the way. Great joy comes with finishing the race God has called you to run. Enjoy the journey and keep your eyes on the prize. One of the greatest testimonies you can have is *I'm still here.* When you speak those words, you are saying, "I did not quit. I did not give up. I am still here."

Prayer of Thanks

Father, I thank You that, with the help of the Holy Spirit, I have staying power. I make the decision today to keep going—to never give up. Help me to run my race with perseverance and discover the joy of finishing each task well.

Determined to Overcome

And He arose and rebuked the wind and said to the sea, Hush now! Be still (muzzled)! And the wind ceased (sank to rest as if exhausted by its beating) and there was [immediately] a great calm (a perfect peacefulness).   MARK 4:39

Thankfully, there is no storm in life that is greater than the power and purposes of God. When you refuse to allow your difficulties to *impress* you, then they will not *oppress* you or *depress* you either. If you put your focus on the Lord, you will hold steady in the storm and arrive safely at your God-appointed destination.

Any time we try to step out and do something for God, the enemy will oppose it. Paul certainly experienced this. He wrote in 1 Corinthians 16:9: "For a wide door of opportunity for effectual [service] has opened to me…and [there are] many adversaries."

Paul experienced opposition, and you will too. I encourage you to make up your mind that you're going to do what God is telling you to do. Don't be double-minded, second-guessing your decision. Determine to push through and refuse to turn back. Trust the Lord, be thankful for His strength, and press on no matter what.

Prayer of Thanks

Thank You, Father, that there is nothing too difficult for You. Help me to lean on You when there is a storm raging around me. I put my focus on You today, and I refuse to be impressed by my problem. I choose to be in awe of You instead.

Join the Party

*A glad heart makes a cheerful countenance, but by sorrow of
heart the spirit is broken.*   PROVERBS 15:13

When Jesus invited people to become His disciples and follow Him, He asked them if they wanted to join His party. I realize He was talking about His group, but I like to think that traveling with Jesus was probably a lot of fun as well as a lot of hard work.

Repeatedly throughout the gospels, we see Jesus invite people to leave their lifestyles and side with His party, and He is still issuing that invitation today. Yes, there is work to do for the kingdom of God, but thankfully we can have fun while we do it.

When we follow Jesus, we are not going to a solemn assembly or a funeral. We are joining His party that is full of life, peace, and never-ending joy!

Prayer of Thanks

*Father, help me to lay aside the burdens and cares of this world
and receive Your joy today. I thank You that You want me to
have fun and enjoy the life You have given me. With Your help, I
will celebrate Your goodness in my life today and every day.*

More Than Partially Forgiven...
Completely Forgiven

So if the Son sets you free, you will be free indeed.

JOHN 8:36 NIV

Satan remembers every tiny thing we have ever done wrong and will do his best to remind us of those things every chance he gets. He is vigilant in his efforts to make us cower under the weight of our own shame. We all sin and come short of the glory of God. No person is without sin, and we all feel guilt at times, but when we keep that guilt long after we have been forgiven, it turns into shame.

Guilt and shame make us feel that God is angry, and so we withdraw from His presence and don't live the life God intended for us. We need to understand and be thankful that God forgives completely—not partially, or almost, but completely! The goodness of God is greater than any bad thing we have ever or could ever do. That should bring a feeling of thanksgiving and a sensation of joy sweeping through our souls!

Prayer of Thanks

Father, I am so thankful that You completely forgive me of my sins when I ask. Regardless of what I have done, forgiveness has been made possible through the sacrifice of Jesus. Thank You that I am righteous in Your sight.

Living with Confidence

Such is the reliance and confidence that we have through Christ
toward and with reference to God.   2 CORINTHIANS 3:4

A person without confidence is like an airplane sitting on a runway with empty fuel tanks. The plane has the ability to fly, but without some fuel, it's not getting off the tarmac. Confidence is our fuel—and this is why the confidence we find in Christ is something to be grateful for.

Our confidence gets us started and helps us finish every challenge we tackle in life. Without confidence, we will live in fear and never feel fulfilled. Confidence allows us to face life with boldness, openness, and honesty. It enables us to live without worry and to feel safe. It enables us to live authentically.

When we know who we are in God, we don't have to pretend to be somebody we're not because we are secure in who we are—even if we're different from those around us. Confidence allows us to live peaceful, joy-filled lives.

Prayer of Thanks

Father, I am thankful for the confidence I have in You. Thank You that I don't have to live an insecure, fearful, worried life. I can soar in my destiny because You give me the strength that I need.

Rejoicing in Progress

For You have been my help, and in the shadow of Your wings will I rejoice.
                                                                    PSALM 63:7

We can be thankful that God wants us to rejoice. In fact, the Bible discusses rejoicing at least 170 times. And if we study the Word, we find that rejoicing is the act of outwardly expressing an emotion.

We may clap our hands when our children show progress, we might shout when our goal is met, or we may laugh when we think about or talk of the goodness of God. We can also rejoice when we make progress in spiritual growth.

The Bible says that the path of the righteous grows brighter and brighter every day (see Proverbs 4:18). If you can look back and say, "I've improved over the last year. My behavior is a little bit better. I'm a little more patient. I'm more giving. I'm a tiny bit less selfish," then you can celebrate. Every improvement deserves some time for rejoicing!

Prayer of Thanks

Father, when I see a measure of progress in my life, help me remember to take some time to rejoice. Thank You for giving me a spirit of joy rather than a spirit of heaviness. I will celebrate and rejoice in You today.

The Power of Doing Good

...how God anointed Jesus of Nazareth with the Holy Spirit and
power, and how he went around doing good and healing all who
were under the power of the devil, because God was with him.

ACTS 10:38 NIV

I firmly believe that when we have problems, we should not worry, but we also need to continue doing the things we know to do. For example, if you have commitments, be sure to keep them. Quite often when people are encountering personal problems, they withdraw from normal life and spend all their time trying to solve the problem. All this unproductive activity prevents them from doing what they should be doing, which is "doing good."

Psalm 37:3 says that we should trust in the Lord and *do good* and we will feed on His faithfulness. The faithfulness of God is something we can all be thankful for! I have discovered that if I continue my study of God's Word, continue praying, keep my commitments, and help as many people as I can, I experience breakthrough much faster. Helping others while we are hurting is actually a very powerful thing to do.

Prayer of Thanks

I thank You today, Father, that I am not subject to my
problems. When I am going through something, I can respond
by helping others around me. I am grateful that with Your help,
I can do good for others; I can make a difference in this world.

A Natural Expression of Thanksgiving

O give thanks to the Lord, for He is good; for His mercy and
loving-kindness endure forever!   PSALM 107:1

Thanksgiving can be a part of who we are deep down in our hearts;
it is a type of prayer and it should flow out of us in a natural way
that is simple and genuine.

Being thankful does not mean merely sitting down at the end
of a day, trying to remember everything we need to be thankful
for because we think we have to thank God in order to make Him
happy, or to satisfy some spiritual requirement, or try to get Him
to do something else for us.

Instead, it means having a heart that is sensitive to God's presence in our everyday lives, and just breathing out grateful prayers
of thanksgiving every time we see Him working in our lives or
blessing us.

Prayer of Thanks

Father, I am thankful that prayer is not some ritual or formula
that I am required to follow. I am grateful that prayer is a
comfortable, ongoing conversation with You based on an
intimate relationship with You. I love You, Father, and I am
excited to give You thanks all day long.

Receiving God's Love

Such hope never disappoints or deludes or shames us, for God's
love has been poured out in our hearts through the Holy Spirit
Who has been given to us.   ROMANS 5:5

Receiving is important in our relationship with God. When we
receive from God, we actually take into ourselves what He is offering. As we receive His love, we then have love in us. Once we are
filled with God's love, we can begin loving ourselves. We begin
giving that love back to God and loving other people.

The Bible teaches us that the love of God has been poured out
in our hearts by the Holy Spirit. That simply means that when the
Lord comes to dwell in our hearts because of our faith in His Son
Jesus Christ, He brings love with Him, because God is love (see 1
John 4:8).

We all need to ask ourselves what we are doing with the love of
God that has been freely given to us. Are we rejecting it because we
don't think we are valuable enough to be loved? Or are we receiving His love with a thankful heart, believing that He is greater
than our failures and weaknesses?

Prayer of Thanks
I am grateful, Father, that You love me and that Your love is
perfect and unconditional. Help me learn to receive Your love
by faith and go through each day knowing that I am valuable
because I am loved by my heavenly Father.

The Source of Happiness

For You, O Lord, have made me glad by Your works; at the deeds
of Your hands I joyfully sing.   PSALM 92:4

Focusing on our problems will prevent us from rejoicing and being glad. Look for the good in your life and your joy will increase. You might have a problem, but if you focus on what's good, then you will discover there are some good things in your life also. The world is full of people and situations that don't please us, so if we are waiting for perfect circumstances to make us happy, we will be waiting forever.

That's why we must learn to base our happiness and joy not on outward circumstances, but on the Lord's presence inside us. Thankfully, we can learn not to fret or have any anxiety about anything, but in everything to give thanks and praise to God. Then the peace that passes all understanding will be ours.

Prayer of Thanks

Father, thank You for the gifts of joy and contentment.
Regardless of the circumstances around me, I choose to praise
You and realize that You are the true source of my joy. Thank
You for Your goodness in my life. I choose to put my hope in
You.

God Says, "I Will Be with You"

...As I was with Moses, so I will be with you; I will not fail you or forsake you.   JOSHUA 1:5

The presence of God in our lives helps us overcome fear. If we know by faith that God is with us, we can be grateful for His presence and we can take on any challenge with confidence and courage. We may not always feel God's presence, but we can be thankful for His Word, remembering that He said He would never leave us or forsake us (see Hebrews 13:5).

In the Bible, the basis for not fearing is simply this: God is with us. And if we know God's character and nature, we know He is trustworthy. We do not have to know what He is going to do, when He is going to do it, or how He is going to do it. Simply knowing He is with us is more than enough.

Prayer of Thanks

Father, I am grateful that You have promised Your presence will never leave me. Thank You that no matter what things look like around me, I don't have to fear because You are with me and You will carry me through.

Access to God

In Whom, because of our faith in Him, we dare to have the boldness (courage and confidence) of free access (an unreserved approach to God with freedom and without fear).

EPHESIANS 3:12

Everything about our spiritual lives depends on our personal faith in God and our personal relationship with Him. We can enjoy that relationship because Jesus' death on the cross gives us free, unhindered access to our heavenly Father. And our faith makes it possible for us to have an intimate, dynamic relationship with Him.

Thankfully, we as ordinary human beings have free access to God at any time through prayer. It is exciting to know we can approach the Creator of the universe boldly without reservations, without fear—and with complete freedom. God loves you and wants a personal relationship with you—how awesome is that! Personal faith in God opens the door to unlimited help from Him.

Prayer of Thanks

Thank You, Father, that I can have a personal relationship with You. Today I come boldly before Your throne of grace, with more than just requests and petitions; I come to you full of gratitude for all that You have done in my life.

Love Shows Respect

Render to all men their dues . . . respect to whom respect is due,
and honor to whom honor is due.   ROMANS 13:7

Love respects the differences in other people. A selfish person expects everyone to be just the way he is and to like whatever he likes, but love appreciates the differences we all have.

Respecting individual rights is very important. If God wanted us to all be alike, He would not have given each of us a different set of fingerprints—we are all created equal, but we are still different.

We all have different gifts and talents, different likes and dislikes, different goals in life—these things make us unique, and we should be grateful for them. Love respects those differences. The person who loves has learned to give freedom to those he loves. Freedom is one of the greatest gifts we can give. It is what Jesus came to give us, and we must also give it to others.

Prayer of Thanks

I am thankful, Father, that You created us all uniquely. Help me to value the differences of others, and help me to love them just like You do.

Overcome Evil with Good

Do not let yourself be overcome by evil, but overcome
(master) evil with good.   ROMANS 12:21

We must not use our personal problems as an excuse to be grouchy and unloving with other people. Always remember that we overcome evil with good. This is why it is so important that we trust God, and while we are waiting on a change in our circumstances, we should remember to do good, do good, and do good!

In the Bible, the apostle Paul shares how even in times when he was suffering, he believed that God would take care of those things that he entrusted to Him (see 2 Timothy 1:12–14). We can be grateful that, like Paul, we are called to give our problems to God and refuse to worry.

A simple formula for victory is trust God, don't worry, do good, and keep meditating on and confessing God's Word, because God's Word is the weapon we have been given by which we can overcome evil and do good.

Prayer of Thanks

Thank You, Father, that no matter what I may be going
through, You give me opportunities to do good for those around
me. I don't have to focus on myself; I can choose to help others.
Let me be an encouragement and a blessing to someone today.

The Way God Created You to Pray

And when you pray, do not keep on babbling like pagans, for
they think they will be heard because of their many words.

MATTHEW 6:7 NIV

Jesus not only loves to teach us—corporately—how to pray (see
Matthew 6:9–13), He also loves to work with us as individuals. He
wants to take us just the way we are, helping each of us discover
our own rhythm of prayer and develop a style of prayer that maxi-
mizes our personal relationship with Him.

We can be grateful that God is far too creative to teach every
person on earth to interact with Him through prayer in exactly
the same way. He is the one who designed us all differently and
delights in our distinctiveness. Of course, there are "prayer principles" that apply to all believers, but God leads each of us as individuals. Don't feel pressure to pray exactly like someone else. If
you pray as the Lord leads you, you'll be amazed at the change it
will make in your prayer life.

Prayer of Thanks

Father, I'm depending on You to teach me how to pray. Thank
You for gifting me with my own personal and distinct way of
communicating. Help me to use what You have given me as I
spend time with You in my daily prayer life.

You Don't Have to Defend Yourself

*When He was reviled and insulted, He did not revile or offer insult
in return; [when] He was abused and suffered, He made no threats
[of vengeance]; but he trusted [Himself and everything] to Him
Who judges fairly.*   1 PETER 2:23

If we want to enjoy peaceful relationships, we will be wise to follow Jesus' example. He was accused of wrongdoing regularly, yet
never once did He attempt to defend Himself. He wasn't bothered
by what other people thought of Him; it did not disturb Him at all.

Jesus could do so because He knew who He was. He did not
have a problem with His self-image. He was not trying to prove
anything. He trusted His heavenly Father to vindicate Him, and,
thankfully, we can do the same. It adds a lot of peace to our lives
when we realize that God is our true defense, and we can remain
calm while He deals with anyone who falsely accuses us.

Prayer of Thanks

*Father, I desire to live in healthy, peaceful relationships. Thank
You for the example of Jesus that shows me I don't have to
defend myself. You are my vindication, and that is all I need.*

Fuel for Even Greater Determination

For a righteous man falls seven times and rises again.

PROVERBS 24:16

When people try something, but are unsuccessful, one of the primary reasons they give up is that they feel like "a failure." The truth is we are never a failure unless we give up. Even though we do our best, we all have times when things just don't work out the way we hope they will. We may fail at one thing, or even a few things, but that certainly does not make us failures in life.

Believe it or not, we should actually be grateful for the failures we encounter because they help prepare us for future success. Failing at some things humbles us and teaches us the lessons we need to learn for the next challenge ahead of us. You don't have to feel defeated from failure; think of failure as fuel for greater determination and success in the future.

Prayer of Thanks

Father, when I am in a difficult situation and tempted to give up, help me to remember that You are with me. Thank You that You give me the strength and determination to keep going. And thank You that no matter what happens, I know You have a good plan for my life.

Created for a Purpose

"For I know the plans I have for you," declares the Lord, "plans
to prosper you and not to harm you, plans to give you hope and
a future."   JEREMIAH 29:11 NIV

As children of God, one of the things we can be grateful for is the
knowledge that God has destined us to do great things. He created
you for a purpose. He has opportunities He wants to give you and
assignments He wants to entrust to you.

I'm sure you've realized by this point in your life that you will
face opposition as you follow God. People who are called to greatness meet great challenges. God never promised us it would be
easy. In fact, He guarantees we will have adversity in this world
(see John 16:33). But He also promises to be with us through difficulties, to fight on our behalf, and to strengthen us to overcome
any obstacle we confront.

No matter what comes your way, keep following the Lord in
faith and with a grateful heart, knowing that He has destined you
to do great things for His glory.

Prayer of Thanks

I thank You, God, that You have given me a hope and a future.
Help me to follow Your leading and walk in my destiny. I trust
Your guidance, and I am thankful for Your presence and power
in my life.

Thankful for Peace

*And let the peace (soul harmony which comes) from Christ rule
(act as umpire continually) in your hearts [deciding and settling
with finality all questions that arise in your minds, in that peaceful
state] to which as [members of Christ's] one body you were also
called [to live]. And be thankful (appreciative), [giving praise to
God always].*   COLOSSIANS 3:15

Peace is our inheritance from Jesus, and this is something to be
thankful for. The Bible teaches that peace is to be the "umpire" in
our lives, settling every issue that needs a decision. To gain and
maintain peace in our hearts, we must choose to follow the guidance of the Holy Spirit and learn when to say no to certain things.

For example, if we don't feel peace about something, we should
never go ahead and do it. And if we don't have peace *while* we are
doing something, then we shouldn't expect to have peace *after* we
have done it.

The presence of peace can help us decide and settle with finality all questions that arise in our minds. If you let the Word of
God have its home in your heart and mind, it will give you insight,
wisdom, and peace.

Prayer of Thanks
*I thank You today, Father, that You have given me peace as
my inheritance. Help me to let go of every worry and anxiety
that would try to weigh me down. Instead, I choose to let peace
guide me through all things in my life.*

Being Who God Created You to Be

So God created man in His own image, in the image and likeness of God He created him; male and female He created them.

GENESIS 1:27

Most people are afraid to be different from everyone else. They are more comfortable following a crowd than daring to follow the leading of God's Spirit. When we follow the example of others, we may please people, but when we step out in faith and follow God's Spirit, we please Him.

There is a fulfillment that comes when we learn to untie the boat from the dock, so to speak, and let the ocean of God's Spirit take us wherever He wills. When we are in control, we strive to decide what will happen next, but when we let God's Spirit take the lead, we are in for a lot of God-ordained surprises in life.

We can be grateful that God has a unique, individual plan for each of us! Let's be determined to be ourselves and refuse to spend our lives feeling inferior just because we are different from someone else.

Prayer of Thanks

Father, thank You for my uniqueness. I am grateful that I don't have to follow the crowd in life—all I have to do is follow You. Today, I will look to You and not to others. Lead me and guide me as I follow You wholeheartedly.

The Source of Your Confidence

I have strength for all things in Christ Who empowers me [I am
ready for anything and equal to anything through Him Who
infuses inner strength into me; I am self-sufficient in Christ's
sufficiency].   PHILIPPIANS 4:13

When we have confidence in God and choose to be secure in
Him, we can progress to living confidently and enjoying the life
He wants for us. Note that I said "confidence in God," not in
ourselves. Usually, when people think of confidence, they think
of self-confidence. There are many voices in society urging you
to "believe in yourself!" That is what we *don't* want to do! Our
confidence must be in Christ alone, not in ourselves, not in other
people, and not in the world or its systems.

Thankfully, we can have a confidence rooted in Christ, knowing that He is everything we need—He is more than enough! The
Bible states that we are sufficient in Christ's sufficiency (see Philippians 4:13). Another way to say it would be, "we have confidence only because He lives in us, and it is His confidence that we
draw from." So go and live with confidence today—confident in
Christ and His presence in your life.

Prayer of Thanks

I am grateful, Father, that I don't have to go through life with
insecurity and a lack of confidence. Because of Your presence
and power in my life, I can experience a new boldness and
a joy like never before. Thank You for Your strength that
empowers me.

It's Never Too Late

Be of good courage and let us behave ourselves courageously for
our people and for the cities of our God; and may the Lord do what
is good in His sight.   1 CHRONICLES 19:13

Are you doing what you really believe you should be doing at this stage in your life, or have you allowed fear to prevent you from stepping out into new things—or maybe higher levels of old things? If you don't like your answer, let me give you some good news: It is never too late to begin again!

Thankfully, you don't have to spend one more day living a narrow life that is controlled by your fears. You can make a decision right now that you will learn to live boldly, aggressively, and confidently. You don't have to let fear rule you any longer. It's important to note that you can't just sit around, waiting for fear to go away. There will be times when you have to feel the fear and take action anyway. Courage is not the absence of fear; courage is action in the presence of fear.

Prayer of Thanks

Father, I am thankful that I don't have to live in fear. I pray that
You will fill me with Your strength and courage to press through
and overcome any fear or uncertainty I may face today.

Set a Goal to Enjoy Every Part of Your Day

Therefore my heart is glad and my glory [my inner self] rejoices;
my body too shall rest and confidently dwell in safety.

PSALM 16:9

There are dozens of things that happen during ordinary, everyday life, and we can enjoy them all if we just make a decision to do it.

Things like getting dressed, driving to work, going to the grocery store, running errands, keeping things organized, sending e-mails, taking the kids to practice, and hundreds of other things. After all, they are the things that life is made up of. Begin doing them with an attitude of gratitude and realize that, through the Holy Spirit, you can enjoy absolutely everything you do every day of your life.

Joy doesn't come merely from being entertained, but from a decision to appreciate each moment that you are given as a rare and precious gift from God.

Prayer of Thanks

Father, thank You for the gift of life, and thank You for every activity that comes with that gift. I pray that You will help me find joy in each part of my day as I live for You. I thank You that I can choose to enjoy even the average, routine parts of my day.

Overlooked Blessings

The lines have fallen for me in pleasant places; yes, I have a good heritage.   PSALM 16:6

Have you stopped to think about how much you have to be thankful for?

If you woke up this morning with more body parts that don't hurt than those that do, you are blessed. If you have food, clothes, and a place to live, you are more secure than 75 percent of the world. If you have money in the bank, in your wallet, or spare change at home, you are among the top 8 percent of the world's wealthiest people. If you have never experienced the danger of battle, the loneliness of imprisonment, the agony of torture, or the pangs of starvation, you are ahead of 500 million people in the world. If you read this message, you are more blessed than two billion people in the world who cannot read.

Don't overlook any blessing—thank God every day for His goodness in your life.

Prayer of Thanks

Father, help me to realize just how blessed I am. Thank You for my health, my home, my family, the advantages I have been given, and the very air I breathe. I choose to focus on what I have rather than what I don't have. Thank You for my wonderful life.

Be Positive

We have thought of Your steadfast love, O God, in the midst of
Your temple.   PSALM 48:9

Positive minds—minds full of faith and hope—produce positive
lives. Negative minds—minds full of fear and doubt—produce
negative lives. In Matthew 8:13, Jesus tells us that it will be done
for us as we have believed. This doesn't mean that you and I can
get anything we want by just thinking about it. God has a perfect
plan for each of us, and we can't control Him with our thoughts
and words, but if we want His plan, we should think and speak in
agreement with His will and plan for us.

I encourage you to think positively about your life and be
thankful for the good things God is doing and going to do. Practice staying positive in every situation that arises; even if you're
going through a difficult situation, stand in faith, believing God
will bring good out of it as He has promised in His Word.

Prayer of Thanks

Father, help me to keep my thoughts and my words focused on
You. I thank You that You have good things in store for my life.
I trust You today.

A Perfect Heart

And I will give them one heart [a new heart] and I will put a
new spirit within them; and I will take the stony [unnaturally
hardened] heart out of their flesh, and will give them a heart of
flesh [sensitive and responsive to the touch of their God].

EZEKIEL 11:19

Although we don't behave perfectly all the time, it is possible for
us to have a perfect heart toward God. That means that we love
Him wholeheartedly, and we want to please Him and do what is
right.

When we receive Jesus as the perfect sacrifice for our sins,
He gives us a new heart and puts His Spirit in us. The heart He
gives us is a grateful, pure, and perfect heart toward Him. I like
to say that He gives us a new "want to." He gives us a desire to
please Him.

All God really wants is for us to love Him, and out of that love,
do the best we can to serve and obey Him. If we do the best we
can each day, even though our best is still imperfect, God sees our
hearts and views us as perfect anyway because of His grace (undeserved favor and blessing).

Prayer of Thanks

I thank You today, Father, that You see the attitude of my heart.
I know that You have given me a new "want to," and with Your
help, I am going to do my best to please You with my actions. I
love You, Father, and I thank You for Your grace in my life.

Loving People, Trusting God

But Jesus [for His part] did not trust Himself to them, because
He knew all [men]; and He did not need anyone to bear witness
concerning man [needed no evidence from anyone about men],
for He Himself knew what was in human nature. [He could read
men's hearts.]   JOHN 2:24–25

Jesus loved people—we see that in His interaction with people,
especially His disciples. He had great fellowship with them—
traveled with them, ate with them, and taught them—but He did
not trust Himself totally to them. Because He knew what was in
human nature.

That does not mean He didn't trust them at all; He just didn't
open Himself up and give Himself to them in the same way He
trusted God and opened Himself up to His heavenly Father. He
didn't expect them to be perfect toward Him and never disappoint Him.

We can be thankful for the example of Jesus because He shows
us how we should live. We should love people, and we can trust
them, but never give them the trust that belongs to God. He is
always trustworthy, and He always has your best interest at heart.

Prayer of Thanks

Father, thank You for the example of Jesus. I love and trust the
people close to me in life, but my ultimate dependence and trust
is in You.

Equipped for Joy

The hope of the [uncompromisingly] righteous (the upright, in right standing with God) is gladness, but the expectation of the wicked (those who are out of harmony with God) comes to nothing.
PROVERBS 10:28

We can be thankful that it is God's will for us to enjoy the life He has provided. The joy of the Lord is our strength. With that knowledge, we can make the decision to enjoy life every day.

Enjoying life does not mean we have something exciting going on all the time; it simply means enjoying the simple, everyday things. Most of life is rather ordinary, but we are supernaturally equipped with the power of God to live ordinary, everyday life in an extraordinary way.

Yes, it takes God's power to enjoy life because all of life is not easy. Many things happen that we do not plan, and some of them are difficult. But Jesus said, "Cheer up, I have overcome the world and deprived it of the power to harm you" (see John 16:33).

Prayer of Thanks
Father, when I am faced with a difficult situation, help me to choose joy in spite of my circumstance. I thank You that Your joy is my strength each and every day.

What Do You Think About Yourself?

And I am convinced and sure of this very thing, that He Who began a good work in you will continue until the day of Jesus Christ [right up to the time of His return], developing [that good work] and perfecting and bringing it to full completion in you.   PHILIPPIANS 1:6

It is important that we have a healthy, scriptural view of ourselves. No one is perfect; we all have growing to do. But thankfully, we can know that we are loved and accepted by God while we are becoming the people He wants us to be.

These thoughts reflect the Bible-based self-image you can have in Christ:

1. I know God created me and He loves me (see Psalm 139:13–14; John 3:16).
2. I have faults and weaknesses, and I want to change. I believe God is working in my life, changing me little by little, day by day (see 2 Corinthians 3:18).
3. Everyone has faults, so I am not a failure just because I am not perfect (see 2 Corinthians 12:9).
4. No matter how often I fail, I will not give up, because God is with me to strengthen and sustain me (see Hebrews 13:5).
5. In myself I am nothing, and yet in Jesus I am everything I need to be (see John 15).
6. I can do all things I need to do—everything God calls me to do through His Son Jesus Christ (see Philippians 4:13).

Prayer of Thanks

Father, I am so thankful that I have a new identity in You. Regardless of what I have been told or how I feel on a given day, I will trust Your Word and believe that everything Your Word says about me is true.

Celebrate Change

Do not conform to the pattern of this world, but be transformed
by the renewing of your mind. Then you will be able to test
and approve what God's will is—his good, pleasing and perfect
will.   ROMANS 12:2 NIV

As children of God, we can be thankful for the change God works
in our lives. Throughout our journey here on earth, God's Spirit
will be working with and in us, helping us change for the better. In
order to make progress, we need to be open to God's work and be
obedient to His guidance.

God wants us to see truth (reality) so we can agree with Him
about any change that is needed, but we don't need to punish ourselves when we see our faults or to feel guilty and condemned. We
can submit to God and learn to celebrate the changes that happen
in our lives. Change and growth is a healthy process that God will
continue as long as we are on earth in our human bodies. Transformation is something to be grateful for!

Prayer of Thanks

I thank You, God, that I don't have to be afraid of change, but
that I can rejoice in it. Help me to be open to Your leading. I am
grateful for Your work in my life.

The Best Way to Live

Some trust in and boast of chariots and some of horses, but we will trust in and boast of the name of the Lord our God.

PSALM 20:7

We can live by trying to take care of ourselves, or we can live by trusting God. Trusting God is the best and most peaceful way to live and, thankfully, it is an option available to us every day.

If you're under pressure because you're trying to take care of yourself, then choose to stop trying to make everything happen yourself, in your own timing, in your own way, according to your own plan. Instead, lean on God in every situation and pray:

Lord, whatever I may desire in life, if You don't want me to have it, I don't want it. If You do want me to have it, I ask You for it and believe You will give it to me in Your time, in Your way, according to Your divine plan.

When you release yourself to God in this way, you will see marvelous things happen in your life.

Prayer of Thanks

Thank You, Father, that I can enjoy Your peace while You guide me and work Your will in my life.

Dealing with Emotional Pain

And after you have suffered a little while, the God of all grace
[Who imparts all blessing and favor], Who has called you to His
[own] eternal glory in Christ Jesus, will Himself complete and
make you what you ought to be, establish and ground you securely,
and strengthen, and settle you.   1 PETER 5:10

When we are hurting emotionally, we may feel angry, frustrated, or discouraged, but we do not have to let any of those feelings control us. We can manage our emotions with God's help, and we can be thankful we are not controlled by our feelings and emotions.

Many people are treated unjustly; they do not deserve the pain they experience. But we can be so glad that even when we go through ugly, painful things, we do have Jesus in our lives to help and strengthen us.

Perhaps you did not have a good start in life, but you can still have a good finish. Let go of the past and take a step into the good life that God sent His Son, Jesus, to purchase for you.

Prayer of Thanks

Father, thank You for helping me overcome any unjust
treatment I may have or ever will experience in my life. I trust
that You are my Vindicator and You always make wrong things
right.

Living in God's Grace

*But he said to me, "My grace is sufficient for you, for my power is
made perfect in weakness."*   2 CORINTHIANS 12:9 NIV

The truth that God wants you to enjoy your life is a blessing that
every believer can be thankful for. But one of the main things that
will keep you from enjoying your life is works of the flesh. A work
of the flesh is our energy, our efforts trying to do what only God
can do.

Trying to do God's job always leads to frustration. Trusting
God to do what only He can do always leads to joy because "what
is impossible with men is possible with God" (Luke 18:27).

The Bible says that God's grace is sufficient for us. Grace is
God's undeserved favor and the power of God to meet our needs
and solve our problems. We become frustrated when we try to
achieve by works a life that God designed us to receive by grace.
So rest in His grace today and be thankful for the joy that grace
promises to bring.

Prayer of Thanks

*I am grateful, Father, for Your grace in my life. Help me to
always receive grace through faith in You and trust You to do
what only You can do.*

Look How Far You've Come

Yet, O Lord, You are our Father; we are the clay, and You our
Potter, and we all are the work of Your hand.   ISAIAH 64:8

It is easy for us to get caught up in looking at how far we have to go
in reaching our goals instead of celebrating how far we have come.
Think about it. How far have you come since you became a Chris-
tian? How much have you changed? How much happier are you?
Are you more peaceful than you were before? Do you have hope?
There is always plenty to celebrate if we look for it.

A thorough study of the Bible shows us that the men and
women who God used in mighty ways always had the attitude of
celebrating what God had done. They did not take His goodness
for granted, but they openly showed appreciation and thankfulness for little things as well as big ones.

Prayer of Thanks
Father, today I choose to be full of thanksgiving for how far You
have brought me. I may not be where I want to be yet, but I
thank You that I'm not where I used to be.

Blessing Those Around You

. . . being mindful of the words of the Lord Jesus, how He Himself said, It is more blessed (makes one happier and more to be envied) to give than to receive. ACTS 20:35

It is the will of God that we give thanks at all times and in everything (see 1 Thessalonians 5:18). Thanksgiving must have an expression in order to be complete. We can say that we are thankful, but do we show it? Are we expressing it? We say "thank you," but there are other ways of showing appreciation, and one of them is to bless others.

Giving to help others is one of the ways we can keep a continual cycle of blessing operating in our lives. God gives to us and we show appreciation by giving to someone else, and then He blesses us some more so we can do it all over again. What we give to others as a result of obedience to God is never lost. It leaves our hand temporarily, but it never leaves our life. We give it, God uses it to bless someone else, and we are blessed in return.

Prayer of Thanks

Thank You, Father, that You bless me so that I may be a blessing to others. Help me look for ways to give to those around me today. I am grateful for Your goodness, and I want to express that gratitude through my generosity to others.

A Key to Effective Prayer

I do not call you servants (slaves) any longer, for the servant does not know what his master is doing (working out). But I have called you My friends, because I have made known to you everything that I have heard from My Father.   JOHN 15:15

One of the most important keys to effective prayer is approaching God as His friend. When we go to God believing that He sees us as His friends, new wonders are opened to us. We experience new freedom and boldness, which are both things to be extremely grateful for.

If we do not know God as a friend, we will be reluctant to be bold in asking for what we need. But if we go to Him as our friend, without losing our awe of Him, our prayers will stay fresh, exciting, and intimate.

A friendship involves loving and being loved. It means knowing that God is on your side, wanting to help you, cheering you on, and always keeping your best interest in mind. God loves you and desires your friendship!

Prayer of Thanks

Father, I am thankful that You have promised to be my friend. Help me to come to You in prayer, knowing that You love me and You are for me. Thank You, God, that I am never alone. You are my friend, and You are with me.

You Can Be as Close to God as
You Want to Be

God has said, "Never will I leave you; never will I forsake you."
                                    HEBREWS 13:5 NIV

Developing your friendship with God is similar to developing a friendship with someone on earth. It takes time. The truth is that you can be as close to God as you want to be; it all depends on the time you are willing to invest in the relationship. I encourage you to get to know Him by spending time in prayer and in the Word and by including Him in all that you do.

Your friendship with God will also deepen and grow as you walk with Him and as you experience His faithfulness. Form the habit of continual, simple, and loving conversation with God. He is always with you and always ready to listen. He is a friend who will never leave you or forsake you. One who is faithful, dependable, loving, and forgiving. That is a friend we can be thankful for!

Prayer of Thanks

Father, I thank You that my relationship with You is developing and growing stronger every day. Thank You that You are dependable and You will never let me down.

Burden-Free Living

Anxiety in a man's heart weights it down, but an encouraging word makes it glad.
                                                    PROVERBS 12:25

In this life, we will always have opportunities to be anxious, worried, and fretful. The devil will see to that, because he knows that anxiety weighs us down. When the devil tries to bring anxiety into our hearts, we can give that anxiety to the Lord in prayer with thanksgiving, making our requests known to Him. When we do that, we will experience the peace of burden-free living.

I encourage you to refuse to be weighed down with worry. Instead, turn to the Lord in prayer, rejoicing in the midst of every circumstance. The Lord is faithful, and He will give the peace and joy He has promised to all those who refuse to give in to worry and fear and instead turn to Him in simple faith and trust.

Prayer of Thanks

Father, when I begin to experience feelings of worry or anxiety, help me to cast my cares on You. Thank You that I don't have to live under heavy burdens any longer. Thank You that I can bring my worries to You so that I can live a life of peace.

The Gift of Right Now

So do not worry or be anxious about tomorrow, for tomorrow will
have worries and anxieties of its own.   MATTHEW 6:34

There is an anointing (God's presence and power) on today. In John 8:58, Jesus referred to Himself as "*I AM*." If you and I, as His disciples, try to live in the past or the future, we are going to find life hard for us because Jesus is always in the present.

Jesus has plainly told us we don't need to worry about anything. All we need to do is seek Him and His ways, and He will add to us whatever we need, whether it is food or clothing or shelter or spiritual growth (Matthew 6:25–33). We don't need to be concerned about tomorrow. Instead, we can concentrate on today and thank God for today's blessings.

Calm down and lighten up! Laugh more and worry less. Don't ruin today by worrying about yesterday or tomorrow—neither of which you can do anything about. Enjoy today while you still can!

Prayer of Thanks
I am grateful, Father, for this day that You have given me. With
Your help, I'm going to live in the present, not in the past or in
the future. I thank You for what you have in store for me today.

What Choice Will You Make?

I call heaven and earth to witness this day against you that I have set before you life and death, the blessings and the curses; therefore choose life.   DEUTERONOMY 30:19

Jesus wants us to experience joy in our souls. It is important to our physical, mental, emotional, and spiritual health. This is why Proverbs 17:22 says, "a cheerful mind works healing." It is God's will for us to enjoy life!

It is time to decide to enter into the full and abundant life that God wills for us. We can be thankful that God allows us to choose what kind of life we want to live. Joy and enjoyment are available, just as misery and sadness are available. Righteousness and peace are available, but so are condemnation and turmoil. There are blessings and curses available, and that is why Deuteronomy 30 tells us to choose.

Make the right choice today. Choose Jesus. Choose joy. Choose peace. Choose life!

Prayer of Thanks

Father, I thank You that I can choose the quality of life I want to live for You. Help me to make wise decisions today. Help me to choose peace and joy. I know that You will give me wisdom and guide me every step of the way. Worry is useless and I choose not to waste my time on it!

The Spirit of a Conqueror

Yet amid all these things we are more than conquerors and gain a
surpassing victory through Him Who loved us.   ROMANS 8:37

Are you living a victorious life in Christ? If you aren't, maybe today is the day for you to begin seeing yourself differently than you have in the past, to see yourself as one who overcomes adversities, not as someone who shrinks back in fear or feels overwhelmed every time a trial comes along.

You see, adversities are not optional, they are part of life, and it takes a conqueror to overcome them. Jesus Himself said that we would face trouble in this world (see John 16:33). Paul understood that obstacles were unavoidable and wrote in Romans 8:37 that we are "more than conquerors" and that we would "gain a surpassing victory."

To be more than a conqueror means that before you ever face adversity, before the battle against you even begins, you already know you will win as long as you trust God and don't give up. That's a promise to be grateful for—you are more than a conqueror in Christ Jesus!

Prayer of Thanks

Father, when I am in a situation that threatens to overwhelm or intimidate me, I will stand on Your Word that says I am more than a conqueror in You. Thank You that I will not be defeated because You are with me, and You are protecting me.

You Are Free from Your Past

It is for freedom that Christ has set us free. Stand firm, then, and do not let yourselves be burdened again by a yoke of slavery.   GALATIANS 5:1 NIV

Many people stay trapped in the past. But there is only one thing that can be done about the past, and that is to forget it. Thankfully, when you ask Him, God forgives and forgets your past... and you can too.

When we make mistakes, as we all do, we can simply ask God's forgiveness and move forward in the freedom Jesus provided for us. Like Paul, we are all pressing toward the mark of perfection, but no one has arrived.

I believe one of the reasons Paul enjoyed his life and ministry is because he made it a priority to leave his past in the past (see Philippians 3:13–14). Like us, he was pressing toward the mark of perfection, admitting that he had not arrived, but he had insight on how to enjoy his life while he was making the trip.

Let's follow Paul's example. Don't get stuck in the past—live in the freedom of forgiveness today!

Prayer of Thanks

I am thankful, Father, that my past is in the past. You have forgiven my sins and given me a fresh start. I accept Your forgiveness and I determine to live my present and my future for Your glory.

Victory over Dread

...Dread not, neither be afraid of them.   DEUTERONOMY 1:29

Dread is a close relative of regret. Dread places us in the future, whereas regret puts us in the past. Dread is also closely related to fear. People often dread doing something for fear of what might happen.

We know that God has not given us a spirit of fear (see 2 Timothy 1:7 KJV), and since He did not give us fear, we know that dread is not from Him either. Thankfully, we can reject feelings of dread, kicking them out of our lives once and for all.

Let this be a day of decision for you—a day when you decide to no longer operate in regret and dread. Become a *now* person. Live in the present, not the past or the future. God has a plan for your life now. Trust Him today. Don't put it off another moment.

Prayer of Thanks

I believe it is Your will, Father, for me to live a life of peace and contentment. Thank You that I don't have to look back with regrets or look ahead with dread. I choose to live in the now You have given me, making the most of each new day.

Praising God all Day Long

Let everything that has breath and every breath of life praise the
Lord! Praise the Lord! (Hallelujah!)   PSALM 150:6

One of the best things we can do throughout the day is to praise
God while we work. No matter what you're trying to build—your
home, your marriage, your business, financial security, an exercise plan, or an intimate relationship with God—do not forget to
worship as you work.

Remember to praise God and thank Him for even small steps of
progress. You don't have to make a production out of your praise;
just keep a thankful heart and an attitude that says, "I love You,
Lord. I worship You. I can't do this without You. I need Your help
today. Thank You for giving me a goal to work toward and for helping me accomplish it."

Prayer of Thanks

I am grateful, Father, for even the smallest steps of progress
You enable me to make in my life. I love You and I know that
You are doing a good work in and through me. Thank You for
everything You have done in my life and everything You are yet
to do.

Jesus Showed Us the Way

Jesus Christ (the Messiah) is [always] the same, yesterday, today,
[yes] and forever (to the ages).   HEBREWS 13:8

In every aspect of life, Jesus is our example—and Jesus always displayed emotional stability. The Bible actually refers to Him as "the Rock," and we can depend on Him to be solid, steady, and stable—the same—all the time. He's always faithful, loyal, mature, and true to His Word.

Jesus is not in one kind of mood one day and in another mood the next day. Thankfully, we can count on Him to be the same today as He was yesterday and the same tomorrow as He is today. Being able to depend on Jesus' stability and consistency is part of what makes a relationship with Him seem attractive to us. If we'll learn to be grateful for the example Jesus set, and follow His lead, we will be able to learn to be stable and enjoy life more.

Prayer of Thanks
I am grateful, Father, that I don't have to be ruled by my emotions. Thank You for the example of Jesus. Help me to be steady and solid no matter what is going on around me. Help me to be more like Jesus.

God Leads Us One Step at a Time

The steps of a [good] man are directed and established by the Lord when He delights in his way [and He busies Himself with his every step]. Though he falls, he shall not be utterly cast down, for the Lord grasps his hand in support and upholds him.

PSALM 37:23–24

As we go through this life, each of us is called to have an individual walk with God. Thankfully, God gives us the direction we need, showing us the way to go, and with His help we follow Him.

A walk with God takes place through one step of obedience at a time. Some people want the entire blueprint for their life before they will make one decision, but God does not usually operate that way; He leads us day by day. Not knowing everything the future holds requires us to live by faith, and that is what God desires.

By faith, we take each step God has shown us, and then He gives us the next one. At times we may fall down, but we can be grateful that God helps us get back up. We continue on by His strength and His grace, knowing that every time we need to make a decision, God will guide us because we have a personal relationship with Him.

Prayer of Thanks

I thank You today, Father, that You are guiding me one step at a time. I trust Your direction for my life. I thank You that Your plan for me is good and You will never lead me astray.

An Act of Love Endures Forever

*If I [can] speak in the tongues of men and [even] of angels, but
have not love (that reasoning, intentional, spiritual devotion such
as is inspired by God's love for and in us), I am only a noisy gong
or a clanging cymbal.*   1 CORINTHIANS 13:1

Most of the things we devote our time and energy to are things
that are currently passing away, things that will not last. We strive
to make money, build businesses, achieve great accomplishments,
be popular, own buildings, cars, and jewelry. We want to expand
our minds and see the world, yet all of these things are temporal.
They will all come to an end.

Only love never comes to an end. An act of love goes on and
endures forever.

Thankfully, God allows us to have a lasting impact when He
asks us to love others. Henry Drummond says that "to love abundantly is to live abundantly, and to love forever is to live forever."
In order to "love abundantly" and "love forever," I encourage you
to first receive God's love for you...then you can walk in love
toward everyone else.

Prayer of Thanks

*Father, I am grateful that I can live my life in such a way as to
have a lasting impact. Thank You for the power of love. Help
me exercise that power and make an eternal impact by showing
love to those around me today. Help me to always know what is
truly important.*

Enjoying Harmonious and Peaceful Relationships

. . . And you shall hold your peace and remain at rest.

EXODUS 14:14

We were created to live in the love and enjoyment of harmonious relationships, free from dissension, confusion, and emotional trauma. God wants our lives to be free from division; He wants us to live in peace with each other; yet such a life often eludes many people. Instead, conflict wreaks havoc in their lives, leaving them wounded and alienated from one another.

But we can be thankful that Jesus gives us His peace. We don't have to live with broken, conflict-filled relationships. We can "hold our peace" in every situation. Psalm 34:14 says we can "crave peace and pursue it" and Matthew 5:9 says we can be "makers and maintainers of peace." As we remain peaceful, God works in our behalf.

Don't let relationship problems plague your life any longer. Determine to end the strife and do all that you can to pursue peace. If you decide to be a peacemaker, you'll be surprised what a difference it will make.

Prayer of Thanks

Father, help me to be a peacemaker in my relationships. I thank You that I no longer waste my time on petty arguments and foolish strife. As far as it depends on me, and with Your help, I am going to have peaceful, harmonious relationships.

God's Word Affects Every
Area of Our Lives

Your word is a lamp to my feet and a light to my path.

PSALM 119:105

While negative thoughts, words, emotions, and relationships can cause stress—and stress can cause sickness—positive thoughts, words, emotions, and relationships can bring health and healing. Consider the following Scriptures:

- *"A calm and undisturbed mind and heart are the life and health of the body..."* (Proverbs 14:30)
- *"My son, attend to my words...for they are life to those who find them, healing and health to all their flesh."* (Proverbs 4:20,22)
- *"Pleasant words are as a honeycomb, sweet to the mind and healing to the body."* (Proverbs 16:24)

We can be thankful for the power of God's Word in our lives. Meditating on Scripture and following God's instruction will cause us to think, speak, and live in a way that brings healing to every part of our lives.

Prayer of Thanks
Father, I thank You for Your Word and the healing it brings to my life. I am grateful that my thoughts, words, emotions, and relationships are all changed by the guidance You give me through Scripture.

Thankful for all God Has Done

Through Him, therefore, let us constantly and at all times offer
up to God a sacrifice of praise, which is the fruit of lips that
thankfully acknowledge and confess and glorify His name.

HEBREWS 13:15

Many people are familiar with the statement, "There is power in praise!" It's true, and when we praise God from our hearts, we exert power in the spiritual realm. God Himself inhabits the praises of His people (see Psalm 22:3).

Praise allows us to remember and express our joy and thanksgiving for all God has done for us . . . and everything He is going to do. It engages our hearts to focus on Him and our mouths to speak about Him.

Thankfully, we can tap into the power that is released through praise—it gives us an opportunity to express how truly thankful we are. We do this because we love God, but also because praise and giving thanks are attitudes that God delights in. Praying with gratitude is the way to see prayer answered.

Prayer of Thanks

Father, I praise You because You are worthy to be praised.
Thank You for everything You have done in my life and
everything You are going to do in the future. I love You, and I
praise You with everything I am.

Today Is a Perfect Day to Bless Others

*And do not forget to do good and to share with others, for with
such sacrifices God is pleased.*   HEBREWS 13:16 NIV

The blessings of God in our lives are certainly something to be
thankful for, but we must also remember that we are blessed in
order to bless others.

Let me suggest an experiment today. Just think: *I am going to
go out into the world today and I will be a blessing to others.* Then get
your mind set before you ever walk out the door that you are going
out as God's ambassador and that your goal is to be a giver, to love
people, and to add benefit to their lives.

You can begin by smiling at the people you encounter throughout the day. A smile is a symbol of acceptance and approval—
something most people in this world desperately search for.
Deposit yourself with God and trust Him to take care of you while
you sow good seed everywhere you go. Make a decision to let God
work through you today!

Prayer of Thanks

*I am so thankful for the blessings in my life, Father. Help me to
use what You have given me to bless others. Today, I choose to
spread Your love, Your joy, and Your blessings to the people I
come in contact with.*

Righteousness in Christ

I will greatly rejoice in the Lord, my soul will exult in my God; for
He has clothed me with the garments of salvation, He has covered
me with the robe of righteousness, as a bridegroom decks himself
with a garland, and as a bride adorns herself with her jewels.

ISAIAH 61:10

Our righteousness in Christ is one of the greatest gifts we can ever
be thankful for. Through faith in Christ we are placed in right-
standing with God. And by faith, we are covered with His robe of
righteousness. In other words, because we are trusting in Jesus
Christ's righteousness to cover us, God views us as right instead of
wrong. His righteousness becomes a shield that protects us from
Satan.

In and of ourselves, we are less than nothing; our righteousness
is like filthy rags, for all have sinned and come short of the glory of
God (see Isaiah 64:6; Romans 3:23). But we are justified and given
a right relationship with God through faith. Knowing we are righteous through the work of Jesus brings peace and joy to our lives
that no one can ever take away.

Prayer of Thanks

I thank You today, Father, that I have right standing with You
and I am pleasing in Your sight because of the work of Jesus. I
am grateful that I know I am accepted, loved, and approved by
You.

Holding on to Hope

And now, Lord, what do I wait for and expect? My hope and
expectation are in You.   PSALM 39:7

God's Word says that He wants us to be blessed (see Deuteronomy 29:9). It states we can and will be blessed in every way when we walk in God's will. Satan wants to keep people fearful and hopeless. Hopelessness steals our God-given peace and joy.

The enemy tells people they will never have anything, their life will never change, and things will never get better. And when people believe his lies, they remain hopeless and discouraged. We receive what we believe, whether it is positive or negative, so it's vitally important for us to have faith in God constantly, like Mark 11:22–24 tells us to do.

Refuse to be hopeless and put your trust in God's Word. Be like Abraham, of whom it is said that although he had no reason to hope, he hoped in faith that God's promises would come to pass in his life. As he waited, he gave praise and glory to God, and Satan was not able to defeat him with doubt and unbelief (see Romans 4:18–20).

Prayer of Thanks

Father, thank You for the power of hope. I am grateful that no matter what the circumstances around me look like, I can place my hope in You and in Your Word. I am at peace today because You are the source of my hope.

Recognize Your Enemy

Be vigilant and cautious at all times; for that enemy of yours, the devil, roams around like a lion roaring [in fierce hunger], seeking someone to seize upon and devour.   1 PETER 5:8

John 10:10 states that "the thief comes only in order to steal and kill and destroy." The passage is referring to Satan and his system. Just as God has a system that He encourages us to live by, and He promises blessings if we do, Satan has a system and he wants us to live by it so he can steal our blessings.

Satan shows us a circumstance and then makes us afraid it will never change. God wants us to believe His Word is true even while we are still in the midst of the circumstance. That's why Scripture says, "Yet amid all these things we are more than conquerors..." (Romans 8:37).

In God's economy, we can believe before we see change or the good things we desire. Jesus gave us peace as our inheritance, but Satan does everything he can to rob us of it. Recognize your enemy, and stand aggressively against him in the peace and power of God.

Prayer of Thanks

Father, though I have an enemy who is trying to rob me of my joy, thank You that I don't have to fear him. You have already defeated the enemy, and Your Spirit lives within me. I recognize I have an enemy, but I thank You that the victory is already mine through Christ.

Relationship vs. Religion

For no person will be justified (made righteous, acquitted, and
judged acceptable) in His sight by observing the works prescribed
by the Law.   ROMANS 3:20

Jesus had much to say about religion, and none of it was good.
Why? Because religion in His day was, and often still is, man's idea
of what God expects. Religion is man trying to reach God through
his own good works.

The Christian faith teaches that God has reached down to man
through Jesus Christ. Thankfully, by placing our faith in Jesus, we
receive the benefits from the work He has done for us. His work—
not our own works of religion, not following rules and regulations
man prescribes—justifies us and makes us right with God.

A Christian is not just someone who has agreed to follow cer-
tain rules and regulations and observe certain days as holy. A
Christian is someone who has had his heart changed by faith in
Jesus Christ.

Prayer of Thanks

I am grateful, Father, that I am free from man-made ideas
of religion. I can relate to You in a personal, intimate way
because of Jesus. Thank You for loving me and for living in a
relationship with me.

When There Seems to Be No Way

Behold, I am doing a new thing! Now it springs forth; do you not perceive and know it and will you not give heed to it? I will even make a way in the wilderness and rivers in the desert.

ISAIAH 43:19

Have you ever faced a situation and said, "There is no way this can ever be"? Maybe some of these thoughts weigh on your mind:

- There is no way I can handle the pressure at work.
- There is no way I can pay my bills.
- There is no way to save my marriage.
- There is no way I can go back to college now.

With God's help, there is *always* a way. This is a beautiful truth to be grateful for. It may not be easy; it may not be convenient; it may not come quickly. You may have to go over, under, around, or through difficulty—but if you will simply keep on keeping on, you *will* find a way. Jesus said in John 14:6, "I am the Way and the Truth and the Life." He is the Way, and He will help you find a way even where there doesn't seem to be one.

Prayer of Thanks
Father, I thank You that You have "made a way in the wilderness." Help me to focus on You and not on my circumstances. Thank You that You are making a way for me today.

Love Never Gives Up

Love never fails [never fades out or becomes obsolete or comes to an end]. 1 CORINTHIANS 13:8

Love never fails. In other words, it never gives up on people. We can be thankful that God never gives up on us, and we can have that same attitude toward others. The apostle Paul describes what love is in 1 Corinthians 13 and mentions that love always believes the best; it is positive and filled with faith and hope.

While Jesus was on earth, He gave a new commandment to His followers: that we love one another (see John 13:34). For this reason, walking in love should be the main goal of every Christian. God is love (see 1 John 4:8) and He never gives up on us. Let's choose to live with that same attitude. Believe in the power of love to change and transform anything and anyone. No person is beyond God's reach!

Prayer of Thanks
I am so thankful, Father, that Your love will never give up on me. Help me, Lord, to have that same attitude toward others. Help me to show Your love to the world around me.

How to Reach Your God-Given Goals

For which of you, wishing to build a farm building, does not first sit down and calculate the cost [to see] whether he has sufficient means to finish it?   LUKE 14:28

Goals are important in life. Paul said that he pressed toward the goal (see Philippians 3:14). As believers, we can be thankful that God helps us set and reach healthy goals in our lives. Many people never accomplish their goals because they do not know how to set them. A popular and easy-to-remember acronym that has been successful in helping countless people reach their goals is the word *smart*:

Specific
Measurable
Attainable
Realistic
Timely

Specific: Make sure your goal is as specific as possible. **Measurable:** Goals that are hard to measure are goals that are hard to meet. **Attainable:** Make sure the goal itself is reachable. **Realistic:** It is important to dream big dreams and aim high, but don't set yourself up for disappointment by trying to reach an unrealistic goal. **Timely:** People who set goals without target completion dates rarely accomplish their objectives.

Prayer of Thanks
Father, I am thankful that I can meet the goals I set with Your help. I pray that You give me wisdom to set healthy goals for my life and the perseverance to reach every goal that I set.

A Time to Remember

And they [earnestly] remembered that God was their Rock, and
the Most High God their Redeemer. PSALM 78:35

There are times to forget and things to forget. For example, when the apostle Paul said that he forgot what was behind, he was talking about not being condemned over past mistakes (see Philippians 3:13). In Isaiah, we are taught not to remember the things of old because God is doing a new thing. That simply means we are not to get stuck in the past.

We hear a lot of teaching about forgetting the past, and although there are times to do that, we should also be taught to remember with gratitude all the good things God has done in the past, passing that gratitude on to future generations. A thankful heart is a heart that remembers God's love and miraculous deeds and shares them with the world.

Prayer of Thanks
Father, I thank You for the amazing things You have done in my past. Help me to always remember Your goodness and use it to build my faith for even bigger and better things to come.

Seek the Giver, Not the Gift

Seek, inquire for, and require the Lord while He may be found
[claiming Him by necessity and by right]; call upon Him while He
is near.   ISAIAH 55:6

One of the many things we can be thankful for in our relationship
with God is that He wants to be our friend (see John 15:15). But
as you grow in your friendship with God, never forget that your
relationship is based on who He is and not on what He can do for
you. Keep seeking His presence, not His presents.

One of the hindrances to a vibrant, mature friendship with
God is focusing on the benefits of friendship with God instead
of focusing on *Him* as our friend. As human beings, we do not
appreciate finding out that certain people want to be our friends
just because we can get them something they want; we feel valued
when we know people want to be friends with us simply because
of who we are and because they actually like us—the same principle applies with God.

Prayer of Thanks

I thank You, God, that You love me and want to be in a
relationship with me. Today, I seek You for who You are, not
for what You can do for me. It is my heart's desire to know You
more and more each day I follow You.

God Wants to Bless You

... They who seek (inquire of and require) the Lord [by right of their need and on the authority of His Word], none of them shall lack any beneficial thing.   PSALM 34:10

Some people have been taught that suffering and lack are virtues in the Christian life. Being able to maintain a good attitude during times of suffering is a virtue that is very important, but continually suffering is not God's will for anybody. We must never see God as a stingy God who would withhold something we need. Consider these verses:

- *"The Lord is my Shepherd [to feed, guide, and shield me], I shall not lack"* (Psalm 23:1).
- *"Let the Lord be magnified, Who takes pleasure in the prosperity of His servant"* (Psalm 35:27).
- *"He will bless those who reverently and worshipfully fear the Lord, both small and great"* (Psalm 115:13).

God is a good Father who loves to bless His children. God wants to bless you and see you enjoy your life! You can simply be thankful, receive it, and aggressively believe for God's best today.

Prayer of Thanks

Father, I thank You that You are good, You love me and want to bless me. Thank You that I don't have to be afraid because You will feed, guide, and shield me.

Praying Bold, Confident Prayers

Since we have such [glorious] hope (such joyful and confident
expectation), we speak very freely and openly and fearlessly.
2 CORINTHIANS 3:12

God is looking for men and women who will pray bold prayers. One of the prayers I hear people pray often is what I call a "just" prayer. A "just" prayer sounds something like this: "Now, Lord, we *just* ask You to protect us," or "Oh, God, if You would *just* help us in this situation." These prayers make it sound as if we are afraid to ask God for very much.

When used this way, the word "just" means *barely enough to get by* or *by a narrow margin*. God wants to give us exceedingly, abundantly, above and beyond all that we can dare to hope, ask, or think (see Ephesians 3:20)—that's something to be grateful for! God wants to hear bold, confident, faith-filled prayers prayed by truly thankful people who are secure in their relationship with Him. Don't be fearful of asking God for too much because He loves you and wants to do more for you than you can imagine.

Prayer of Thanks

Father, I am so thankful that You allow me to pray bold,
confident prayers. I know You are not a God of just enough—
You are a God of more than enough. I take the limits off of
You today, and I trust You to do something big in my life.

Draw Near to God

Come close to God and He will come close to you. JAMES 4:8

Many times people draw away from God because of their sins and failures. Do you ever hear or study God's Word and end up feeling condemned? God's Word is meant to convict us of sin and convince us to do things God's way, but it is never intended to make us feel guilty or bad about ourselves.

When God reveals sin in your life, let it draw you to Him for help and forgiveness, never let it drive you away from Him. Remember, Jesus didn't die for perfect people who never make mistakes, but He died for sinners. He paid for our sins so we might receive His forgiveness and mercy and then actually learn from our mistakes.

We can be grateful and thankful that the Lord didn't push us away because of our faults. Instead, He draws us to Him and begins to change us into what He wants us to be. All we have to do is be willing to be changed. Just ask Him and trust Him to do it. He is faithful. He will finish the work He has started in your life.

Prayer of Thanks

I thank You today, Father, that You draw me to Yourself despite my sins and my failures. Help me not to draw away from You when I make mistakes. Instead, help me choose to come to You in faith, believing that You love me and want to help me.

Thankful to Be Free from Confusion

For God is not the author of confusion but of peace, as in all the
churches of the saints.   1 CORINTHIANS 14:33 NKJV

Confusion is not from God. When we are confused, it is because
we are trying too hard to reason things out in our own minds
instead of trusting Him. He offers us peace, not confusion. When
you feel confused, you should realize that something about your
approach to life is wrong. Perhaps you have moved out of grace
and into your own works. That simply means you may be trying
to solve your own problems instead of relying on God. But thankfully, you can give up your efforts and entrust yourself totally to
the Lord, leaving your situation entirely in His hands.

Once you turn from your own efforts and reasoning to the
grace of God, you open a channel of faith through which He can
begin to reveal to you what you need to know in order to handle
that problem or situation. Enter God's rest, and then you will find
the guidance you need.

_____

Prayer of Thanks

I am grateful, Father, that You give me peace instead of
confusion. I will live in Your grace each day, knowing that You
can handle whatever situation or circumstance I may face.
Thank You for Your peace—I receive it today.

A Life of Adventure

Whatever may be your task, work at it heartily (from the soul), as [something done] for the Lord and not for men.

COLOSSIANS 3:23

We were never created to live a boring life. God put a craving for adventure in us, and adventure means trying something we have never done before. If you are going to be adventurous, you may need to step out into something new. Don't sit on the sidelines of life and watch the brave people live exciting lives—join them. Step out of your "boat of safety" and see if you can walk on water as Peter did (see Matthew 14:26–31).

I assure you, if you are stepping out into God's will for you, He will make you able to succeed. You do not have to feel able, and you do not have to have experience. All you need is the desire to be obedient to God, a thankful attitude, and a heart full of faith. God is not looking for ability; He is looking for availability. He is looking for somebody to say, "Here I am, God, send me. Here I am, use me. I want to serve You, God. I want to do all that You want me to do."

Prayer of Thanks

Father, I am thankful that You want me to enjoy an amazing, adventure-filled life. Whatever You have for me to do, I pray that You will make it clear. Thank You for the opportunities You are sending my way and the boldness You are giving me to make the most of them.

Be Assured of God's Love for You

And so we know and rely on the love God has for us. God is love.
Whoever lives in love lives in God, and God in them.

1 JOHN 4:16 NIV

The key to trusting God is to know and believe you are loved by
Him. To grow in God and be changed, we need to trust Him. Often
He will lead us in ways that we cannot understand, but thankfully,
even in those times, we can have a tight grip on His love for us—
His never-ending love.

The apostle Paul was convinced that nothing would ever be able
to separate us from the love of God in Christ Jesus (see Romans
8:38–39). We should and can have that same absolute assurance
of God's never-ending love for us as individuals.

Accept God's love for you, and make that love the basis for your
love and acceptance of yourself. Receive His affirmation, knowing
that you are changing and becoming all that He desires you to be.
Then start enjoying yourself—where you are—on your way to full
spiritual maturity.

Prayer of Thanks

Father, thank You for the gift of Your love. No matter what
happens, no matter what I may go through, knowing that You
love me and You gave Your only Son for my salvation is all that
I need. I am so grateful for Your love, and I love You in return.

Mighty to Save

Surely the arm of the Lord is not too short to save, nor his ear too dull to hear.   ISAIAH 59:1 NIV

Thankfully, God's arm can reach us no matter where we are, and we can have the joy of knowing that He delights in helping us. God hears us when we call on Him, and we have the privilege of trusting Him instead of trying to solve our own problems. Ephesians tells us that we should do what the crisis demands and then abide in Christ (see Ephesians 6:13).

When we attempt to do what only God can do, we end up frustrated and feeling miserable. For example, only God can change people, because only He has the ability to change a person's heart. I wasted many years trying to change myself, my husband, my children, and other relatives and friends, but nothing worked until I stopped trying in the flesh and began to trust God. You can believe and trust God, and while you do, He will work, and you can enjoy the wait.

Prayer of Thanks

Father, I thank You that You delight in helping me and that You are working in my life. Help me avoid my own fleshly effort and put my trust in You. I am grateful that the arm of the Lord is mighty to save in my life.

Following God's Lead

He refreshes and restores my life (my self); He leads me in the
paths of righteousness [uprightness and right standing with
Him—not for my earning it, but] for His name's sake.

PSALM 23:3

God never leads us anywhere that He cannot keep us. If God is
leading you to deal with some unpleasant situation in your life,
don't run from it; trust that God is going to help you and be thankful that you are not alone. He promises to be with you at all times
and never to leave you or forsake you.

Surrender can be frightening when we first begin to practice
it, because we don't know exactly what the outcome will be if we
yield ourselves to God's will. However, once we have surrendered
and we begin to experience the peace that passes understanding,
we learn quickly that God's way is better than any plan we could
ever devise, and we are thankful for His leading. Cast your care on
Him today, and let Him take care of you.

Prayer of Thanks

Father, when I am not sure what to do or where to go, I thank
You that You have promised to lead me. I submit my will
and my plans to You, and I will follow Your plan for my life
wholeheartedly.

Safe and Secure

So we take comfort and are encouraged and confidently and boldly
say, The Lord is my Helper; I will not be seized with alarm [I will
not fear or dread or be terrified]. What can man do to me?

HEBREWS 13:6

A confident person feels safe. He believes he is loved, valuable, cared for, and protected by God's will for him. When we feel safe and secure, it's easy to step out and try new things.

During the initial construction on the Golden Gate Bridge, no safety devices were used, and twenty-three men fell to their deaths. For the final part of the project, however, a large net was used as a safety precaution. Twenty-five percent more work was accomplished after the net was installed. Why? Because the men had the assurance of their safety, so they were free to wholeheartedly serve the project.

When people feel safe, they are free to take a chance on failing in order to try to succeed. As children of God, we are safe and secure, knowing God loves us and has a good plan for our lives. Therefore, we can live with thanksgiving and confidence as we step out boldly each and every day.

Prayer of Thanks

I thank You, God, that You are always there to catch me when I
fall. Today, I choose to live with confidence because I know I am
safe and secure in Your love. I know nothing will happen to me
that I can't handle because You are with me.

Developing the Habit of Being Thankful

Thank [God] in everything [no matter what the circumstances
may be, be thankful and give thanks], for this is the will of God
for you [who are] in Christ Jesus [the Revealer and Mediator of
that will].   1 THESSALONIANS 5:18

We all have many things to be thankful for in this life. The problem is that we get into the bad habit of taking them for granted, and sadly we often only see what we don't have.

Because we are so used to having plenty of clean water and healthy food, good clothes and nice homes, convenient transportation and excellent education, freedom and safety, and security, we forget that millions of people around the world do not enjoy these wonderful blessings.

I believe that maintaining an attitude of gratitude is something we need to do on purpose. Take time daily to think about your blessings and voice your gratitude to God for His continual goodness in your life. Make gratitude a habit!

Prayer of Thanks

Father, I pray that You will help me develop a habit of
thankfulness. I don't want to take any blessing in my life
for granted. Help me fully realize how You have blessed me,
and I will be extremely grateful for You and Your provision in
my life.

God Will Never Stop Loving You

Your mercy and loving-kindness, O Lord, extend to the skies,
and Your faithfulness to the clouds.   PSALM 36:5

God is not angry and wrathful, just waiting to punish us for each of our mistakes. Aren't you grateful for that? If we spend our time believing that God is angry with us, we are focusing on what we have done wrong instead of what God has done right in sending His Son to pay for our sins. It is true that we all sin, and God doesn't like sin because of the damaging effects it has on His children. But we must always remember that God is good, kind, merciful, slow to anger, forgiving, faithful, and just.

If you receive God's love right in the midst of your imperfection, it will empower you to change your ways with His help. God does love you. He has never stopped loving you and He never will.

Prayer of Thanks

I thank You today, Father, that You have always loved me and You always will. Let the truth of Your love guide me in every decision I make today. I thank You that I can enjoy my life, because I know that You are for me and Your love will never leave me.

Enjoying People

... You shall love your neighbor as [you do] yourself.

MATTHEW 22:39

God has created all kinds of people with many different tempera-ments and personalities, and He enjoys them all. Variety seems to be something that God really delights in.

If you haven't given this any thought, take a little time and look around you. God created variety, and He says that what He has created is good; therefore, I urge you to accept those who are dif-ferent from you and learn to enjoy them as God does.

We encounter a lot of people. Some of them by choice, but a lot of them just end up in our lives as we go through our day. If you want to enjoy each day of your life, be thankful for and choose to enjoy the people you interact with each and every day. If there is someone in your life you are struggling with, try to focus on the good things about them, and start thanking God for them instead of disliking them.

Prayer of Thanks

Father, help me to love and accept the people in my life the way that You do. Thank You that You have made us all different and yet You love us all the same. Today, I choose to appreciate and enjoy the people You bring across my path.

The Beautiful Truth

*The Lord is merciful and gracious, slow to anger and plenteous in
mercy and loving-kindness.*   PSALM 103:8

The promise that God is not mad at us is the most freeing truth
we will ever find. God knows that we will sin, but He provided the
forgiveness of our sins in Jesus. The beautiful truth is that when
we no longer focus on our sin, we find that we do it less and less.
As we focus on God's goodness, we become more and more like
Jesus.

God, through Christ, has totally taken care of the problem of
sin—that's something to be thankful for! God urges us not to sin,
but He knew we would due to the weakness of our flesh, so He
took care of the problem by sending His Son as the sacrifice for
our sins.

Jesus paid for everything that we have done and ever will do
wrong, and He opened up a new way for us to live and serve God.
Not in fear or guilt, but in freedom, love, and intimacy. Receive
God's love, mercy, and forgiveness today and be thankful for it!

Prayer of Thanks

*Father, I am so grateful that You are not mad at me. I am
thankful that You still love me even when I sin. And thank You
for the sacrifice of Jesus, making it possible for me to be in
relationship with You today.*

How to Enjoy a Peaceful Life

For let him who wants to enjoy life and see good days . . . keep his tongue free from evil . . . Let him turn away from wickedness and shun it, and let him do right. Let him search for peace . . . [Do not merely desire peaceful relations with God, with your fellowmen, and with yourself, but pursue, go after them!]   1 PETER 3:10–11

If you want to walk in peace, 1 Peter 3:10–11 gives some helpful instruction. This passage shows four specific principles for those who want to enjoy life and live in peace.

- Keep your tongue from evil: God's Word clearly states that the power of life and death is in the mouth. We can bring blessing or misery into our lives with our words.
- Turn away from wickedness: We should take action to remove ourselves from any wicked environment.
- Do right: The decision to do right closes the door to doing wrong. Don't be weary in doing what is right, for in due season you will reap a harvest (see Galatians 6:9).
- Search for peace: Notice that we must search for it, pursue it, and go after it. Crave peace enough to make whatever changes are necessary to have it.

If you'll live by these principles and choose to be thankful for the peace God provides, then your relationships, attitude, and health will be transformed by the truth of God's Word.

Prayer of Thanks

Father, when I am in a situation that threatens to steal my peace, help me to remember that I can choose peace. I am thankful that You have given me Your peace and that it keeps me from being upset and frustrated.

Disappointed? Get Reappointed

A man's mind plans his way, but the Lord directs his steps and
makes them sure.   PROVERBS 16:9

Disappointment occurs when our plans are thwarted by something we have no control over. We can be disappointed by unpleasant circumstances or by people who let us down. When we are disappointed, our emotions initially sink, and then sometimes they flare up in anger. But, thank God, we don't have to be led by emotions.

The next time you are disappointed, pay attention to the activity of your emotions, but instead of letting them take the lead, make the decision to manage them. There is nothing unusual or wrong about initial feelings of disappointment, but it is what we do from that point forward that makes all the difference in the world.

With God on our side, even though we will experience disappointments in life, thankfully, we can always get "reappointed." Trusting that God has a good plan for us and that He orders our steps is the key to preventing disappointment from turning into despair.

Prayer of Thanks

Father, I am so grateful that when I deal with a
disappointment, I can trust that You have a better plan than
mine. Thankfully, I can trust that You are working even when
things don't work out the way I had planned.

God Is Your Reward

After these things, the word of the Lord came to Abram in a vision, saying, Fear not, Abram, I am your Shield, your abundant compensation, and your reward shall be exceedingly great.   GENESIS 15:1

In the world's system, you work hard and then you get your reward. When we follow God's plan and love and obey Him, we also get a reward. God does many wonderful things for us, but the greatest reward we get is an intimate relationship with Him. Trusting God always brings a wonderful reward.

When you get weary and doing what is right is difficult, just look forward to your reward. Jesus didn't look forward to what He would endure on the cross, but He didn't focus on His difficulty. Instead He focused on the good that would come in due time.

Look at Hebrews 12:2: "... He, for the joy [of obtaining the prize] that was set before Him, endured the cross, despising and ignoring the shame, and is now seated at the right hand of the throne of God."

Prayer of Thanks

I thank You, God, that You are my reward. You are the One I turn to, and I know You will always make a way for me. In good times and bad, I will look to You.

It's Wise to Take a Break

The whole earth is at rest and is quiet; they break forth into
singing. ISAIAH 14:7

God has created all things for our enjoyment and it begins by enjoying Him. He also wants us to enjoy one another and He wants us to enjoy ourselves. We can be thankful that God wants us to enjoy life, and we can allow that realization to affect how we go through our day.

Next time you have a desire to take a short break from your work and go for a walk in the park, go ahead and do it without feeling guilty or unspiritual. Your work will still be there when you return. If you have been working hard and feel you need a day off, then take it. You will be more fruitful if you take time to be refreshed. If you don't want to end up with all kinds of regret about things you wish you would have done, then get started today making every moment count. Work is good, but it does need to be balanced with rest and taking time to do things you enjoy.

Prayer of Thanks

I am grateful, Father, that You gave us the example of rest.
When I'm feeling stressed out and overworked, help me to
remember that it is wise to rest and be refreshed. Thank You for
the peace and joy that comes when I choose to rest in You.

Know Who You Are

Namely, the righteousness of God which comes by believing
with personal trust and confident reliance on Jesus Christ
(the Messiah). [And it is meant] for all who believe.

ROMANS 3:22

God's Word assures us that we have tremendous value because of who we are—God's beloved children. What you do is not always perfect. But you can still know who you are—a child of God whom He loves very much. Your worth and value come from the fact that Jesus died for you, not because you do everything perfectly (see Romans 3:22–23; 4:5).

You are special to God, and He has a good plan for your life (see Jeremiah 29:11). You have been purchased with the blood of Christ (see Acts 20:28). The Bible refers to the "*precious blood of Christ*," indicating that Christ paid a high price to ransom you and me (see 1 Peter 1:19). Believe that you are God's beloved child and never stop thanking Him that you are. That truth will bring healing to your soul and freedom to your life.

Prayer of Thanks

I am grateful, Father, that I have tremendous worth and value
in Your sight. Thank You for the blood of Jesus that purchased
my salvation. And thank You that I am forever Your child.

Count the Cost

For which of you, intending to build a tower, does not sit down
first and count the cost, whether he has enough to finish it.

LUKE 14:28 NKJV

When we make a commitment to walk in love, it usually causes a shift in our lifestyle. Many of our ways—our thoughts, our conversation, our habits—begin to change. For instance, we may be accustomed to spending all our extra money on ourselves only to discover that walking in love requires that we spend some of it on others. We may also experience the same thing when it comes to how we use our time.

Love often requires sacrifice on our part, just as Jesus sacrificed in order to show His love for us. Love is tangible. It is not just an emotional feeling, a spiritual thing that cannot be seen or touched—love is evident to everyone who comes in contact with it. That's how God's love has always been for us. One of the greatest things we have to be grateful for is that God *demonstrated* His love for us (see Romans 5:8).

Prayer of Thanks

I thank You, Father, that You demonstrated Your love by
sending Jesus to die for my sins—He paid the ultimate price. I
pray that You will give me an opportunity to walk in love today
by doing something helpful for someone else.

God's Mercy Is New Every Day

It is because of the Lord's mercy and loving-kindness that we are
not consumed, because His [tender] compassions fail not. They
are new every morning; great and abundant is Your stability and
faithfulness.   LAMENTATIONS 3:22–23

One of the things we can praise God for daily with a heart full of gratitude is that He is determined to have an intimate relationship with each of us. The only way He can do that is if He extends grace, mercy, and forgiveness to us continually. And the only way we can have that relationship with Him is if we learn to continually receive His grace, forgiveness, and mercy.

In case you are wondering, you have not used up all of God's mercy for you. There is still an abundant amount available to you, and there will be as long as you live. God's mercy is new every day! And it is a gift that can only be enjoyed if it is received freely. So thank God for His mercy today, live boldly by His grace, and be all He created you to be.

Prayer of Thanks

Father, thank You for Your mercy, Your compassion, and Your
loving-kindness that never fails. I celebrate Your goodness
today, and I am so grateful that I can have a personal, intimate
relationship with You.

Stable People Get Promoted

Not that I am implying that I was in any personal want, for I
have learned how to be content (satisfied to the point where
I am not disturbed or disquieted) in whatever state I am.

PHILIPPIANS 4:11

Many people feel able and qualified to do a particular thing, and
yet they live frustrated lives because the right doors don't seem to
open. Why is that? The truth is they may be "able, but not stable."
God has given them abilities, but perhaps they have not made the
effort to mature in stability of character.

God must be able to trust us, and other people must be able
to depend on us, in order for God to increase our level of responsibility. When we are stable and mature, our lives are marked by
consistency and thankfulness. We continue to operate in the fruit
of the Spirit even when we must endure situations or people that
are not what we would like them to be.

Life is not problem-free, and it never will be. Let circumstances
do what they will—but as far as you're concerned, be determined
to remain stable and thankful in the Lord.

Prayer of Thanks

Thank You, Father, for the way You help bring strength and
maturity to my life. Help me to be both "able and stable," so
that I might accomplish all You have called me to do.

A Deeper Level of Prayer

. . . Not My will, but [always] Yours be done.   LUKE 22:42

Asking God for what we need and desire in the natural realm is definitely not wrong, but we should not major on those things. God's Word says that He knows what we need before we ask Him (see Matthew 6:8), so all we need to do is simply ask and let Him know that we are trusting Him to take care of everything that concerns us.

After we ask God for our daily physical needs, we can focus the majority of our prayer time on talking to Him about our spiritual needs, such as spiritual maturity, developing and displaying the fruit of the Spirit, obedience, and walking in love, to name a few. We also have the privilege of praying for other people and being part of their victories.

God is inviting you to a deeper walk with Him and that means you want His will even more than you want your own.

Prayer of Thanks

I thank You, Father, that You hear me every time I pray. Even though I have daily needs that I bring to You, help me to enter a deeper level of prayer. I pray that Your will would be done in my life and in the world around me.

No Longer a Victim

He heals the brokenhearted and binds up their wounds [curing
their pains and their sorrows].   PSALM 147:3

You may have been a victim at one point in your life, but you don't
have to remain one. You can be emotionally healthy and whole
in your soul. The Word of God promises that God will heal your
wounds. He will help you . . . He's waiting to help you.

We all have painful issues from the past that we need to deal
with. Many of them were not our fault, and it isn't fair that we
should suffer because of other people's behavior. Perhaps you were
teased mercilessly as a child and still feel insecure or sensitive
because of that old pain. Maybe someone you loved left you without explanation, or you may have been abused in some way. Whatever the source of your pain, be thankful that God loves you and
wants to heal you. You don't have to spend your life as a victim;
you can have victory and even help bring victory to others.

Prayer of Thanks
Father, I thank You that You are a healer. You have not left me
to suffer in the pain of the past—You are healing my wounds
and giving me the strength to move forward. Today is a new
day, and I am going to enjoy every minute of it!

Our Thoughts Affect Our Attitude

[Let your] love be sincere (a real thing); hate what is evil [loathe all ungodliness, turn in horror from wickedness], but hold fast to that which is good. Love one another with brotherly affection [as members of one family], giving precedence and showing honor to one another.   ROMANS 12:9–10

If we allow our thoughts about a person to be negative, our attitude and behavior toward that person will also be negative. In order to love people, we must make a decision to think good thoughts about them.

God's Word teaches us to always believe the best of people. Our love should be sincere. If we are praying for an individual but thinking negative thoughts about what he is like and how he will probably never change, our prayers will be negated by our negative thinking.

It is important to have a loving attitude toward people, an attitude that is filled with mercy and kindness. A right attitude begins with right thinking. We can be grateful God has that attitude toward us, and we can be determined to have the same attitude toward others.

Prayer of Thanks

Father, I thank You that You love me enough to think good thoughts about me. Help me to have that same attitude when dealing with the people in my life. I want to be more like You today.

Love Displays Patience

Love endures long and is patient.   1 CORINTHIANS 13:4

Love is patient. It is not in a hurry. It always takes time to wait on God, to be grateful for His goodness, and to fellowship with Him. A person whose life is marked by love is patient with people. For example, he takes the time to listen to the elderly person who is lonely and wants to talk. He is willing to listen to the same story four or five times just to show kindness.

The patient person is long-suffering. He can put up with something uncomfortable for a long period of time without complaining. He has the power to endure whatever comes with a good attitude. Patience is a wonderful virtue, but it is a virtue than can only be developed under trial. In other words, we need something to be patient about in order to develop patience, so let's start thanking God each time we need to exercise patience instead of complaining about it.

Prayer of Thanks

Father, as I go through my day today, help me to be patient with those around me. Thank You that You give me the strength and ability to demonstrate godly character. Today, with Your help, I choose to be kind and patient every chance I get.

Because He Lives

We were buried therefore with Him by the baptism into death,
so that just as Christ was raised from the dead by the glorious
[power] of the Father, so we too might [habitually] live and behave
in newness of life.   ROMANS 6:4

There is a popular song titled "Because He Lives," and it is about the fact that Jesus' death and resurrection give us the power and privilege to live life today in victory. Because He lives, we can face whatever comes our way, knowing that God will never allow us to go through more than we can bear, and that He always provides a way out.

Because Jesus lives, we can also have a new attitude toward ourselves. We can stop expecting ourselves to be perfect and learn to enjoy ourselves even in the midst of making mistakes. Jesus died for our mistakes and is alive today to help us grow in Him and be changed by His Word and Holy Spirit. Be grateful for the sacrifice of Jesus, and get a new attitude about yourself! Stop thinking that your failures and mistakes are too much for God. He has cast all of your sins behind His back (see Isaiah 38:17). He isn't looking at them, so you don't need to look at them either!

Prayer of Thanks
I thank You, Father, that Jesus is alive and that the same Spirit who raised Him from the dead dwells in me. Help me face every challenge in life boldly, put my guilt and sin behind me, and embrace Your mercy and forgiveness.

He's Done It Before, He Can Do It Again

David said, The Lord Who delivered me out of the paw of the lion
and out of the paw of the bear, He will deliver me out of the hand
of this Philistine. And Saul said to David, Go, and the Lord be
with you!   1 SAMUEL 17:37

If we remember the miracles God has done in the past with awe and a thankful heart, we will not so easily fall into worry and fear when we have new challenges to face. When David was facing Goliath, he remembered the lion and the bear he had already slain with God's help. Because he remembered what God had done, he had no fear of his situation with Goliath.

Are you facing something right now that looks like a giant in your life? If so, remember God's goodness, be thankful for what He has done before, and choose to believe He can do it again. Write down three things that God has done for you in the past and focus on them instead of your problem. Nothing is impossible for God. Take some time to think about and talk about God's miraculous work. Then you will find courage filling your heart.

Prayer of Thanks

With all my heart, I thank You, Father, for the wonders You
have done in the past. And today, I stand in faith, believing
that You will work mightily in my life once again. Thank You for
being the same yesterday, today, and forever.

God Does Not Forget You

...Yes, they may forget, yet I will not forget you. Behold, I have indelibly imprinted (tattooed a picture of) you on the palm of each of My hands; [O Zion] your walls are continually before Me.   ISAIAH 49:15–16

Our faith increases when we understand that God remembers us. We can be grateful that we are never forgotten. He keeps one eye on us all the time. It doesn't matter if others have forgotten us or abandoned us; what really matters is that God never will. He remembers all of our prayers. He keeps our tears in a bottle, and does not forget the cry of the humble, poor, and afflicted (see Psalm 56:8; 9:12).

We may never understand why some difficult things happen the way they do, but no matter what happens, God is still God and He has not forgotten you. He has your picture tattooed on the palm of His hand!

Prayer of Thanks

When I realize, Father, that You will never forget me, my heart is filled with gratitude. I'm thankful that I'm always on Your mind and that You have a wonderful plan for my life.

The Value of Self-Control

Live discreet (temperate, self-controlled), upright, devout
(spiritually whole) lives in this present world.   TITUS 2:12

As believers in Jesus Christ, God has given us a new nature, but
at the same time, we also have to deal with the old nature. When
we allow the old nature to rule, we follow feelings, when in reality, we should operate in self-control. Self-control is a fruit of our
new nature and, thankfully, it is something that can be developed.
Much like we build muscles by using them, we can develop self-
control by using it.

Freedom in Christ is a gift to be thankful for, and exercising
self-control is a form of freedom, not a type of bondage. You don't
have to do what you feel like doing. You're free to do what you
know is wise. Discipline and self-control will help you be what
you say you want to be but never could be without the help of
God's guidance and grace.

Prayer of Thanks
Father, I am so thankful that I don't have to be ruled by
emotions or impulses. Thank You that, with Your help, I can
live a self-controlled, overcoming life in Christ.

Your Emotions Don't Have a Vote

If any of you is deficient in wisdom, let him ask of the giving God
[Who gives] to everyone liberally and ungrudgingly, without
reproaching or faultfinding, and it will be given him.

JAMES 1:5

Learn not to ask yourself how you *feel* about things, but instead
ask yourself if doing or not doing something is right for you. This
is wisdom, and wisdom is a gift from God to be thankful for. You
can choose to live by wisdom and decide to do what you know is
right.

There may be a certain thing you want to do badly. It might be a
purchase you want to make that you know you cannot afford. Your
feelings vote yes, but your heart says no. Tell your feelings they
don't get to vote. They are too immature to vote and will never vote
for what is best for you in the long run. Don't let emotions rule
your life and you will enjoy life more.

Prayer of Thanks

I am grateful, Father, that You give me the wisdom I need to
make healthy, life-giving choices. Instead of giving my emotions
the final say, I am going to look to You and to Your Word for
direction in my life. Thank You that Your Word is a lamp unto
my feet and a light unto my path.

Getting the Most Out of Your Marriage

Do to others as you would have them do to you.   LUKE 6:31 NIV

I wonder how many millions of people think, *I just don't feel the way I once did about my spouse. I wish I still felt excited about our marriage—that the romantic feelings would come back.* This is when we need to remember: wishing does not do any good; only action changes things.

If you don't feel you are getting anything out of your marriage, perhaps you are not putting enough into it. We usually give our spouses the unfair and unrealistic responsibility of making us happy rather than being grateful for them and choosing to make them happy. In the process, selfishness causes both of you to be unhappy. But you can change that! If you want your marriage or any other relationship to improve, just start being grateful for that person and try to bless them every chance you get.

Prayer of Thanks

Father, thank You for my spouse and for their unique gifts and abilities. Help me to appreciate them and focus on their strengths. Today, I choose to be a blessing and let You take care of everything else.

Let Peace Lead the Way

... To all of you that are in Christ Jesus (the Messiah), may there be peace (every kind of peace and blessing, especially peace with God, and freedom from fears, agitating passions, and moral conflicts).   1 PETER 5:14

The Bible teaches that God will lead us by the presence of peace. Thankfully, peace is the umpire in our lives that lets us know if we are in God's will or out of it. You will not experience peace if God is leading in one direction and you are pulling in another; you will feel frustrated and conflicted.

God will not force you to do what is right, but He will show you what to do if you seek Him and ask for His guidance. Then He will leave the choice to you. If you make right choices, you will reap good results that will cause you to be extremely grateful.

If you really want change in your life, take the step to follow God even if doing so is difficult for you. Be led by peace and trust that His plan for your life is better than you could even imagine.

Prayer of Thanks

Thank You, Father, for Your peace that passes all understanding. When I listen for Your voice and follow Your instruction in my life, I know that I will live with a peace and joy beyond compare.

Are You Distracted or Determined?

*"Few things are needed—or indeed only one. Mary has chosen
what is better, and it will not be taken away from her."*

LUKE 10:42 NIV

In order to enjoy the present moment and the gifts it contains,
we need to have balanced attitudes toward work. Luke 10:38–42
tells the story of Jesus' visit to the home of two sisters, Mary and
Martha.

Martha was overly occupied and too busy (see Luke 10:40).
But Mary sat down at Jesus' feet and listened to what He had to
say. Martha was distracted with much serving; Mary was thankful
Jesus was there and was determined not to miss the beauty of the
present moment. And Jesus said that Mary made a better choice
than Martha did.

Jesus did not tell Martha not to work; He told her not to be
frustrated and have a bad attitude while she worked. Jesus wants
us to work hard, but He also wants us to be wise enough to realize
when we should stop all activity and not miss the miracle of the
moment.

Prayer of Thanks

*Thank You, Father, for the way You teach me to live my life
in balance. Help me to do the work You have given me to do
without letting it become a distraction to my relationship
with You. Thank You that I can enjoy moments at Your feet
each day.*

The Beauty of Praise

I will recount the loving-kindnesses of the Lord and the
praiseworthy deeds of the Lord, according to all that the Lord has
bestowed on us, and the great goodness to the house of Israel,
which He has granted them according to His mercy and according
to the multitude of His loving-kindnesses.   ISAIAH 63:7

One of the ways *Vine's Expository Dictionary of Old & New Testament Words* defines "praise" is *telling a tale* or *a narration*. In other words, praising God is simply recounting or telling aloud the great things He has done. Praise is beautiful because it magnifies the goodness of God and strengthens us and all those who hear us, enabling us to deal with some of the more unpleasant things in life.

If we are doing nothing more than sitting at lunch with a friend and speaking about some wonderful things God has done with gratitude in our hearts, we are praising Him. In fact, the Bible says God likes those conversations, and when He hears them, He gets out His book of remembrance and records them (see Malachi 3:16). He does not record our murmuring, grumbling, or complaining, but He records the words we speak when praise is on our lips. Talk to someone today about something good God has done for you!

Prayer of Thanks

Father, I am thankful that my relationship with You is
not a complicated list of religious rituals. I can praise You
simply by telling others about Your goodness. Thank You for
Your blessings in my life—I will praise You all day long.

Jesus Was Perfect for You

If we confess our sins, he is faithful and just and will forgive us our
sins and purify us from all unrighteousness.   1 JOHN 1:9 NIV

Perfectionism is fueled with the tyranny of the *shoulds* and *oughts*. It is the constant nagging feeling of never being good enough. We think things like, *I should pray better, read the Bible more, and be kinder.* We instinctively want to be pleasing to God, and we are deeply afraid we aren't. As a result, we believe God is disappointed with us because we don't measure up.

But the pathway to God is not perfection. Some people in a crowd asked what they needed to do to please God, and the answer Jesus gave was, "Believe in the One Whom He has sent ..." (John 6:29). More than anything, God wants us to trust Him and believe His Word. You can stop struggling to attain perfection and be thankful that you are righteous before God because of Jesus. You don't have to buy or earn God's love. It isn't for sale—it's free!

Prayer of Thanks
Father, help me to realize that I don't have to earn Your love
or approval. I thank You that I am acceptable in Your sight
because the sacrifice of Jesus has given me Your righteousness.
I will live my life to please You today, not because I have to earn
Your love, but because I want to show my love for You.

Growing in Maturity

Rather, let our lives lovingly express truth [in all things, speaking truly, dealing truly, living truly]. Enfolded in love, let us grow up in every way and in all things into Him Who is the Head, [even] Christ (the Messiah, the Anointed One).   EPHESIANS 4:15

God does not expect us to be perfect. In fact, it is precisely because we never could be perfect that He sent Jesus to save us and the Holy Spirit to help us in our daily lives. If we could do it by ourselves, we would not need help. Thankfully, Jesus came to forgive our imperfections and to wipe them away in God's sight. We actually are perfect through Jesus, but we can never be perfect in our own performance.

Jesus did say, "Be perfect, even as your Father in heaven is perfect" (Matthew 5:48 NLT), but study of the original language reveals that He meant that we should grow into complete maturity of godliness in mind and character. God is not disappointed that we have not arrived at manifesting perfect behavior, but He does delight in finding us growing into maturity.

Prayer of Thanks

Father, I am so thankful that You help me grow into spiritual completeness and maturity. I'm not perfect, but because of Your work, I thank You that I'm okay and I'm on my way!

God Is Good... all the Time

...No one is [essentially and perfectly morally] good—except
God only.   LUKE 18:19

God is good. Goodness is one of His many wonderful character
traits to be grateful for. And because goodness is part of His character, we can expect Him to respond in that way every time. God
is not good only sometimes; He is good all the time. He is good to
people who don't deserve it. He helps us even when we have done
dumb things, if we will just admit our mistakes and ask boldly for
His help.

We can always ask God for help: "If any of you is deficient in
wisdom, let him ask of the giving God [Who gives] to everyone
liberally and ungrudgingly, without reproaching or faultfinding,
and it will be given him" (James 1:5).

What good news! God will give us wisdom when we have
trials—He will show us the way out. Thankfully, all we need to
do is ask, and He will give without finding fault with us. Amazing!

Prayer of Thanks

Father, when I am in a situation where I need Your wisdom and
Your provision, I ask that You will provide exactly what I need.
I thank You that goodness isn't just something You display, it is
Your very nature. I love You, and I thank You for Your goodness
today.

The Apostle Paul's Thanksgiving List

Now thanks be to God for His Gift, [precious] beyond telling [His indescribable, inexpressible, free Gift]!   2 CORINTHIANS 9:15

Like Jesus, Paul thanked God for many things. He thanked Him that people received him as a minister. He thanked God for his partners. He thanked Him for the churches he founded. He thanked Him for the people in the churches.

In 2 Corinthians 2:14, Paul's grateful heart is on display when he says: *"But thanks be to God, Who in Christ always leads us in triumph [as trophies of Christ's victory] and through us spreads and makes evident the fragrance of the knowledge of God everywhere."*

Paul knew that it is by God's grace that we receive every good thing that He chooses to bestow upon us. We can follow Paul's example and dedicate our lives to giving thanks to God that He has made us trophies of Christ's victory.

Prayer of Thanks

I thank You, Father, for Christ's victory that makes my salvation and my life in You possible. Like Paul, I want to live each day thankful for Your power and wonderful work in my life. Help me to never forget Your grace is poured out to me.

A Contented Heart Is a Grateful Heart

But godliness with contentment is great gain.   1 TIMOTHY 6:6 NIV

Being content and being grateful go hand-in-hand. People who are discontent have never developed a habit of being appreciative and thankful for the daily blessings in their lives. Think about this: If you were in the hospital right now, you would be content with something as simple as sitting in your own home in your favorite chair, but when you were at home in your chair, perhaps you were not content then either. We always think we will be content when . . . but why not choose to be content right now?

Even if you don't have what you want or need right now, keep a positive attitude and remain hopeful. Be content with what God has given you, refuse to focus on what you don't have, love others, and stay hopeful concerning every area of your life.

Prayer of Thanks

I thank You, God, that You have given me so many daily blessings. Help me to be content and not to take any of them for granted. Even as I wait on You for the things I am praying for, I choose to be grateful for the blessings I live in each and every day.

God Meets all Your Needs Abundantly

So Abraham called the name of that place The Lord Will Provide.
And it is said to this day, On the mount of the Lord it will be
provided.   GENESIS 22:14

It is important to develop an abundant mind-set—one that
believes God will always provide whatever we need and is thankful in advance that He will do so.

All throughout Scripture, God promises to provide for His
children. In fact, in the Old Testament, one of the Hebrew names
of God is "Jehovah-Jireh," which means *The Lord Our Provider.*
You and I are God's children. He is our Father, and He delights
in providing for us just as natural parents delight in helping their
children.

Clearly, all the resources of heaven and earth are at our heavenly Father's disposal, so there is nothing we need that He cannot
provide. He loves us and wants to take care of us. In fact, there is
no one He would rather share His blessings with than His children. Start thanking God that everything you need is on its way to
you right now!

Prayer of Thanks

Father, I am so thankful that You are Jehovah-Jireh. Regardless
of how I feel or what my situation looks like, I will look to You
and thank You in advance that You will provide for my every
need in Your perfect timing.

Turning Any Situation
Around for Good

As for you, you thought evil against me, but God meant it for good,
to bring about that many people should be kept alive, as they are
this day.   GENESIS 50:20

Whatever may have happened to us in the past, it does not have
to dictate our future. Regardless of what people may have tried
to do to us, God can take it and turn it for good. Romans 8:28
(NIV) says, "In all things God works for the good of those who
love him..."

In Genesis 37–50, Joseph's brothers meant evil against him.
They devised a plan to destroy him by selling him into slavery in
Egypt. But in the end, Joseph became second in command to Pha-
raoh and was used by God to save many lives.

Whatever happens in your life, remember that God is on your
side. He will build your life, your reputation, your family, and your
career. Be thankful that He is with you, put your confidence in
Him, and prepare to be amazed at how He can turn every situation
around for His glory!

Prayer of Thanks

I am grateful, Father, that You can turn any and every
situation in my life around for good. Help me today to focus on
You rather than my past. And thank You that You can take even
the most painful parts of life and fashion something beautiful
from them.

The Heart of an Eagle

That is why I would remind you to stir up (rekindle the embers
of, fan the flame of, and keep burning) the [gracious] gift of
God, [the inner fire] that is in you.   2 TIMOTHY 1:6

Do you ever feel like an eagle in a chicken yard? You know in your
heart that there is much more within you than you are experienc-
ing and expressing in your life right now. You feel certain God has
a great purpose for your life—and you cannot escape or ignore the
inner urge to "go for it."

I encourage you today to fan the flame inside you. Fan it until
it burns brightly. Never give up on the greatness for which you
were created, and never try to hide your uniqueness. Instead, be
thankful for it, and be thankful that God has something special in
store. Realize your hunger for adventure is God-given; wanting to
try something new is a wonderful desire; and embracing life and
aiming high is what you were made for. You are an eagle!

Prayer of Thanks

Father, thank You for the dreams and desires You have placed
in my heart. Thank You that You have a destiny for me. Today,
I will dare to dream of all the wonderful things You have in Your
plan for my life.

Prayer Doesn't Have to Be Long

*Call to me and I will answer you and tell you great and
unsearchable things you do not know.*   JEREMIAH 33:3 NIV

The length of our prayers really makes no difference to God. All
that matters is that we pray the way He is teaching us to pray and
that our prayers are Spirit-led, heartfelt, thankful, and accompa-
nied by faith. Throughout the Bible, there are incredibly brief, but
powerful, prayers. Here are a few of them:

- Moses prayed for his sister: *"Heal her now, O God,
  I beseech You!"* (Numbers 12:13).
- Elijah prayed: *"O Lord my God, I pray, let this child's soul
  come back to him"* (1 Kings 17:21 NKJV).
- Jesus prayed: *"Father, forgive them, for they do not know
  what they do"* (Luke 23:34 NKJV).

There will be times when you'll pray longer prayers than others,
but there is no correlation between how many minutes or hours we
pray and whether God hears us. Just one word spoken to Him in
faith from a sincere heart can reach His heart and move His hand.

Prayer of Thanks

*Thank You, Father, that I can pray to You from my heart, no
matter how long or short that prayer may be. I am grateful that
I can just be myself when I'm with You.*

The Awesome Power of God

Let be and be still, and know (recognize and understand) that I
am God. I will be exalted among the nations! I will be exalted in
the earth!   PSALM 46:10

If we aren't careful, it is easy to lose sight of the greatness of God.
We tend to think of Him and His abilities from our limited perspective. But we must never forget that when the Lord rises up,
every knee shall bow and every tongue confess that Jesus Christ
is Lord, to the glory of God the Father (see Philippians 2:10–11).

We serve a great and mighty God, and we can be thankful that
His greatness is at work in our lives. I encourage you to spend
more time in worship and praise, and less time in planning and
trying to tell God what He needs to do. Thank Him for His goodness and the fact that His power is at work in your life.

Prayer of Thanks

Father, help me to realize just how powerful and mighty You
are. Thank You that no enemy can defeat You and nothing can
stop Your work or Your plan in my life.

Listening When God Speaks

*The sheep that are My own hear and are listening to My voice; and
I know them, and they follow Me.*   JOHN 10:27

It's important that we don't think that prayer and fellowship with
God is us doing all the talking. We can also spend time with Him
listening. Prayer is a two-way street. Not only does God hear us,
but thankfully, He speaks to us too.

A great exercise to practice while listening to God is to ask Him
if there is anyone He wants you to encourage or bless—then be
still and listen. You will be surprised at how quickly He responds.
He will fill your heart with godly thoughts and goals. You will
more than likely have some people come to mind and some creative ideas on how to bless and encourage them. These "ideas"
and "thoughts" are God speaking to you. God speaks in many different ways, but one thing is for sure: We will miss His voice if we
don't learn to listen.

God has ideas to present to you that you haven't even considered. Listen carefully to Him with a heart that is thankful for His
presence. Then follow the advice given in John 2:5—"Whatever
He says to you, do it."

Prayer of Thanks

*Father, I thank You that You still speak to Your people. I pray
that You will show me someone who needs encouragement
today. Thank You for speaking to me and allowing me to be a
blessing in someone's life.*

A Beautiful Exchange

God made him who had no sin to be sin for us, so that in him we might become the righteousness of God.

2 CORINTHIANS 5:21 NIV

The beautiful exchange that takes place when we give our lives to God is something we can always be grateful for. Salvation means that we offer God what we have, and He gives us what He has.

He takes all of our sins, faults, weaknesses, and failures, and gives us His ability, His righteousness, and His strength. He takes our diseases, and sicknesses, and gives us His healing and health. He takes our messed-up, failure-filled past and gives us the hope of a bright future.

In ourselves we are nothing; our own righteousness is like filthy rags or a polluted garment (see Isaiah 64:6). But in Christ, we have a future to be thankful for—one worth looking forward to. The term "in Christ" very simply means that we have placed our faith in Him concerning every aspect of our lives. We are in covenant with Almighty God. What an awesome thought!

Prayer of Thanks

Father, when I am feeling inferior or condemned, help me to remember who I am in Christ. Thank You that I'm forgiven, accepted, righteous, strong, and able because I am found in You.

God Can Use the Most Unlikely of People

For God selected (deliberately chose) what in the world is foolish
to put the wise to shame, and what the world calls weak to put the
strong to shame.   1 CORINTHIANS 1:27

God often chooses those who are the most unlikely candidates for the job. By doing so, He has a wide open door to show how His grace and power can change human lives.

Each of us has a destiny, and there is absolutely no excuse not to fulfill it. We cannot use our weakness as an excuse, because God says that His strength is made perfect in weakness (see 2 Corinthians 12:9). We cannot use the past as an excuse, because God tells us old things have passed away and all things have become new (see 2 Corinthians 5:17).

How God sees us is not the problem; often it is how we see ourselves that keeps us from succeeding. If you'll see yourself as God sees you, grateful for His transforming power, no obstacle can stop you from His purposes. You are recreated in God's image and resurrected to a brand-new life. Your destiny is just waiting for you to claim it!

Prayer of Thanks

I thank You, God, that You choose the weak things of the world
to shame the wise. Thank You that there is no excuse that can
keep me from fulfilling my destiny in You. My life is Yours; have
Your way through me.

Everybody Can Help Somebody

*See that none of you repays another with evil for evil, but always
aim to show kindness and seek to do good to one another and to
everybody.*   1 THESSALONIANS 5:15

Wishing for something does not produce the results we desire.
Whatever God leads you to do, aggressively pursue what needs to
be done to achieve those results.

I once heard a story about four people named Everybody, Somebody, Anybody, and Nobody. There was an important job to be
done, and Everybody was sure Somebody would do it. Anybody
could have done it, but Nobody did. Somebody got angry about
that because it was Everybody's job. Everybody thought Anybody
could do it, but Nobody realized that Everybody wouldn't do it.
In the end, Everybody blamed Somebody when Nobody did what
Anybody could have done.

The moral of the story is simple: If you see that something
needs to be done and you have the ability to do it, be thankful
for the opportunity God has given you and go be the change that
everyone else is waiting for.

Prayer of Thanks

*Father, I am so thankful for the strengths and gifts You have
given me. Show me what You want me to do, and help me go
after it with all my heart. With Your help, I know that I can
make a difference.*

Keep Moving Forward

*Wait and hope for and expect the Lord; be brave and of good
courage and let your heart be stout and enduring. Yes, wait for and
hope for and expect the Lord.* PSALM 27:14

If we are going to do anything great for God, and if we are determined never to give up on our dreams, we have to take chances;
we have to be courageous. When we face situations that threaten
or intimidate us, we need to pray for boldness and a courageous
spirit. Feeling fear is never a problem as long as we have more
courage than fear!

The spirit of fear will always try to keep us from going forward.
For centuries, the enemy has used fear to try to stop people, and
he is not going to change his strategy now. But thankfully, we can
defeat fear. We are more than conquerors through Him who loves
us (see Romans 8:37). Courage is not the absence of fear; it is
pressing forward while the feeling of fear is present. When you feel
afraid, ask God to strengthen you, be thankful that He will, and
move forward in His strength!

Prayer of Thanks

*Thank You, Father, for the gift of boldness. I am grateful for the
dreams You have given me and the determination to pursue
them. I choose to never give up on the dreams You have placed
in my heart.*

Stronger and Stronger in the Lord

. . . I will strengthen and harden you to difficulties, yes, I will help
you; yes, I will hold you up and retain you with My [victorious]
right hand of rightness and justice.   ISAIAH 41:10

Consider your life. Are there situations you now handle well that would have previously made you feel fearful and anxious? Of course there are. As you have been walking with God, He has been strengthening you and hardening you to difficulties—you can be thankful that you are stronger than you used to be.

In the same way, I can assure and encourage you that some of the things bothering you right now will not affect you the same way in five years. We often struggle when we do certain things for the first time, but after gaining some experience, that struggle is no longer present. We can press through obstacles and never allow circumstances to control us. Instead, trust the Lord and know that He is working in your life in every situation.

. *Prayer of Thanks*

Father, help me to learn from You in every situation I face. I
thank You that I am stronger than I used to be, and I thank
You that You are making me even stronger through my present
circumstances. I put my trust in You, knowing that nothing is
too difficult for You.

Grace and Thankfulness

For it is by free grace (God's unmerited favor) that you are
saved (delivered from judgment and made partakers of Christ's
salvation) through [your] faith. And this [salvation] is not of
yourselves [of your own doing, it came not through your own
striving], but it is the gift of God.   EPHESIANS 2:8

It's difficult—if not impossible—to be truly grateful and thankful
until we fully understand the grace of God. Grace is unmerited
favor, but it is also God's power made available to us so we can do
with ease what we could never do on our own. Once we grasp the
fact that every good thing we have comes to us by the goodness of
God, what is left for us but gratitude and thanksgiving?

It is hard to give credit to God when we think that we deserve
whatever we receive from Him. But it is hard not to give credit to
God when we know that we do not deserve anything we receive
from Him—it's all by His grace. Our lives should merely be a
thankful response to that.

Prayer of Thanks

Father, I am thankful for Your grace. Without Your grace for
my life, I would be without hope. But because of Your grace and
power, I am grateful that I can accomplish the plans that You
have for me.

The Opportunity to Show His Power

So he said to me, "This is the word of the Lord to Zerubbabel:
'Not by might nor by power, but by my Spirit,' says the Lord
Almighty."   ZECHARIAH 4:6 NIV

I was at war with myself for many years. I did not like myself and tried to change myself continually. The more I struggled to change, the more frustrated I became, until the glorious day when I discovered Jesus accepted me just as I was. He, and only He, could make me what He wants me to be.

Don't rate yourself as unusable just because you have some weaknesses. God gives each of us the opportunity to be one of His successes. Our weakness gives Him the opportunity to show His power and His glory.

Instead of wearing yourself out trying to get rid of your weaknesses, give them to Jesus and be thankful that He is going to demonstrate His strength in you. Take your eyes off what you think is wrong with you and look to Him. Draw strength from His boundless might. Let His strength fill up your weaknesses. You cannot successfully change yourself, but you can trust God to do it for you.

Prayer of Thanks
I thank You, Father, that I don't have to be frustrated in life,
trying to change myself in my own efforts. Help me today to
release my weakness to You, knowing that in my weakness,
You show Yourself to be strong.

Quick to Forgive

*Be gentle and forbearing with one another and, if one has
a difference (a grievance or complaint) against another, readily
pardoning each other; even as the Lord has [freely] forgiven you,
so must you also [forgive].*   COLOSSIANS 3:13

The world is filled with pain and hurting people; and my experience has been that hurting people hurts others. The devil works
overtime among God's people to bring offense, strife, and disharmony, but we can be thankful that God gives us a tool to disappoint and defeat the devil: We can be quick to forgive.

Forgiveness closes the door to Satan's attack so that he cannot
gain a foothold that might eventually become a stronghold. It can
prevent or end strife in our relationships with others. No wonder
Scripture tells us over and over that we are to forgive those who
hurt or offend us. Jesus made forgiveness a lifestyle, and He taught
us to do the same. This is essential to living a joy-filled life.

Prayer of Thanks

*Father, I am so thankful for the forgiveness You have given me
through Jesus and for the grace to be able to forgive others.
Regardless of what others have done to hurt or offend me, today
I choose to forgive those who have caused me pain. Thank You
for helping me to live out that forgiveness each new day.*

Accept Your Children for Who They Are

Rear them [tenderly] in the training and discipline and the counsel and admonition of the Lord.   EPHESIANS 6:4

Love and acceptance are the greatest gifts parents can give their children. Acceptance liberates our children and allows them to be who God designed them to be. Love sees the gifts in our children, thanks God for those gifts, and seeks to help them use those gifts for God's glory.

In order to have harmonious and positive relationships with our children, it is absolutely critical that—even when correcting them—we accept them for who they are and that we embrace their unique personalities. Love does not try to force our children to be what we want them to be. It helps them be what God wants them to be, and to overcome their weaknesses and thrive in using their strengths.

Prayer of Thanks

I thank You today, Father, for the children You have given me and the unique gifts and personalities each one has. Give me wisdom to raise them to the best of my ability for Your glory. I am so grateful that You have placed them in my life.

Change and Transition

For I am the Lord, I do not change; that is why you, O sons of Jacob, are not consumed.   MALACHI 3:6

Everything changes except God—we can be thankful that He is the constant, unchanging source of our lives. Letting all the changes around us cause us to be upset won't keep changes from occurring. People change, circumstances change, our bodies change, our desires and passions change. One certainty in this world is change.

Most changes take place without our permission. But thankfully, with the help of the Holy Spirit, we can choose to adapt. If we refuse to make the transition in our minds and attitudes, then we are making a huge mistake. Our refusal to adapt doesn't change the circumstances, but it does steal our peace and joy. Remember, if you can't do anything about it, cast your care upon the Lord (see 1 Peter 5:7) and trust that He will take care of you.

Prayer of Thanks

I am grateful, Father, that when everything seems to be changing and unsure around me, I can trust that You will never change. Help me to look to You instead of my circumstance. I thank You that You are the foundation of my life.

Following God One Step at a Time

*The steps of a [good] man are directed and established by the
Lord when He delights in his way [and He busies Himself with his
every step].*   PSALM 37:23

If you want God to use you, do not let the fear of failure stop you
from obeying Him as He leads you. Thankfully, God not only
sees where you are, He sees where you can be. He not only sees
what you have accomplished, He sees what you will do with His
help. God is always leading us to greater things and wants us to
look forward to the future. Don't fear the unknown because God
knows everything, and you are safe with Him.

Following God is often like walking in a fog. We can only see
one or two steps in front of us, but as we take those steps, the next
ones become clear. As we trust the Lord, we will have an exciting
journey that will make life adventurous and enjoyable—every step
of the way.

Prayer of Thanks

*Father, thank You that You are directing and establishing my
steps. I trust You to lead me one step at a time into the destiny
You have for me. Thank You that You have good things planned
for my life.*

Words Are Fuel for Emotions

He who guards his mouth and his tongue keeps himself from
troubles.   PROVERBS 21:23

Words fuel good moods or bad moods; in fact, they fuel our attitudes and have a huge impact on our lives and our relationships. If we speak positive and good things, then we minister life to ourselves. We increase the emotion of joy. However, if we speak negative words, then we minister death and misery to ourselves; we increase our sadness and our moods plummet.

But, thankfully, we can control what words we speak and the quality of our lives. Why not help yourself first thing every day? Don't get up each morning and wait to see how you feel and then talk about every feeling you have to anyone who will listen. If you do that, you are giving your emotions authority over you. Instead, get up praising God for His goodness in your life. Let words of thankfulness fuel a life of peace and joy.

Prayer of Thanks

Father, thank You that I can choose what kind of attitude I am
going to have by choosing to speak words of life each day. No
matter how I feel or what is going on around me, I'm going to
encourage and strengthen my spirit, not my flesh.

Thankful for the Process of Transformation

And all of us, as with unveiled face, [because we] continued to behold [in the Word of God] as in a mirror the glory of the Lord, are constantly being transfigured into His very own image in ever increasing splendor and from one degree of glory to another; [for this comes] from the Lord [Who is] the Spirit.

2 CORINTHIANS 3:18

Transformation doesn't happen overnight, and the process can seem very slow at times. But that doesn't change the fact that one of the benefits of living in a relationship with Jesus is the freedom to forget the past and move ahead into what God has for us.

When you are tempted to condemn yourself over the progress you think you should be making, turn your focus back on Jesus and be thankful that He is doing His work in your life in His perfect timing. Remind yourself, "God loves me and He has a good plan for my life. I haven't arrived yet, but I'm okay and I'm on my way!" Remember that through faith you have been made right with God, and even though you have not arrived at perfection, you are making progress.

Prayer of Thanks

Thank You, Father, that You are transforming my life in Your perfect timing. I trust You, and I choose not to feel condemned or frustrated anymore. You are at work in my life, and I am grateful for that.

God Has Good Things for You

He who did not withhold or spare [even] His own Son but gave
Him up for us all, will He not also with Him freely and graciously
give us all [other] things? ROMANS 8:32

Some people seem to have the idea that to be a Christian they have to give up everything they enjoy, but that is not true. God is love, He is good, and He wants us to enjoy good things. The Bible says God gives us all things ceaselessly to enjoy (see 1 Timothy 6:17). God loves us so much, He sent His Son, Jesus, to earth to take our sins and give us life, and life more abundantly (see John 3:16; 10:10). That's something to be forever grateful for! Anything God teaches us not to do is only for our benefit. We obey His commands for our own good according to the Word of God.

When we receive Jesus, we receive the kingdom of God within us, and that kingdom is righteousness, peace, and joy in the Holy Spirit (see Romans 14:17). We can choose to continue living with misery, depression, discouragement, fear, worry, anxiety, guilt, and condemnation, but Jesus wants us to receive freedom from those things. God doesn't want us carrying them around any longer. Through Jesus, we can live the joyful, overcoming, abundant life we were meant to live.

Prayer of Thanks

Father, help me to realize that You have nothing but good things
in store for my life. Thank You that even when You correct and
instruct me, You are showing me a better way to live. I am grateful
for Your goodness and the joyful life I can experience in You.

Failure or Stepping-Stone?

Blessed (happy, to be envied) is the man who is patient under trial and stands up under temptation, for when he has stood the test and been approved, he will receive [the victor's] crown of life which God has promised to those who love Him.   JAMES 1:12

No one sets out or wants to fail. But "failure" can be an important stepping-stone on the way to success. Failure certainly teaches us what not to do, which is often as important as knowing what we are to do! Making failure positive is all about how we look at it. We can learn to be thankful for our failures.

Many stories have circulated about how many times Thomas Edison failed before he invented the incandescent light bulb. I have heard he tried 700 times, 2,000 times, 6,000 times, and 10,000 times. No matter how many attempts he made, the number is staggering. But he never gave up. Edison is reported to have said that in all his efforts, he never failed—not once; he just had to go through many, many steps to get it right! It takes that kind of determination if you are really going to do anything worthwhile.

Prayer of Thanks
Father, I am thankful that You can take even the failures in my life and do something amazing with them. I believe in faith that You are doing something powerful in my life. I thank You in advance for what I'm learning, even in the tough times.

Developing Godly Courage

*Seek the Lord and His strength; yearn for and seek His face and to
be in His presence continually!*   1 CHRONICLES 16:11

Giving in to a fear of failure will surely keep you from reaching
your full potential in life. The good news is, you have no reason to
fear failure. First of all, God is with you. And second, there is no
such thing as failure if you simply refuse to quit.

Every time you are tempted to fear, be thankful for the times
God has been with you and helped you in the past, and remember
that He is with you now. He will not fail you or forsake you. He is
your God; He will help you and hold you in His hand. He is hardening you to be able to face difficulties. He is building in you the
strength, stability, and character you need to press through to the
good things He has in store for you, and He is developing in you
the courage to never give up.

God may allow us to go through difficulties in order to stretch
and expand our capacity for faith. If you have great faith in God,
you will be able to accomplish great things in your life.

Prayer of Thanks

*Father, when I am in a situation where I begin to feel the fear
of failure, I thank You that I don't have to give in to that feeling.
I choose to stand firm instead of run. Thank You that You are
with me and I have nothing to fear.*

Getting Off the Performance Treadmill

In this the love of God was made manifest (displayed) where
we are concerned: in that God sent His Son, the only begotten
or unique [Son], into the world so that we might live through
Him.   1 JOHN 4:9

As long as we are on what I call the "performance treadmill," we will inevitably suffer with disappointment in ourselves. We will feel that we have not performed as expected. We did not get an A on our spiritual tests, we fell short of our goals, we lost our tempers, and now we are disappointed with ourselves, and we are sure that God is disappointed too.

The truth that we can be grateful for is that God already knew that we wouldn't perform as expected when He chose to love us. And it is His love that is the basis for our relationship with Him, not our works. When our relationship with God is a solid foundation in our lives, we will be free to do the best we can, and not get stressed out about our imperfections. It's time to get off the treadmill and run in the freedom of His grace.

Prayer of Thanks

I thank You, Father, that You are not disappointed with me.
You knew what You were getting when You chose me. Thank
You for choosing me anyway and for loving me perfectly in the
midst of my imperfections.

Taking a Peace Inventory

*And He came and preached the glad tidings of peace to you who
were afar off and [peace] to those who were near.*

EPHESIANS 2:17

Do you enjoy a peaceful atmosphere most of the time? Are you thankful and able to keep your peace during the storms of life? Are you at peace with God? Are you at peace with yourself? These are important questions. It is good to take a "peace inventory," checking various areas of our lives to see if we need to make adjustments anywhere.

Jesus said He gave us His peace (see John 14:27). If He gives us His peace, we can gratefully walk in it and enjoy it. The minute we sense that we are losing our peace, we need to make a decision to calm down. I have found that the sooner I calm down, the easier it is to do so. If I allow myself to become extremely upset, it not only takes a toll on me emotionally, mentally, and physically, but it is more difficult to return to peace.

Jesus has provided peace for our lives, but we must appropriate it, not letting our hearts get troubled or afraid. We cannot just passively wait to feel peaceful. We are to pursue peace and refuse to live without it.

Prayer of Thanks

*Father, thank You for the gift of peace that You have given me.
As I do an inventory of my life, I choose to receive Your peace
and live in it each day. I am so grateful that with Your help I
can be at rest and enjoy Your peace.*

The Gift of Repentance

If My people, who are called by My name, shall humble themselves,
pray, seek, crave, and require of necessity My face and turn from
their wicked ways, then will I hear from heaven, forgive their sin,
and heal their land.   2 CHRONICLES 7:14

When I am headed in the wrong direction, I thank God for the ability to turn around and go in the right direction. That is actually what true repentance is. It is not just a feeling of being sorry, but also a decision to turn and go in the right direction from now on.

We get into trouble through making a series of wrong decisions, and with God's help, we will get our lives straightened out by a series of right decisions. It took more than a day to get into trouble, and it will take more than a day to get out.

Anyone who is ready and willing to make a real investment of time and right choices can see his or her life turn around for the better. God's mercy is new every day. He is waiting to give you mercy, grace, favor, and help; all you have to do is be thankful for that mercy and say "yes" to whatever God is asking of you.

Prayer of Thanks

Thank You, Father, for the new starts You provide in my life.
Help me realize when I do wrong, then help me repent and
begin again. I am so grateful for Your mercies that are new
every morning in my life.

Let God Change You

Create in me a clean heart, O God, and renew a right, persevering,
and steadfast spirit within me.   PSALM 51:10

When God shows us a fault, thankfully, He does not expect us to
fix it in our own strength. He only wants us to acknowledge it, to
agree with Him, to be sorry for it, and be willing to turn away from
it. He knows—and we need to know—that we cannot change ourselves. But He will change us if we study His Word and cooperate
with His Holy Spirit.

Change of all types is worth celebrating because it is required
for progress. The process may not bring joy, but later on it will
produce the peaceful fruit of righteousness that God desires and
that we can enjoy (see Hebrews 12:11). Give yourself permission
to lighten up, and don't be so concerned about your own perfection. Do what you can do, and let God do what you cannot do.

Prayer of Thanks

Father, help me to be open to Your refining work in my life. I
love You and I open my heart to receive Your instruction. Have
Your way in my life today. Thank You for changing me to be
more like You!

The Power of Laughter

*In the world you have tribulation and trials and distress
and frustration; but be of good cheer [take courage; be
confident, certain, undaunted]! For I have overcome the world.
[I have deprived it of power to harm you and have conquered it
for you.]*   JOHN 16:33

Praise God for laughter—what a wonderful gift! Laughter has tremendous power, and this is something everyone would be wise to do more of. We as Christians tend to be so anxious about everything—our sins, expecting perfection from ourselves, our personal growth, and trying to meet people's expectations. We can carry heavy burdens that Jesus never intended us to carry.

If we would just laugh a little more—*be of good cheer*, "cheer up"—we would find that a little bit of laughter makes our load much lighter. In the world we live in it is easy to find plenty to worry about, but we can choose to purposely find things to laugh about. Take every opportunity you can find to laugh and laugh and laugh!

Prayer of Thanks

*Father, I thank You that Your joy is my strength and that
laughter is a good medicine. Help me not to carry burdens that
You never intended me to carry. Help me to relax and enjoy the
power of laughter.*

God Cares for You

Casting the whole of your care [all your anxieties, all your worries, all your concerns, once and for all] on Him, for He cares for you affectionately and cares about you watchfully.   1 PETER 5:7

God cares about everything that concerns you, and He wants to personally take care of you. Don't make yourself miserable worrying about things that God wants you to release to Him. When we are anxious today about what may happen tomorrow, or things that happened yesterday, we waste the day God has graciously given us.

The next time you are tempted to get anxious or upset about something—especially about something in the past or the future—think about something God has done for you lately and choose to be grateful. Learn from God's goodness in your past and prepare for your future, but live in the present, remembering that no matter what happens, He always loves you and wants what is best for you.

Prayer of Thanks

Father, I am so thankful that You love me and You care about my life. Today, I choose to not let worry ruin what You have planned for me. I am going to remain grateful that You are with me and You will never leave me.

Get Ready to Get Involved

But he answered, "You give them something to eat."

MARK 6:37 NIV

One time, I was asking God to help a friend who was going through a very difficult time. She needed something, so I asked God to provide it. To my surprise, His answer to me was, "Stop asking Me to meet the need; ask Me to show you what you can do."

God wants us to be ready to get involved. He has blessed us with gifts, talents, and abilities. We need to not only be thankful for those things, but we need to use them to bless others.

As you go through your day, I encourage you to pray and watch for opportunities to do what you believe Jesus would do if He were still on earth in bodily form. If you are a Christian, Jesus lives in you now and you are His ambassador. Make sure you represent Him well. Be thankful for your blessings and look for ways to be a blessing to others around you.

Prayer of Thanks

Father, help me to see the needs of those around me. Thank You that You have blessed me in so many ways. Today I pray that You will show me ways I can share those blessings with others.

The Wonder of God's Mercy

Praised (honored, blessed) be the God and Father of our Lord
Jesus Christ (the Messiah)! By His boundless mercy we have been
born again to an ever-living hope through the resurrection of Jesus
Christ from the dead. 1 PETER 1:3

The mercy of God toward each of us is something that we can always be thankful for. Charles Spurgeon once said, "God's mercy is so great that you may sooner drain the sea of its water or deprive the sun of its light or make space too narrow, than diminish the great mercy of God."

Wow! Think about that. Can any one of us drain the sea? We might be able to drain a bathtub or a pool...but not the sea! That gives you an idea of God's immense mercy toward us.

Although God does hate sin, and injustice makes Him angry, He is not an angry God! He is full of mercy, not holding our sins against us. We can never do so much wrong that there is no more mercy left for us. Thankfully, where sin abounds, grace does much more abound.

Prayer of Thanks

Father, I am thankful for Your mercy in my life. Even when You
are displeased with my sin, I know that You love me and You
hear my prayer. Thank You that You forgive my sins and stand
ready to help me begin again.

Don't Get Stuck in a Moment

Restore to me the joy of Your salvation and uphold me with a
willing spirit.   PSALM 51:12

Your future has no room for your past, and I encourage you not to get stuck in a moment or a time frame in your life that is over. Millions of people miss today because they either refuse to let go of the past or they worry about the future. Things in life like abuse and pain—things that happened to me and to millions of others—are unfortunate to say the least. Such abuses are traumatic and they do affect us, but we can recover.

God is a Redeemer and a Restorer—that's something we can be thankful for every day. He promises to restore our souls. There is a beautiful hope in knowing that if we invite Him in and cooperate with His healing process, God will restore us and give us a lifetime of new, joy-filled, divine moments with Him.

Prayer of Thanks

Father, I thank You that I never have to live stuck in the past.
You are a Redeemer and a Restorer, and You want to bring
healing in my life. Thank You that my past is over and I have a
beautiful future to look forward to.

Your Perfect Heavenly Father

If you then, evil as you are, know how to give good and advantageous gifts to your children, how much more will your Father Who is in heaven [perfect as He is] give good and advantageous things to those who keep on asking Him!

MATTHEW 7:11

If someone had an angry father, it is quite natural to view Father God as angry too. Hopefully you are one of the blessed ones who had an awesome earthly dad, but for many, that is not the case.

Children who grow up with angry, absent, or abusive fathers often don't feel safe. They have a feeling of impending doom or danger hanging over them most of the time. But, thank God, your heavenly Father is different from earthly fathers. If your father was absent, you need to know that God will never leave you. If your father was abusive or angry, your heavenly Father wants to give you a double reward for your former trouble (see Isaiah 61:7).

No matter how unfaithful your father may have been to you, I urge you not to let it ruin your life. Make a decision to believe the truth that your heavenly Father is faithful and loves you dearly.

Prayer of Thanks

Father, I thank You that I can look to You to be the parent I never had. Help me to forgive the injustices I endured as a child, and help me to move on to a new, happy, and peaceful life with You. I am grateful that You are a perfect heavenly Father.

Made to Encourage Others

Therefore encourage (admonish, exhort) one another and edify
(strengthen and build up) one another, just as you are doing.

1 THESSALONIANS 5:11

One of the best things you can do for someone is encourage them
and build them up. Say something positive to the people around
you about who they are or how much you appreciate them. Or tell
them how much God loves them and wants to bless them. Encouragement is powerful. It makes people feel better in every way.

I remember one time when I got a text message from my young-
est son. All it said was, "I love you, Mommy!" At that moment, I
literally felt refreshed by his words. They gave me the extra dose of
strength I needed that day.

Think about the people you're going to be around today. Be
thankful that they are in your life, and ask God to help you speak
encouraging words to them. You might be surprised at what a difference it will make, not only for them, but for you too.

Prayer of Thanks

Father, as I am going through my day, I pray that You will show
me ways I can encourage and build people up. Thank You for
the opportunities You give me to make a difference in the lives
of others. I want to seize my opportunities today.

Wisdom and Revelation

I keep asking that the God of our Lord Jesus Christ, the glorious Father, may give you the Spirit of wisdom and revelation, so that you may know him better. I pray that the eyes of your heart may be enlightened in order that you may know the hope to which he has called you, the riches of his glorious inheritance in his holy people, and his incomparably great power for us who believe.   EPHESIANS 1:17–19 NIV

Rather than focus on negative things in life, the Bible teaches us to see good things in Christ with the "eyes of your heart." Ephesians 1:17–19 says that the Spirit of wisdom and revelation are important so we may:

* Have knowledge of God, or know God Himself. This is not knowledge gained through education, but revelation.
* Know the hope of our calling, the eternal plan of God and how we fit into it. We can be thankful that God has called us to be His sons and daughters, and as such, we have an inheritance.
* Know that revelation knowledge of God's power is available to us. We can do anything God asks us to do because of the greatness of His power.

Give thanks today that you can know God, have hope, and live in His power!

Prayer of Thanks

I thank You, Father, that You have given me hope in Christ Jesus. Today, I will focus on the good things in my life and listen for Your voice. Thank You that You lead and guide me in the wisdom and revelation of Your Word and Your Holy Spirit.

More Than Things

And my God will liberally supply (fill to the full) your every
need according to His riches in glory in Christ Jesus.

PHILIPPIANS 4:19

Many times, we think of needs in terms of the basic necessities
of life—food, shelter, clothing, and finances to purchase these
things. These represent our physical needs, but God created us to
need more than this. Our needs are varied.

We don't simply need money, nourishment, a roof over our
heads, and clothes to wear. We also need wisdom, strength,
health, friends, and loved ones; and we need the gifts and talents
and abilities to help us do what we are supposed to do in life. We
need many things, and thankfully, God is willing to meet *all* of our
needs as we obey and trust Him. We must believe that He wants
to provide for us and then develop an attitude of thanksgiving for
what He has done and is doing.

Prayer of Thanks

Father, I thank You today for the gift of Your provision. You
don't just meet some of my needs, You meet all of my needs.
Thank You for Your complete and total provision that carries
me through every day of my life.

Releasing the Weight of Worry

And who of you by worrying and being anxious can add one unit
of measure (cubit) to his stature or to the span of his life?

MATTHEW 6:27

It is one thing to know that we should not worry, but it is quite another to be thankful for that truth and then actually stop worrying. One of the things that helped me let go of worry was finally realizing how utterly useless it is. Let me ask you: How many problems have you solved by worrying? Has anything ever gotten any better as a result of you worrying about it? Of course not.

The instant you begin to worry or feel anxious, give your concern to God in prayer. Release the weight of it and totally trust Him to either show you what to do or to take care of it Himself. Prayer is a powerful force against worry. I'm reminded of an old gospel chorus called "Why Worry When You Can Pray?" When you're under pressure, it's always best to pray about your need instead of fretting or complaining about it.

Prayer of Thanks
Father, I thank You that I don't have to live a life full of worry. I
thank You that I can come to You in prayer the moment I begin
to worry about something and I can cast my care on You. Help
me make the wise choice to stop worrying and start trusting
You today.

Winning the Battle of the Mind

[Inasmuch as we] refute arguments and theories and reasonings and every proud and lofty thing that sets itself up against the [true] knowledge of God; and we lead every thought and purpose away captive into the obedience of Christ (the Messiah, the Anointed One).   2 CORINTHIANS 10:5

Satan has declared war on God's children, and our minds are the battlefield in which the war is won or lost. Satan loves to put wrong thoughts into our minds—thoughts that are not in agreement with God's Word—hoping we will meditate on them long enough for them to become reality in our lives. We can cast down those wrong thoughts and bring every thought captive into the obedience of Jesus Christ.

Be thankful that you can choose your own thoughts and that you are not a prisoner to whatever kinds of thoughts just fall into your mind. Think good things that agree with God's Word on purpose. Think about God's love for you and the good plan He has for your life. Think about how you can be a blessing to other people and how you can be a blessing to God by simply being available for Him to work through. Thinking right thoughts will close the door to wrong ones, and in the process, it also closes the door to the devil.

Prayer of Thanks

I thank You, Father, that I am Your child and I am greatly blessed. Today, I choose to think God-honoring thoughts, focusing on Your goodness in my life. I am grateful that I can choose what thoughts I am going to dwell on.

God Leads Us by Peace

*Now may the Lord of peace Himself grant you His peace (the
peace of His kingdom) at all times and in all ways [under all
circumstances and conditions, whatever comes]. The Lord [be]
with you all.*   2 THESSALONIANS 3:16

People often do things they don't have peace about, and then they
wonder why they have big messes in their lives. If we follow God's
Word and are thankful for His direction and leading, we will enjoy
blessed and peaceful lives. The Bible warns us that we will live in
turmoil if we follow our own will and walk in our own ways (see
Deuteronomy 28:15–33).

I hear people say things like this too often:

- "I know I shouldn't do this, but…"
- "I know I shouldn't buy this, but…"
- "I probably shouldn't say this, but…"

These words reflect an uncomfortable feeling deep inside, a
"knowing" that the action they are taking is not right or good for
them, but they won't surrender their wills to God's leading.

Thankfully, when we feel this lack of peace, we can decide to
release our plans and submit to God's good plan for our lives.

Prayer of Thanks

*I thank You, Father, that You lead me in peace. Help me be
sensitive to the leading of Your Spirit as You set the course for
my life. Thank You for the peace that comes with knowing You
are in control and You have a good plan for me.*

Learning to Expect God's Goodness

Every good gift and every perfect (free, large, full) gift is from above; it comes down from the Father.   JAMES 1:17

God delights in providing for His children. We must realize that He loves to bless us and simply learn to live with gratitude for His goodness. Here is a list of things to think and speak regarding God's provision in your life:

- All of my needs are met according to God's riches in Christ Jesus (see Philippians 4:19).
- God blesses me and makes me a blessing to others (see Genesis 12:2).
- I give and it is given unto me, good measure, pressed down, shaken together, and running over (see Luke 6:38).
- God richly and ceaselessly provides everything for my enjoyment (see 1 Timothy 6:17).
- I serve God, and He takes pleasure in my prosperity (see Psalm 35:27).

Prayer of Thanks

Father, I am grateful for Your abundant provision in my life. I am thankful that You provide for my every need. Help me to trust Your goodness in my life and learn to look to You first to meet my every need.

Expressing the Unconditional
Love of God

Hatred stirs up contentions, but love covers all transgressions.
                                                        PROVERBS 10:12

Thankfully, God does not require us to earn His love, and we must not require others to earn ours. We must realize that love is something we are to become; it is not something we do and then don't do. We cannot turn it on and off, depending on whom we want to give it to and how they are treating us.

Sometimes we pray to be able to love the unlovely, and then do our best to avoid every unlovely person God sends our way. Some people are sent into our lives for the sole purpose of being sandpaper to us. Not only do others have rough edges, but so do we. Learning to walk in love with unlovely people is an important tool God uses to develop our spiritual maturity.

Believe it or not, we should be thankful for all the difficult people in our lives because they help us: they sharpen and refine us for God's use.

Prayer of Thanks

Father, I am grateful for the chance to love people in the same unconditional way that You love me. Help me to love everyone—even those people who are difficult to get along with. I thank You that You are using them to sharpen and refine me for Your use.

Prayer Is Just Like Breathing

Also [Jesus] told them a parable to the effect that they ought always to pray and not to turn coward (faint, lose heart, and give up).
                                                          LUKE 18:1

Prayer can be like breathing—regular, easy, second-nature—and we can pray our way through life as part of the way we live. In fact, just as our physical lives are sustained by breathing, our spiritual lives should be maintained by praying.

We can pray out loud or we can pray silently. We can pray sitting down, standing up, or lying on the floor. We can pray while we are moving or while we are being still. We can pray while we are shopping, waiting for an appointment, participating in a business meeting, doing household chores, driving, or taking a shower. These are good times to offer prayers of thanksgiving. We can pray things like, "Thank You, Lord, for everything You're doing," or, "Praise God, I know You're with me in this situation." Prayer is simply talking with God and expressing your heart to Him, and that can be done anytime, anywhere.

Prayer of Thanks

Father, thank You for the gift of prayer. Regardless of what my day looks like, I am so grateful that I can take a moment to pray in every situation, confident that You hear and answer me.

The One with You Is Greater

Be strong and courageous. Be not afraid or dismayed before the
king of Assyria and all the horde that is with him, for there is
Another with us greater than [all those] with him.

2 CHRONICLES 32:7

The attitude you and I can have in the face of our problems is one
of peace and trust. Rather than looking at our past failures, our
present difficulties, or our future fears, we can look to the Lord,
thankful for His wisdom, strength, and power. We can remind
ourselves that no matter how many problems may be facing us,
the One who is with us is greater than all those opposing us.

If we depend totally on ourselves or on other people, we set
ourselves up for failure and disappointment. The best thing we
can do in any situation is lean on God. People may fail and disappoint us, but we can thank God that He will never fail us or
forsake us.

Prayer of Thanks

I am grateful, Father, that You will never fail me or forsake
me. Thank You for the relationships in my life, but help me to
remember to come to You for help before I go to any person. You
are my number one source of help and strength.

Grace, Grace, and More Grace

But where sin increased and abounded, grace (God's unmerited favor) has surpassed it and increased the more and superabounded.

ROMANS 5:20

We can never have a problem that is too big for the grace of God. If our problem gets bigger, thankfully, God's grace gets bigger too. If our problems multiply, so that we go from one to two to three or more, the grace of God also multiplies so that we are able to handle them.

No matter what our problems may be, or how many we are facing, we can put our faith in God to solve them. It just takes a grateful heart, confident that our God is big enough to handle whatever we face. What is impossible with man is possible with God.

If there is something that we are supposed to be doing, the Lord will give us the ability to do it. There is no way that He is going to lead us into a situation without empowering us to do what He has called us to do. Whatever you might be facing today, God's grace (enabling power) is yours, and you can do what is required through Christ Who is your strength.

Prayer of Thanks

Father, when I am faced with multiple problems at once, I thank You for Your grace that is sufficient for me. I am grateful that there is no problem, or amount of problems, too difficult for You.

How to Experience Real Change

Therefore we do not become discouraged (utterly spiritless,
exhausted, and wearied out through fear). Though our outer
man is [progressively] decaying and wasting away, yet our
inner self is being [progressively] renewed day after day.

2 CORINTHIANS 4:16

Change does not come through struggle, human effort without
God, frustration, self-hatred, self-rejection, guilt, or works of the
flesh. Change in our lives comes as a result of having our minds
renewed by the Word of God and by trusting God to work in us
according to His will. God, Who began a good work in you, will
complete it (see Philippians 1:6).

As we agree with God and really believe that what He says is
true, it gradually begins to manifest in us. We begin to think differently, then we begin to talk differently, and finally we begin to
act differently. This is a process that develops in stages, and we
must always remember that while it is taking place, we can be
thankful and have an attitude that says, "God is changing me little
by little, and I can enjoy myself while He is working."

Prayer of Thanks

Father, thank You for changing me and making me what You
want me to be. Thank You for completing the good work You
have begun.

Finding God's Will

Therefore do not be vague and thoughtless and foolish,
but understanding and firmly grasping what the will of the
Lord is.   EPHESIANS 5:17

Most Christians want to know God's will for their lives. Let me share with you what at least a portion of God's will is. I cannot tell you whether or not His will is for you to move to Minneapolis, or where you are to send your children to school, or whether you are supposed to get the lead role in the Easter play at church. But I can give you one absolutely certain way to know and obey God's will for your life: Be thankful.

Be thankful—all the time, no matter what you are going through. That's right; just keep a grateful heart in every circumstance. Sometimes thanksgiving comes easily while other times it is difficult, but if you will develop and maintain an attitude of thanksgiving, you'll be in God's will. How can I be so certain? Because 1 Thessalonians 5:18 says, "In everything give thanks; for this is the will of God in Christ Jesus for you" (NKJV).

Prayer of Thanks

I thank You today, Father, that even while I wait for the
specifics of Your will in my life, I can know Your broader will
for my life—to always be thankful. Today I choose to live in
Your will with a grateful heart, and I know You will reveal Your
purposes for my daily life.

Joy with Each New Step

. . . If only I may finish my course with joy.   ACTS 20:24

The apostle Paul wanted to be all God wanted him to be, and he desired to do all God wanted him to do—but he wanted to do it with joy. We should learn to be joyful about our progress, not depressed about how far we still have to go or oppressed by a legalistic attitude about it. We can be thankful for everything God has done and everything He is still going to do. We can learn to look at the positive, not the negative.

One of the side effects of a legalistic approach to God is that people can never be satisfied unless they keep all of the Law. If they fail in one point, they are guilty of all (see James 2:10). Life is sometimes filled with failure, disappointment, and frustration. But one of the benefits of our New Covenant relationship with Christ is the fact that we can be led by the Holy Spirit instead of rules, and we can be joyful during the journey. Our joy is not to be found in our performance, but in Jesus Himself.

Prayer of Thanks

Father, I am thankful that You give me joy for the journey. Even as I am learning and growing in You, I can experience joy each new day. Thank You that I don't have to live under the Law; I am living in Your grace and Your joy every step of the way.

The Best Relationship You Can Have

Behold, I stand at the door and knock; if anyone hears and listens
to and heeds My voice and opens the door, I will come in to him and
will eat with him, and he [will eat] with Me.   REVELATION 3:20

We have the great privilege of developing a relationship with God
and inviting Him to be a vital part of everything we do, every day.
That starts with simple prayer—just talking to Him and sharing
your life with Him as you go about the things you have to do. Be
thankful that His presence is with you, and include Him in your
thoughts, in your conversations, and in all your everyday activities.

When you let God out of the Sunday-morning box that many
people keep Him in, letting Him invade your Monday, Tuesday,
Wednesday, Thursday, Friday, Saturday, and all day Sunday as
well, you'll be amazed at what a difference it will make. Don't try
to keep God in a religious compartment; He wants to have free
access to every area of your life. He wants to be involved in every
part of your life. He desires an intimate relationship with you.

Prayer of Thanks

I thank You, God, that You love me enough to want to be in
relationship with me. I want to share every part of my life with
You. Help me to remember that You are with me every minute
of the day.

Secure Enough to Say "No"

Now am I trying to win the favor of men, or of God? Do I seek to
please men? If I were still seeking popularity with men, I should not
be a bond servant of Christ (the Messiah).   GALATIANS 1:10

Have you ever felt that you could not be everything that everybody wanted you to be? Have you ever known deep down inside
that you really needed to say "no" to a lot of people—but the fear
of displeasing them had your mouth saying, "I'll try," while your
heart was screaming, "I can't do it!"?

Sometimes, insecure people say "yes," when they really mean
"no." Those who succeed at being themselves don't allow others to
control them. They are led by a bold heart that knows God loves
them, not by the fear of displeasing others or being rejected by
them.

We should not get angry at people because they place demands
on us, because in reality it is our responsibility to order our lives.
Thankfully, we can be secure in Christ and bold enough to say
"no" to people when we know it is the right thing to do.

Prayer of Thanks

When I am in a situation, Father, where I am tempted to
overcommit to something or someone even though I don't have a
peace about it, help me to be secure enough to say "no." I thank
You that my security is found in You, not in pleasing others.

Developing Great Faith

And Jesus, replying, said to them, Have faith in God [constantly].
MARK 11:22

Little faith can become great faith as we use it. As we take steps to trust God, we experience His faithfulness and that, in turn, encourages us to have greater faith. As our faith develops and grows, our problems have less power over us and we worry less—that's something to be grateful for.

We can choose to think about what God can do instead of what we cannot do. If we continually think about the difficulty of our situation, we may end up in despair, and that means we feel unable to find a way out. We feel trapped, and then it is easy to panic and begin to do irrational things that only make the problem worse. But the Bible tells us that God always provides the way out (see 1 Corinthians 10:13). Even though you might not see the way out right now, one does exist and God will reveal it as you trust Him.

Prayer of Thanks

Father, I thank You that my faith can grow stronger as I put my trust in You. You are greater than any problem I will ever face. When I focus on You, I know that worry and despair will fade away. Thank You for Your faithfulness and Your work in my life.

What Does the Bible Say About It?

Now the Berean Jews were of more noble character than those in Thessalonica, for they received the message with great eagerness and examined the Scriptures every day to see if what Paul said was true.   ACTS 17:11 NIV

There are many things that influence our thoughts, and our own desire is one of them. I have discovered when I desire something in a strong way, it is easy for me to think God is telling me to get it. For this reason, we must always check to see if what we feel led to do lines up with the Word of God. God does often lead us by desire, but we want to be sure it is not merely fleshly desire.

Any idea, prompting, or thought that comes to us needs to be compared to the truth of Scripture. The Bible is written as a personal letter to each of us. God speaks to us, ministers to our needs, and directs us in the way we should go in His written Word. So if we think we have heard a word from God, we can check to see if it lines up with Scripture and be thankful that we have the infallible Word of God to live by.

Prayer of Thanks

Father, I am thankful for the truth of Your Word. When I feel a prompting in my spirit, I am grateful that I can make sure it lines up with Scripture. Today, I will listen for Your voice and live in accordance with what You tell me and what You have written in Your Word.

The Best Kind of Friends

The man of many friends [a friend of all the world] will prove himself a bad friend, but there is a friend who sticks closer than a brother.   PROVERBS 18:24

We can love everybody, but we cannot be close friends with everybody. People who are upset with you for wanting to move on with God are often those who do not want to go on with Him themselves. Choose to form close relationships with other Christians who share the same values you have. A mature believer in Christ can help you reach new levels of maturity, but a carnal believer may be used as a temptation to cause you to compromise your faith.

God is faithful in all areas, and thankfully, we can ask Him to give us friends who will add to our lives instead of subtract from them. Always be thankful for good friends, for they are indeed a gift from God.

Prayer of Thanks

Father, when I find myself feeling lonely, help me to remember that You will provide the people in my life who will be an encouragement to me. I thank You that You provide everything I need, including friends.

The Gratitude That Comes with Grace

But by the grace (the unmerited favor and blessing) of God I am
what I am, and His grace toward me was not [found to be] for
nothing (fruitless and without effect).   1 CORINTHIANS 15:10

If you and I think that we deserve what we receive from God because we have earned it by our good works—our great amount of prayer, our daily Bible-reading, our giving—then we are not going to be thankful or grateful. On the contrary, we are going to think that whatever blessing we receive is proof of our own personal holiness.

But when we understand that every blessing we receive is only because of the grace of God, and never because we deserve it, our hearts are transformed. We are filled with gratitude for the goodness of God. There is nothing that can cause us to overflow with thanksgiving and praise more than a revelation of the grace of God that has been freely poured out upon our lives.

Prayer of Thanks

Father, I am grateful today for Your goodness in my life. I
know that I haven't done anything to deserve it; You simply
bless me because You love me. Thank You for Your perfect,
unconditional love.

Let Your Light Shine

Let your light so shine before men that they may see your moral
excellence and your praiseworthy, noble, and good deeds and
recognize and honor and praise and glorify your Father Who is
in heaven.   MATTHEW 5:16

Before we purchase something, we like to check its quality. As
we shop, we read labels or we look for certain trademarks (brand
names) that have a reputation for being of good quality. That is
what people should be able to do with us as disciples of Christ.
Love is the trademark (distinctive sign or characteristic) of a
Christian. People should be able to identify us not only by what we
say, but by how we behave.

As believers, we have a great opportunity to show the world
who Jesus is. We do that by walking in His love—the love of the
Father that was revealed and expressed in His Son Jesus and is
now manifested in us. The Word says, "*Let your light so shine before*
men," and nothing shines brighter than love. Keep in mind that
you have the privilege of personally representing Jesus, and be
thankful that He will use you to draw people to Him.

Prayer of Thanks

Father, thank You for the example Jesus gave us of how to love
others. And thank You for the opportunity I have to share Your
love with everyone I come into contact with today. Help me
shine brightly in a dark world.

But What if I Miss God?

And your ears will hear a word behind you, saying, This is the way;
walk in it, when you turn to the right hand and when you turn to
the left.   ISAIAH 30:21

Sometimes we experience hesitation in life because we are afraid we might "miss God," or do something wrong as we try to follow Him. Let me encourage you by telling you that if you miss God's will for you somehow, you don't have to worry—He'll find you. I think we all get lost in life at times and need the mercy of God to show up and get us back on the right track. Today, you can thank God that He is faithful to straighten out any crooked path in front of you.

If you are afraid of making wrong decisions about your direction in life, all you have to do is remember how much God loves you and look at the testimonies of the people who have gone before you. The Bible is full of miraculous stories of God's guidance and provision.

When we take a step of faith after praying and seeking God, if we *do* make a mistake, then God will help us get back on track. Thankfully, God can make that so-called mistake somehow work out for our good.

Prayer of Thanks

I thank You, Father, that You see my heart. If I miss Your voice
and Your direction in my life, I thank You that You'll find me
and get me going in the right direction. I trust Your guidance
and I choose today not to live in fear of missing You.

The Strength to Deal with Change

The name of the Lord is a strong tower; the [consistently] righteous man [upright and in right standing with God] runs into it and is safe, high [above evil] and strong.   PROVERBS 18:10

Many people don't like change. Former U.S. president Woodrow Wilson said, "If you want to make enemies, try to change something."

Often when we grow weary or simply become bored with a situation, we get restless and begin to pray: "Oh, God! Something has to change!" Then, when God tries to bring change into our lives, we say, "Lord, what are You doing? I don't think I can take this change!" We often find ourselves caught in the tension between wanting change and fearing change.

Thank God, He never changes. Because He is always the same, we can trust Him through any changing circumstances or situation (see Hebrews 13:8, Malachi 3:6). This should give us great courage and comfort when we face changes in our lives. We do not need to fear change; we can handle it, because God remains the same.

Prayer of Thanks

Father, I am so thankful that I don't have to fear change. You never change and You are my strong tower. I stand on the firm foundation of Your Word and I will live in peace, even when things are changing all around me.

Praying a "Right Now" Prayer

And this is the confidence (the assurance, the privilege of boldness)
which we have in Him: [we are sure] that if we ask anything (make
any request) according to His will (in agreement with His own
plan), He listens to and hears us.   1 JOHN 5:14

We often hear about a prayer need or think about a situation and say to ourselves, *I need to pray about that later when I pray.* That thought is a stall tactic of the enemy. Why not pray right that minute? Procrastination is one of the major things that the devil uses to keep us from ever doing the right thing. Never put off until later what you can do right now!

Prayer would be easy if we just followed our hearts, but Satan wants us to procrastinate because he is hoping that we will forget the matter entirely.

A grateful heart is already focused on the Lord and ready to pray at any moment. Praying as we sense the desire or need to pray is easy to do, and it is the way we can pray continually and stay connected to God in every situation throughout the day.

Prayer of Thanks

Father, I thank You for the power of prayer. When there is a
prayer need that comes to my attention, I'm going to talk to You
about it immediately. Thank You that You are always ready to
hear my prayer.

Humbly Leaning on the Lord

For God sets Himself against the proud (the insolent, the
overbearing, the disdainful, the presumptuous, the boastful) [and
He opposes, frustrates, and defeats them], but gives grace (favor,
blessing) to the humble.   1 PETER 5:5

Humility is knowing we cannot succeed by trusting in ourselves and our own human effort. Instead, we trust in God, thankful that He does what we cannot. As we follow the leading of the Holy Spirit and lean on Him at all times, He always equips us to do what we should be doing. Most human failure comes from people trying to do things in their own strength without relying on God.

I have found that when I feel frustrated, it is because I am exerting fleshly effort trying to do something that only God can do. I suggest that when you feel frustrated that you stop and ask yourself if you are doing the same thing. Works of the flesh equal frustration, and works of the flesh mean that I am working without God.

We can live the joyful, overcoming life God has for us when we realize God helps those who know they cannot help themselves—those who realize they are totally dependent on Him and are grateful that He will provide everything they need.

Prayer of Thanks

Father, I am thankful that I do not have to depend on my own strength or best effort to get through life. Thank You that You are here to guide me and help me each day. I trust You and I place my life in Your hands.

Laying Down Your Life

Anyone who loves his life loses it, but anyone who hates his life in this world will keep it to life eternal. [Whoever has no love for, no concern for, no regard for his life here on earth, but despises it, preserves his life forever and ever.]   JOHN 12:25

When we believe God is asking us to do something, we often begin with the questions: *What am I going to have to give up if I do this? If I do this, what will it cost me? If I do this, how uncomfortable am I going to be?*

The truth is that anything we do for God requires an investment. Part of loving Him involves a willingness to lay our lives down for Him. If God has been asking you to do something and you have been procrastinating because you know it will require sacrifice on your part, I urge you to go ahead and do it. Nothing feels better than knowing you have fully obeyed the Lord.

Do not be afraid of sacrifice when God calls you or puts something in your heart that He wants you to do. His plan for your life is greater than anything you can imagine. Be thankful that His plan is best and determine that you will pay the price and pass the test. I assure you, it is worth it.

Prayer of Thanks

I thank You today, Father, that no sacrifice I make for You will ever be without great benefit for my life. Fill me with the faith and strength to do all that You call me to do. I choose to obey Your voice in every single area of my life.

Going Through Is Better
Than Getting Stuck

When you pass through the waters, I will be with you, and through
the rivers, they will not overwhelm you. When you walk through
the fire, you will not be burned or scorched, nor will the flame
kindle upon you.   ISAIAH 43:2

We will all go through trying situations in life, some more difficult than others. Many times, we think the phrase "I'm going
through something" is bad news, but if we view it properly, we
realize *going* through is good; it means we are not stuck! We may
be facing difficulties, but we can be thankful that at least we are
moving forward.

We will face a variety of things, but those things we go through
are the very circumstances, challenges, and situations that make
us people who know how to overcome adversity. We do not grow
or become strong during life's good times; we grow when we press
through difficulties without giving up. When we do what we know
is right even when it is difficult, uncomfortable, or inconvenient,
we grow spiritually and we are strengthened.

Prayer of Thanks
I am grateful, Father, that even when times are tough, I can
depend on You to carry me through. I am grateful that I can
face any challenge because You are with me.

The Expectation of Joy

You will show me the path of life; in Your presence is fullness of joy,
at Your right hand there are pleasures forevermore.

PSALM 16:11

Joy in life is a wonderful thing to have. We may want to see changes in our circumstances, but we don't have to allow unpleasant situations to make us miserable. We can be grateful that joy makes some of those less-desirable circumstances more bearable. Even when you are going through something that is difficult, you can release joy in your life by *expecting* something good to happen.

Joy can vary in intensity from calm delight to extreme hilarity. It is closely connected to our expectations (what we think and believe). One meaning of joy is: "The passion or emotion excited by the acquisition or expectation of good."* In other words, our joy is affected by how much we expect good things to happen to us. Don't fear or expect bad things to come your way. Pray, believe, and expect God's best for your life—then watch your joy increase.

Prayer of Thanks

Father, I thank You for Your joy. Today I will live in a faithful
expectation of Your goodness in my life. I will rejoice in Your
love and Your faithfulness.

---

* American Dictionary of the English Language, 1st ed. Facsimile of Noah Webster's 1828 edition, permission to reprint by G. & C. Merriam Company, copyright 1967, 1995 (renewal), by Rosalie J. Slater, s.v. "joy."

Exercising the Muscle of Self-Control

Make every effort to add to your faith goodness; and to goodness,
knowledge; and to knowledge, self-control; and to self-control,
perseverance; and to perseverance, godliness.

2 PETER 1:5–6 NIV

One of the biggest mistakes we make is to think we have no control over how we feel or what we do. God has given us a spirit of discipline and self-control, and it is called *self*-control because God gives us this tool to control ourselves. We all have it, but do we use it?

Anything we have but never use becomes dormant and powerless. Do you work out regularly? Why do you do that? You exercise to keep your bones and your muscles strong—to guard your health. Thankfully, God has given us self-control, and we can use it to guard our spiritual, emotional, and physical health. But we have to use that muscle in order for it to work properly. When we do, we begin to experience a new level of strength that only self-control can bring. Self-control is your friend, not your enemy. It helps you be the person you truly want to be.

Prayer of Thanks

Father, thank You that I have self-control. Help me to live a
self-controlled life and follow Your Spirit rather than my flesh.
Thank You that with Your help, I can have victory over the flesh
and live in the freedom of Your Spirit.

Talk Yourself into a Better Mood

*Death and life are in the power of the tongue, and they who
indulge in it shall eat the fruit of it [for death or life].*

PROVERBS 18:21

The words you say determine much of your attitude and outlook
on life. If you will make a decision that you are going to say as
little as possible about your problems and disappointments in life,
they won't dominate your thoughts and your mood. It's time we
stopped focusing on our problems and started focusing on the
goodness of God.

If you talk as much as possible about your blessings and hopeful expectations with a thankful attitude, your frame of mind will
match them. Be sure each day is filled with words that fuel love,
peace, and joy, not anger, depression, bitterness, and fear. Talk
yourself into a better mood! Find something positive to say in
every situation, remaining thankful for the blessings of God that
are all around you.

Prayer of Thanks

*Thank You, Father, for every blessing You have given me. I
choose to focus on You and Your provision in my life, rather
than focusing on my problems or needs. I know that You are
going to provide for me, and so I will keep my focus, my faith,
and the words I speak centered around You.*

The First Step in Planning

A man's mind plans his way, but the Lord directs his steps and
makes them sure.   PROVERBS 16:9

Many times we make a plan, and then pray for it to work. But God
wants us to pray first and ask Him for His plan. After we have
His plan, then He wants us to trust Him to bring it to pass. We
can live with an attitude of praise and thanksgiving, knowing that
God's plans always succeed.

Activity birthed out of the flesh, our own effort without God,
actually prevents God from showing Himself strong in our lives.
The Bible describes that kind of activity as "works of the flesh."
I've come to realize that works of the flesh are "works that don't
work." That is not the way to live the higher life that God has prepared for us. Pray first, ask God for His plan, and trust Him to
work in your life.

Prayer of Thanks
Father, thank You for the gift of prayer. Instead of leaning on
my understanding today, I am going to come to You first and
ask that You show me Your plan for today and for my life.

Refusing to Strike Out

*What then shall we say to [all] this? If God is for us, who [can be]
against us? [Who can be our foe, if God is on our side?]*

The story is told of a little boy who was overheard talking to himself in his backyard. He was wearing a baseball cap and carrying a ball and bat: "I'm the greatest hitter in the world," he announced. Then he tossed the ball into the air, swung at it, but missed. "Strike one!" he yelled. He picked up the ball and said again, "I'm the greatest hitter in the world!" He tossed the ball into the air. He swung again and missed. "Strike two!" he yelled. He straightened his cap and said one last time, "I'm the greatest hitter in the world!" He tossed the ball up into the air and swung at it. He missed. "Strike three! Wow!" he exclaimed. "I'm the greatest *pitcher* in the world!"

A thankful, positive, never-give-up attitude will change your outlook and change your life.

Prayer of Thanks

*Father, help me to see life in a new way. I thank You that
because You are with me, I never have to feel like a failure
again. You have a plan for my life. If I swing and miss, it just
means that You have something better in store.*

Standing Firm

Therefore put on God's complete armor, that you may be able to resist and stand your ground . . . and, having done all [the crisis demands], to stand [firmly in your place]. Stand therefore [hold your ground].

EPHESIANS 6:13–14

Faith stands firm, but fear takes flight and runs away. We are letting fear rule us if we run from what God wants us to confront. When the Israelites were afraid of Pharaoh and his army, God told Moses to tell them to "fear not; stand still . . . and see the salvation of the Lord" (Exodus 14:13).

We will never see or experience God's delivering power if we run from things in fear. Stand still and see what God will do for you. Trust Him, be thankful for His faithfulness, and give Him a chance to show His power and goodness to you.

When fear knocks on the door, send faith to answer. Don't speak your fears; speak faith. Say what God would say in your situation—say what His Word says, not what you think or feel.

Prayer of Thanks

Help me, Father, to stand firm when I feel anxious or afraid. I thank You that because You are with me, I have nothing to fear. Today, I will choose to stand firm rather than shrink back when I feel fear in my life.

Strength and Weakness

*When the righteous cry for help, the Lord hears, and delivers them
out of all their distress and troubles.* PSALM 34:17

We all have some strengths and some weaknesses. This is true
even of the people we read about in the Bible. Paul wrestled with
his weaknesses (see 2 Corinthians 12:9), but he learned to be
grateful for them because through them, he discovered Christ's
strength and grace would be sufficient.

If we want to fully enjoy the life God has given us, we must
realize Christ's grace is sufficient for our weaknesses too—and be
grateful that it is! With the help of the Holy Spirit, we can know
who we are in Christ and not be condemned because of our weaknesses. Lean on the Lord, and trust that His grace and strength
are far greater than our weakness.

Prayer of Thanks

*Father, I am so thankful that in my weaknesses You show
yourself strong. Your strength and Your grace are sufficient for
me just as they were for Paul. Thank You for Your daily strength
in my life.*

Don't Get Distracted, Simply Pray

You shall not need to fight in this battle; take your positions,
stand still, and see the deliverance of the Lord . . . Fear not nor
be dismayed. Tomorrow go out against them, for the Lord is
with you.   2 CHRONICLES 20:17

Many times God tells us to do something or gives us an assignment and we begin doing it. But then the enemy comes against us, and when we turn to fight him, we turn away from God. Suddenly, the enemy has all our attention. We spend our time fighting him instead of praying and asking God to intervene.

I want you to know this: The enemy is really not your problem; he is God's problem. You will waste your time if you turn your attention away from your God-given assignments and opportunities and begin to focus on the enemy.

Satan knows that if he can distract you, he can ultimately defeat you. God is your defender; He promises to fight your battles for you. So when the enemy begins to stir up a storm in your life, be thankful God has the victory and do these simple things: pray and trust God.

Prayer of Thanks

Father, thank You for the power of prayer. Instead of trying to
fight my own battles, I turn them over to You today. I am so
grateful that, when the enemy comes in like a flood, I am more
than a conqueror through You (see Romans 8:37).

The Resurrection Side of the Cross

I want to know Christ—yes, to know the power of his resurrection
and participation in his sufferings, becoming like him in his death.

PHILIPPIANS 3:10 NIV

We can learn to live on the resurrection side of the cross. Jesus wasn't just crucified; thankfully, He was raised from the dead so that we might no longer be stuck in sin, living lowly, wretched, miserable lives.

Often we see a crucifix in a church with Jesus hanging on it. I know it is done to remember and honor Him, and I am not against it, but the truth is that He is not on the cross any longer. He is seated in heavenly places with His Father, and He is enjoying resurrection living.

We can thankfully celebrate that Jesus came to lift us out of the ordinary, out of negative thinking, guilt, shame, and condemnation. He came to take our sin to the cross and defeat it. It has no power over us any longer because we are forgiven—the penalty has been paid. We can live on the resurrection side of the cross and be seated in heavenly places with Him through faith.

Prayer of Thanks

Father, help me to experience the resurrection power of Jesus
in my life. Thank You that Jesus conquered sin and death,
and because Your Spirit lives in me, I can live an overcoming,
victorious life too.

Happiest When Helping

And God is able to bless you abundantly, so that in all things
at all times, having all that you need, you will abound in every
good work.   2 CORINTHIANS 9:8 NIV

A study on the principle of the Golden Rule was conducted by
Bernard Rimland, director of the Institute for Child Behavior
Research. Each person involved in the study was asked to list 10
people he knew best and to label them as happy or not happy.
Then they were to go through the list again and label each one
as selfish or unselfish. Rimland found that all the people labeled
happy were also labeled unselfish. "The happiest people are those
who help others," he concluded.

God gives us the ability and opportunities to help others all
throughout the day. When we take the time to be a blessing, it
causes us to focus less on what we don't have, feel grateful for
what we do have, and experience a new level of joy in the process.
Don't let a day go by without helping someone.

Prayer of Thanks

Father, I am thankful that You give me opportunities every
day to be a blessing to others. You've blessed me with so much.
I want to use what You have given me to bless someone else
today.

God Is in Love with You

In this is love: not that we loved God, but that He loved us and
sent His Son to be the propitiation (the atoning sacrifice) for
our sins.   1 JOHN 4:10

The Bible is a record of God's amazing grace and love. The heroes
we admire were people just like us. They failed miserably at times,
and yet they found love, acceptance, forgiveness, and mercy as free
gifts from God. His love drew them into intimate relationships
with Him, empowered them to do great things, and taught them
to enjoy their lives.

We can be grateful that just as they experienced that acceptance, we can experience it too. God doesn't approve of sin, but
He does love sinners and will continue to work with us toward
positive change.

Don't waste years living with a fear that God is angry with you.
Thankfully, you can receive the amazing, passionate love of God
and know that He is not disappointed with you as long as you
continue to believe in Him. Your faith pleases Him, and it is what
He requires (see John 6:28–29). God loves us because He chooses
to and not because we deserve it. Be thankful today that you are
loved unconditionally!

Prayer of Thanks

I thank You, Father, that You love and accept me. I can look
into Your Word and see that You used men and women who
were flawed and imperfect. If You could use them, I know that
You can use me too.

A Believing Heart Is a Thankful Heart

Jesus replied, This is the work (service) that God asks of you: that
you believe in the One Whom He has sent [that you cleave to,
trust, rely on, and have faith in His Messenger].   JOHN 6:29

I think we all know—but need to be reminded on a regular basis—
that God desires a thankful people, not a murmuring, grumbling,
faultfinding people.

It is interesting to note as we study the history of the nation of
Israel that this kind of negative attitude was a major problem that
caused them to wander in the wilderness for 40 years before enter-
ing the Promised Land. We may call it by many names, but God
called it "unbelief."

God's attitude is that if His people really believe Him, then no
matter what happens in life, they will know that He is big enough
to handle it and to make it work out for their good. Words of faith
are filled with joyful expectation, and not with murmuring, faultfinding, and complaining. Joy and peace are the results of a thankful, believing attitude.

Prayer of Thanks

Father, I thank You that You are reminding me that there is
blessing in a thankful, believing heart. Help me to trust in You
no matter what the circumstances around me look like. I know
You will provide for my every need.

Choosing Your Words Carefully

Even a fool when he holds his peace is considered wise; when he closes his lips he is esteemed a man of understanding.

PROVERBS 17:28

The book of Proverbs is filled with Scriptures about holding your tongue because there is wisdom in discretion. Sometimes the wisest thing you can say is nothing at all. Before you start talking about things you feel strongly about, ask yourself how much you really need to say. Get quiet and listen to what *God* is saying. You'll never regret saying what He wants you to say, the way He would say it.

I want to encourage you to concentrate on positive things and be thankful for these things. That will close the door to negative words and attitudes. As Romans 12:21 says, we overcome evil with good. In other words, if we stay busy doing right things, then there will be no room for the wrong ones. So make it your goal to do what is good before God, and enjoy the freedom and victory it brings to your life.

Prayer of Thanks

Father, I am so thankful that I can live in the wisdom You provide. Help me know when to speak up and when to be quiet. If it's a conversation I should stay out of, I thank You that You will help me exercise self-control and be disciplined enough to do so.

Desire Unity

Behold, how good and how pleasant it is for brethren to dwell
together in unity!   PSALM 133:1

Bickering between God's people is nothing new. It was a problem in the early Church, just as it is now. Paul strongly encouraged and urged the church toward unity and wrote in Philippians 2:2: "Fill up and complete my joy by living in harmony and being of the same mind and one in purpose, having the same love, being in full accord and of one harmonious mind and intention."

Where there's unity, there's blessing and anointing. When people are thankful for each other and choose to live in unity, they will experience the power of agreement. But the power of God can't work in our lives if we stay bitter and angry toward people. His love can't flow through us if we're holding on to strife and resentment. Peace equals power, and no peace equals no power.

————————

Prayer of Thanks
I thank You today, Father, for the power we can experience
when we decide to come together in unity. Today, I choose
to put aside strife and arguments in order to pursue peace
and unity. I am grateful that You will help me do this in Your
strength.

Carried in His Arms

I will say of the Lord, He is my Refuge and my Fortress, my
God; on Him I lean and rely, and in Him I [confidently]
trust!   PSALM 91:2

At various points in our lives, all of us feel we're getting "out of
our depth" or "in over our heads." There are problems all around:
A job is lost, someone dies, there is strife in the family, or a bad
report comes from the doctor. When these things happen, our
temptation is to panic because we feel we've lost control.

But think about it: The truth is that we've never been in control
when it comes to life's most crucial elements. The only thing that
holds us up—and the thing we can be most grateful for—is the
grace of God, our Father, and that won't change. God is never out of
His depth, and therefore, we're safe when we're in life's "deep end"
because we can trust that He will always carry us in His arms.

Prayer of Thanks

Thank You, Father, that You are a refuge for me. I know that
because You are with me, I can feel safe and secure. Thank You
that no matter how difficult life may seem, I can be at peace
because You will never let me go.

An Attitude of Obedience

*Sacrifice and offering You do not desire, nor have You delight in
them; You have given me the capacity to hear and obey [Your law,
a more valuable service than] burnt offerings and sin offerings
[which] You do not require.*   PSALM 40:6

God delights in our obedience. He wants to lead and guide us,
but it does no good if we are not prepared to listen and obey. He
has given us the capacity both to hear Him and to obey Him. God
does not require a higher sacrifice than heartfelt obedience.

Some of what God asks you to do will be exciting, and some
will not, but we should be equally prepared to follow Him either
way. We can be thankful knowing that what He tells us to do will
work out for good, if we will just do it His way.

If you want God's will for your life, I can tell you the recipe in
its simplest form: *Pray and obey.* God has given you the capacity to
do both.

Prayer of Thanks

*Father, I am thankful that You speak to my heart and guide me
in the way I should go. Regardless of how difficult it may seem,
I want to obey Your voice and trust that Your plan for my life is
best. Thank You for loving me and speaking to my heart.*

Separating Your "Who" from Your "Do"

But God shows and clearly proves His [own] love for us by the fact
that while we were still sinners, Christ (the Messiah, the Anointed
One) died for us.   ROMANS 5:8

God wants us to be assured of His love and never allow anything
to separate us from it. With a heart full of gratitude, we can rest in
the knowledge that God loves us in the good times, and He loves
us in the hard times. God loves us on the days we act right, and
He loves us on the days we don't act right. Thankfully, God's love
is unconditional.

He loves us based not on what we do, but on who we have
become in Christ. In other words, we need to know that we are
God's beloved children, and how to separate our "who" from our
"do." We won't *do* everything right all the time, but we are still in
right-standing with God through Christ. God still loves us every
moment of every day. That is something worth celebrating!

Prayer of Thanks

Father, I am grateful that Your love for me is based on who I
am in Christ, not on what I do each day. Even though I want to
please You with my actions, I thank You that Your love for me
is deeper than that. You love me as Your child, and nothing can
take away Your love.

The Best Friend You'll Ever Have

No one has greater love [no one has shown stronger affection] than to lay down (give up) his own life for his friends.   JOHN 15:13

Jesus is the best friend you will ever have. Whether or not you feel He is there, He is there for you to depend on in every area of your life. Lean on and trust Him with all your heart and mind. He will take you in the right direction and make your paths straight. You can talk to Him about everything.

Thank Him for the blessings He has given you—including the blessing of His presence. He always understands you and never rejects or condemns you. Nothing is too big for Him to handle, and for that matter, nothing is too small. Although we don't always *feel* God's presence, when we put our trust in Him, we see the result of Him working in our lives.

Prayer of Thanks

Thank You, Father, for the friend I have in Jesus. I believe that I am never alone and I have the best friend I could ever hope for in Christ Jesus. Thank You for Your daily love and presence in my life.

Let God In

*For the eyes of the Lord run to and fro throughout the whole
earth to show Himself strong in behalf of those whose hearts are
blameless toward Him.*   2 CHRONICLES 16:9

The closer you grow to God, the easier it is to develop a lifestyle of
making the right choices. Philippians 2:12 says to work out your
own salvation with fear and trembling. This means after your salvation when you are born again, you build your relationship with
God by studying, learning, praying, and fellowshipping with God.
You invite Him into every *area* of your life.

God is not willing to live in what I call a "Sunday morning
box." He wants to invade every day of your life and be involved in
everything you do. Be grateful that God is your partner in life. He
delights in helping you, and He especially enjoys just being with
you! Acknowledge God in all your ways and He will direct your
steps (see Proverbs 3:6).

Prayer of Thanks

*Father, I desire to give every part of my life to You. I thank
You that Your power is too great to be confined to any one
part of my life. Today, I choose to submit every part of my life
and everything I have—my time, energy, talents, finances,
relationships, and emotions—to You.*

Refuse to Be Offended

Good sense makes a man restrain his anger, and it is his glory
to overlook a transgression or an offense.   PROVERBS 19:11

We have many opportunities every day to get offended; each time we must make a choice. If we choose to live by our feelings, we will never flow in the all-important facet of love called forgiveness. Forgiveness is the antidote for offense, and we can be very thankful that God has provided it as a way for us to keep our peace.

I once read that 95 percent of the time when people hurt our feelings, it was not what they intended to do. We always seem to assume people are attacking us, while the truth is, they are probably just being insensitive to how their behavior is affecting us. Rarely do people stay awake at night planning to be offensive to the people they meet the next day. Stress levels are high in the world today, and frequently people hurt us due to the pressure they feel inside themselves.

"Drop it, leave it, and let it go," is what *The Amplified Bible* says we are to do with offenses (see Mark 11:25). It is important to forgive quickly. Thankfully, the quicker we forgive, the easier it is to do. God is love, and He forgives and forgets. In order to be like Him, we can develop the same habit.

Prayer of Thanks

Father, I am thankful that You have forgiven me of all my sins.
I pray that You will help me follow Your example and forgive
those people who have hurt me. Thank You for Your strength that
makes it possible for me to forgive others and live without offense.

It's Impossible for Love to Fail

But I tell you, Love your enemies and pray for those who persecute
you.   MATTHEW 5:44

It is difficult to keep showing love to those individuals who take
from us all we are willing to give and who never give anything
back. But I want to encourage you not to give up. We are not
responsible for how others act, only how we act.

The truth is that God did not give up on us. How could He? He
is love, and love never quits—aren't you thankful for that? Love is
always right there, doing its job. Love knows that if it refuses to
quit, it will ultimately win the victory.

Some people may refuse to receive our love no matter what we
do. But that does not mean that love has failed. Love upholds us. It
gives us joy. It pleases God when we walk in love.

Prayer of Thanks

Father, when I am faced with a person who doesn't seem to
receive love, help me to keep showing them love anyway. I know
that no act of love is ever wasted. Thank You that love never
fails.

Don't Worry About the Future

So do not worry or be anxious about tomorrow, for tomorrow will have worries and anxieties of its own. Sufficient for each day is its own trouble.   MATTHEW 6:34

Worry, fear, and dread are classic "peace stealers." All of them are a total waste of energy; they never produce any good results. And we can resist each of them in the power of the Holy Spirit.

God has equipped us to handle life as it comes, but if we spend today worrying about tomorrow, we find ourselves tired and frustrated. God will not help us worry. Each day has enough for us to consider; we don't need to anticipate tomorrow's situations while we are still trying to live out today.

The only solution to worry is total abandonment to God and His plan. Even when unpleasant things happen, we can thank God that He has the ability to make them work out for our good if we continue to pray and trust Him (see Romans 8:28).

Prayer of Thanks

Father, I am so thankful that I can choose not to worry. Regardless of my circumstances, I can focus on You and trust Your plan for my life. Thank You that You are working all things together for my good.

God's Faithful Provision

Look at the birds of the air; they neither sow nor reap nor gather
into barns, and yet your heavenly Father keeps feeding them. Are
you not worth much more than they?   MATTHEW 6:26

God is faithful, and because faithfulness is embedded in His character, He cannot fail us or let us down. Experience with God gives us experience with His faithfulness. We all have needs, but we can be thankful that He meets those needs time and again. He may not always do what we would like, but He does do the right thing. He may not be early, but He is never too late.

I have seen God come through multitudes of times during the years I have been serving Him. I can truly say *God is faithful*. He has given me needed strength, answers that came just in time, right friends in right places, open doors of opportunity, encouragement, needed finances, and much more. And He will do the same for you! There is nothing we need that God cannot provide.

Prayer of Thanks

I thank You today, Father, that You are faithful. Your provision
is always exactly what I need and exactly when I need it. Help
me to look to You for provision in my life. Thank You that You
are more than enough for me.

Keep Doing What Is Right

And as for you, brethren, do not become weary or lose heart in doing right [but continue in well-doing without weakening].

2 THESSALONIANS 3:13

History is filled with examples of people who are famous for doing great things—yet if we study their lives, we find that they failed miserably before they succeeded. Their real strength was not their talent as much as it was their tenacity. Consider these examples:

- NBA legend Michael Jordan was once cut from his high school basketball team.
- After his first audition, Fred Astaire received the following assessment: "Can't act. Slightly bald. Can dance a little."
- Best-selling author Max Lucado had his first book rejected by 14 publishers.
- Walt Disney was fired from a newspaper because he lacked ideas.

These people succeeded in a variety of different endeavors, but they had one thing in common: perseverance. A refusal to give up is one of the symptoms of confidence, and thankfully, confidence can be yours in Christ. Keep doing what you believe to be the right thing for you, and eventually you will enjoy the breakthrough you desire.

Prayer of Thanks

I am grateful, Father, that failure can be a learning tool. Help me today to have the confidence and perseverance needed to carry on, even through failure. I thank You that, with You in my life, I will always win as long as I don't quit.

The Free Gift of God's Love

For He foreordained us (destined us, planned in love for us)
to be adopted (revealed) as His own children through Jesus
Christ, in accordance with the purpose of His will [because it
pleased Him and was His kind intent].   EPHESIANS 1:5

There is only one thing you can do with a free gift, and that is receive it and be grateful. I urge you to take a step of faith right now and say out loud, "God loves me unconditionally, and I receive His love!" You may have to say it a hundred times a day before it finally sinks in, but when it does, it will be the happiest day of your life.

To know that you are loved by someone is the best and most comforting feeling in the world. God not only loves you, but He also provides other people who will truly love you. When He does provide, be sure to remain thankful for those people. Having people who genuinely love you is one of the most precious gifts in the world.

Take time to thank God for His love and all the people who love you! It is His gift to you and, I believe, one of the most valuable gifts that you will ever receive.

Prayer of Thanks

Father, thank You for the free gift of Your love. I am grateful
that You love me unconditionally and You have put people in
my life who love me too. I don't take Your love for granted and,
though I can never repay Your love, I want to live my life for You
in return.

Faith over Fear

Now faith is the assurance (the confirmation, the title deed) of the things [we] hope for, being the proof of things [we] do not see and the conviction of their reality [faith perceiving as real fact what is not revealed to the senses].   HEBREWS 11:1

"I will not fear" is the only acceptable attitude we can have toward fear. That does not mean we will never feel fear, but it does mean we will not allow it to rule our lives. The Bible says that God has not given us a spirit of fear (see 2 Timothy 1:7).

Fear is not from God, but faith is! We should remember to do everything with a spirit of faith. Faith is confidence in God and a belief that His promises are true. Faith will cause a person to go forward, to try new things, and to be aggressive.

Be firm in your resolve to do whatever you need to do, even if you have to "*do it afraid*"! To "do it afraid" means to feel the fear and do what you believe you should do anyway. Stand in faith, be thankful for God's promises, and boldly pursue what God has put in your heart to do.

Prayer of Thanks

Thank You, Father, that I can live in faith and not in fear. Regardless of the difficulty of the situation I may be facing, I will choose to do what You have called me to do, even if I have to "do it afraid." Thank You for giving me the strength that I need.

Love Isn't Always Convenient

I will not sacrifice to the Lord my God burnt offerings that cost me nothing. 2 SAMUEL 24:24 NIV

If God wants us to help people, why doesn't He make it easy and inexpensive? Let me answer that question with another question. Did Jesus sacrifice anything to purchase our freedom from sin and bondage? Of course He did. He sacrificed everything—and we are eternally thankful for our salvation! One of the ways we can show our gratitude is by giving to help others.

I have learned that true giving is giving in a way that affects us. Giving away our clothes and household items that are old and we are finished with may be a nice gesture, but it is not sacrificial giving. Real giving occurs when we give somebody something that we want to keep, or something that will definitely cost us.

God gave us His only Son because He loves us, so what will love cause us to do? Don't let inconvenience or sacrifice keep you from truly loving others.

Prayer of Thanks

I am grateful, Father, that You loved me so much that You sent Your Son, Jesus, to die for my sins. Help me to remember that love is not self-serving, but it is selfless and sacrificial.

Simplicity and Decisions

But above all [things], my brethren, do not swear, either by heaven or by earth or by any other oath; but let your yes be [a simple] yes, and your no be [a simple] no, so that you may not sin and fall under condemnation.   JAMES 5:12

Decision-making can be simple if we refuse to be double-minded. After making a decision, stand firm, let your "yes" be "yes" and your "no" be "no." Indecision and double-mindedness not only bring confusion and complication, but, as James noted, they also cause condemnation (see James 5:12).

If we believe in our hearts that we should do something and then allow our heads to talk us out of it, it is an open door for condemnation. We often labor over decisions when actually we just need to decide. Pray for God's wisdom and guidance, and then make decisions without worrying about them. Thankfully, you don't have to live in fear of being wrong. If your heart is right and you make a decision that is not in accordance with God's will and end up going astray, He will forgive you, find you, and get you back on course.

Prayer of Thanks

Father, help me to avoid complicating the process of decision-making. I thank You that You see my heart and You will correct my course if I take a wrong step. I thank You that I can simply follow what I believe You are leading me to do and trust You to protect me in the process.

Having a Childlike Approach to Life

Whoever will humble himself therefore and become like this little child [trusting, lowly, loving, forgiving] is greatest in the kingdom of heaven.   MATTHEW 18:4

One thing we all know about children is that they enjoy life. A child can literally enjoy anything. A child can turn work into a game so he is able to enjoy it.

I recall asking my son to sweep the patio when he was about 11 or 12 years old. I looked outside and saw him dancing with the broom to the music playing on the headset he was wearing. I thought, *Amazing! He has turned sweeping into a game. If he has to do it, he is going to enjoy it.*

We should all have that attitude. We may not choose to dance with a broom, but we should choose an attitude of thanksgiving in everything we do and always enjoy all aspects of life.

Prayer of Thanks

When I am in a situation that doesn't seem like a lot of fun naturally, help me, Father, to make the most of it. I thank You that I can enjoy every part of my life, knowing that the joy of the Lord is my strength.

Strengthened Through Praise

Let them confess and praise Your great name, awesome and
reverence inspiring! It is holy, and holy is He!   PSALM 99:3

There is tremendous power in praise. We gain more and more strength, our faith increases, and the things that are coming to defeat us are destroyed as we praise God. Enjoying good praise and worship music is one of the tools we have available to help us live in an atmosphere of praise.

Every time we have an opportunity—even a minute or two while walking through a parking lot into a store, or waiting in line to pay for an item—take the opportunity to praise and worship God. After a while, praise becomes so natural that it flows out of us without a deliberate decision on our part. We find ourselves singing and thanking God as an automatic response to our awareness of His goodness, mercy, and grace.

Prayer of Thanks

Father, help me get to a place where my natural reaction is praise. Thank You that I can look to You and Your goodness rather than the cares of the world. I am grateful for Your presence and power in my life.

Partnering with God

Be unceasing in prayer [praying perseveringly].

1 THESSALONIANS 5:17

Prayer is the greatest privilege of our lives. It's not something we have to do; it's something we get to do! Prayer is one of the ways we partner with God to see His plans and purposes come to pass in our lives and in the lives of those we love. It is the means by which we human beings on earth can actually enter into the awesome presence and power of God.

Prayer allows us to share our hearts with God, to listen for His direction, to express our thanksgiving, and to know how to discover and enjoy all the great things He has for us. I have heard it said that "all failure is a failure to pray." Communicating with God is indeed the greatest privilege I know, and it is also the simplest privilege I know. Don't make prayer complicated or difficult. Keep it simple and enjoy every moment spent with the Lord in prayer.

Prayer of Thanks

Father, I thank You for the great privilege of coming to You in prayer. It is amazing to think that I can enter into Your presence with thanksgiving today. Thank You, Lord, for hearing my prayer and for guiding me as I go through my day today.

Shine On!

*The Lord make His face to shine upon and enlighten you
and be gracious (kind, merciful, and giving favor) to you.*

NUMBERS 6:25

As you go through your day, ask the Lord to make His face shine
upon you. Ask Him to lift up His countenance upon you and give
you peace. Ask Him to shine His glory upon you, as He did with
Moses. Then let that light so shine before others that they may see
it and glorify your heavenly Father (see Matthew 5:16 KJV).

Letting your light shine can be as simple as putting a smile
on your face. Practice smiling at others and you will find most of
them smiling back. The light of God's glory is in you, but if you
never show it outwardly, people won't be blessed. It is amazing
what will happen if you will just be thankful, smile, and be nice to
people. Show favor as often as you can to as many as you can. By
so doing, you will receive favor, because we are told that whatever
we sow is what we will reap (see Galatians 6:7).

Prayer of Thanks

*I thank You, Father, for the opportunity I have to be a light in
a dark world. Let Your light and Your life shine through me for
others to see. I am grateful that with Your help, my life can be a
blessing to others.*

The Trap of Ingratitude

Let this same attitude and purpose and [humble] mind be in you
which was in Christ Jesus: [Let Him be your example in humility.]

PHILIPPIANS 2:5

As human beings, we all struggle with selfishness and ingratitude.
We can pray and believe God for something, and even be very
thankful and grateful for it when we receive it. But it doesn't take
us very long until we are no longer thankful and grateful for them,
but actually come to think we are entitled to them.

If we aren't careful, we can even develop a demanding attitude in our relationship with the Lord. We can become upset and
aggravated when the Lord doesn't give us everything we think
we are entitled to. As His children, we do have an inheritance,
but a humble attitude is necessary to receive it. A humble attitude
pleases God and will keep our hearts grateful for every blessing we
receive.

Prayer of Thanks

Father, I am so thankful for Your work in my life. Please help
me to keep a humble attitude, never demanding Your goodness.
Thank You that You pour out Your favor in my life, not because
I've earned it, but simply because You love me and You want to
bless me.

Great Expectations

*I waited patiently and expectantly for the Lord; and He inclined to
me and heard my cry.*   PSALM 40:1

Sometimes we expect *nothing*; we merely wait to see what happens
and *nothing* does because we have been expecting *nothing*. At other
times, we may fall into the trap of expecting to be disappointed
because we have been disappointed time and time again in the
past, so we are afraid to hope for anything. However, God wants
us to have a faith-filled expectation of His goodness, because He
can do exceedingly, abundantly above all that dare to ask or think
(see Ephesians 3:20).

Developing a very thankful attitude for God's present goodness
in your life will open the door for God to do even more. Let Him
know that you expect to see His goodness in your life, not because
you deserve it, but because He is good!

The Bible teaches us that God is waiting to bless people, but
He is looking for someone who is expecting and believing for His
favor (see Isaiah 30:18).

Prayer of Thanks

*I thank You today, Father, that You promise in Your Word that
You love me and You have a great plan for my life. I am grateful
for Your abundant provision, and I stand in faith waiting with a
positive expectation of Your goodness.*

Staying in Peace

So repent (change your mind and purpose); turn around and
return [to God], that your sins may be erased (blotted out,
wiped clean), that times of refreshing (of recovering from the
effects of heat, of reviving with fresh air) may come from the
presence of the Lord.   ACTS 3:19

Peace with God is maintained by never attempting to hide sin.
Because hiding sin just causes condemnation and guilt, and neither of those are productive in any way. God knows everything
anyway, so it is useless to think we can hide anything from Him.
When we make mistakes, we shouldn't withdraw from God, but we
should come near to Him, thankful that He promises to restore us.

To repent means to turn away from sin and return to the highest place. God is not surprised by our weaknesses and failures.
Actually, He knew about the mistakes we would make before we
made them. All we need to do is admit them because He is faithful
to forgive us continually from all sin (see 1 John 1:9). God is waiting for you with open and outstretched arms—always run to Him!

Prayer of Thanks

I am grateful, Father, that You forgive my sins and You bring
healing and restoration into my life. I choose to reject the
condemnation of the enemy and come to You when I sin and
fall short. Thank You that You forgive me and love me through
it all.

God's Way Is Always Better

You will guard him and keep him in perfect and constant peace
whose mind [both its inclination and its character] is stayed on
You, because he commits himself to You, leans on You, and hopes
confidently in You.   ISAIAH 26:3

We may not always get things our way in life, but we can trust that
God's way is better. God is a good God, and He said that He has
good things planned for His children: "For I know the thoughts
and plans that I have for you, says the Lord, thoughts and plans
for welfare and peace and not for evil, to give you hope in your
final outcome" (Jeremiah 29:11).

We do not have to be afraid of harm, because God is not an
angry judge; He is not mean. He is good. We can rejoice with
thanksgiving, knowing that everything good in life comes from
God. He wants us to trust Him, and when we take a step of faith
to do so, we will see the goodness of God manifested in our lives.
The more we surrender, the better life becomes.

Prayer of Thanks

Father, when I find myself disappointed by my circumstances,
help me to remember that You are in control. I thank You that
Your plan for my life is so much better than my own plan. I
trust You and Your direction for my life.

You Have the Mind of Christ

For who has known or understood the mind (the counsels and
purposes) of the Lord so as to guide and instruct Him and give
Him knowledge? But we have the mind of Christ (the Messiah)
and do hold the thoughts (feelings and purposes) of His heart.

1 CORINTHIANS 2:16

In 1 Corinthians 2:16, we are told we have the mind of Christ.
This statement overwhelms many people. If these were not the
words of the Bible, they wouldn't believe it. But Paul was not saying we're perfect or we'll never fail. He was telling us that we can
think spiritual thoughts because Christ is alive within us. Thankfully, we no longer have to think the way we once did; we can
begin to think as He does.

Another way to look at this is to point to the promise God
spoke through Ezekiel: "A new heart will I give you and a new
spirit will I put within you, and I will take away the stony heart
out of your flesh and give you a heart of flesh. And I will put my
Spirit within you" (Ezekiel 36:26–27).

Your mind, heart, and spirit are new in Christ. You are growing
spiritually and becoming more like Him each day—that's something to be thankful for!

Prayer of Thanks

Thank You, Father, that You have given me the mind of Christ.
I no longer have to dwell on anxious, fearful, insecure thoughts.
Because of Jesus, my mind is renewed and I can think positive,
joyful, faith-filled thoughts about my life.

Fickle Feelings

And those who belong to Christ Jesus (the Messiah) have crucified the flesh (the godless human nature) with its passions and appetites and desires.　　　　　　　　GALATIANS 5:24

Feelings are very fickle. They are always changing; they come and go like the waves in the ocean. They are up, then down, and seem to be controlled by some unseen force that we don't understand. If we are wise, we don't go sailing in the ocean when it is wild with waves that appear dangerous, and neither should we follow our emotions when they are wildly changing.

Thankfully, we don't have to be controlled by our feelings. We can live submitted to the Word of God instead. The best thing to do when you're feeling overly emotional is wait for your feelings to settle before taking any action. Take the helm and sail your own ship. Don't just get into the boat with nobody at the helm and merely hope that the waves of life take you somewhere good. Instead of following feelings, trust God and follow His Word if you really want to experience a joyful life.

Prayer of Thanks

Father, I thank You for the gift of Your Word. I am grateful that I don't have to live controlled by my feelings. I choose instead to live according to the promises and instruction in the Word of God.

Condemnation or Conviction

For God did not send the Son into the world in order to judge
(to reject, to condemn, to pass sentence on) the world, but that
the world might find salvation and be made safe and sound
through Him.   JOHN 3:17

There is an important difference between condemnation (guilt) and true conviction from God.

Condemnation manifests as a heavy burden that requires us to pay for our faults and mistakes and pushes us down. Conviction is the work of the Holy Spirit, who is showing us that we have sinned and inviting us to confess our sins, to receive forgiveness and God's help to improve our behavior in the future. Condemnation makes the problem worse; conviction is intended to lift us out of the problem.

If you feel conviction, simply thank God for speaking to you, confess your sin to Him, and turn away from that sin. Then... receive God's forgiveness and let go of it! God forgives and forgets, and if you want to experience the joy of redemption that God wants us all to experience, you'll need to let go of it too.

Prayer of Thanks
Thank You, Father, that there is no condemnation in Christ
Jesus. When You convict me of sin, help me to bring it to
You in repentance without feeling burdened by guilt and
condemnation. You have forgiven me, so I choose today to
forgive myself as well.

The Wonderful Person God
Says You Are

He has made everything beautiful.   ECCLESIASTES 3:11

When we receive Jesus as our Savior, He takes our sin and gives us His righteousness (see 2 Corinthians 5:21). I doubt that many of us understand the full impact of that. At no cost to us, we are made right with God. We can feel right instead of wrong!

Why not take a step of faith today and try saying or thinking something good about yourself. I am not encouraging a wrong kind of pride, but I am encouraging you to be bold enough to believe you are the wonderful person God says you are.

In Psalm 139, David confessed that he knew God had made him, and then he said, "Wonderful are Your works, and that my inner self knows right well" (v. 14). David was thankful that he had been created by God in a wonderful way—you have been too! Be bold enough to believe that today.

Prayer of Thanks

Father, help me to experience the joy of knowing who I am in Christ. You have created me uniquely and saved me completely. I thank You that I am beautiful in Your sight.

Pray Without Ceasing

Pray at all times (on every occasion, in every season) in the Spirit, with all [manner of] prayer and entreaty. To that end keep alert and watch with strong purpose and perseverance, interceding in behalf of all the saints (God's consecrated people).   EPHESIANS 6:18

To pray at all times is to "pray without ceasing" (1 Thessalonians 5:17 NKJV), but how do we do that? We do it by keeping an attitude of thanksgiving and total dependence upon God as we go about our everyday lives, turning our thoughts toward Him in the midst of doing all the things we have to do.

I believe that God really wants us to live a lifestyle of prayer and that He wants to help us stop thinking about prayer as an event and begin to see it as a way of life, as an internal activity that undergirds everything else we do. He wants us to talk to Him and listen to Him continually—to pray our way through every day with our hearts connected to His.

Prayer of Thanks

Father, I am so grateful that You are always available. I can call on You in prayer all throughout the day, and I will never get a "busy" signal. Help me grow in prayer and let it be one of the greatest enjoyments in my life.

Thankful for God's Correction

Those whom I love I rebuke and discipline. So be earnest and
repent.   REVELATION 3:19 NIV

God views conviction, correction, and discipline as something to
be celebrated rather than something to make us sad or frustrated.
Why should we celebrate when God shows us that something is
wrong with us? Enthusiasm sounds like a strange response, but in
reality, the fact that we can see something that we were once blind
to is good news.

When we make enough progress in our relationship with God
that we begin to sense when we are out of His will, then that is
something to be thankful for. It is a sign of progress and should
be celebrated joyfully. The longer we serve God and study His
ways, the more sensitive we become to His will. We eventually
grow to the place where we know immediately when we are saying
or doing something that is not pleasing to God, and we have the
option of repenting and making a fresh start.

Prayer of Thanks

I am grateful, Father, that You love me enough to bring
correction and instruction into my life. Thank You that You are
transforming me and making me more like Your Son, Jesus.

Will I Have Enough?

Now to him who is able to do immeasurably more than all we
ask or imagine, according to his power that is at work within us.

EPHESIANS 3:20 NIV

One of the strongest and most persistent fears that people experience is the fear that they won't have enough of what they need. We want to feel safe in every area of life. We want to be secure in our belief that we will have what we need when we need it. This fear can lead to an ungrateful heart, because it brings the feeling that there is never enough. It is best to ask God for what we want and need and then focus on what we do have instead of what we don't have.

God's Word says that we are not to fear because He is with us. It is just that simple: "Fear not [there is nothing to fear], for I am with you" (Isaiah 41:10). Thankfully, He has everything we need and He loves us. So like any loving parent, He will provide for us. He has promised to never leave or forsake us. We can be thankful that He never sleeps, He is ever-present, and He keeps watch over us with loving care.

Prayer of Thanks

Father, I am thankful that You provide all that I need and so much more. I refuse to live in fear, wondering if I will have enough. Thank You that You are a God who does immeasurably more than I could ask or imagine.

Sowing Seeds of Victory

Roll your works upon the Lord [commit and trust them wholly
to Him; He will cause your thoughts to become agreeable to
His will, and] so shall your plans be established and succeed.

PROVERBS 16:3

If you're not happy with the situation you're in right now, will you make the effort to change it? Do you want to be in the same situation this time next year? Or do you want something different? If you want to have something different, ask for the Lord's direction and then start moving that way. You can choose to pay the price on this end to have what you want later on.

You will have to spend some of this year moving toward your goals for next year. As you move forward, you'll need to make tough choices, and you'll come to some painful crossroads. But when you reach these places, press through. If you press through, you can be thankful that God is with you to help and strengthen you. If you begin working toward your goal now, you'll have the victory you long for later on.

Prayer of Thanks

Father, I pray that You will help me be disciplined enough each day to move toward my goals. I thank You that You have a good plan for my life, and if I'll do my part, You will always do Your part.

Victory Is Worth the Cost

For by You I can run through a troop, and by my God I can leap
over a wall.   PSALM 18:29

Throughout the Bible, we find the commands of God always come
with the promise of reward. God is not a taker; He is a giver. He
never tells us to do anything unless it is for our ultimate benefit.
I assure you: Everything God ever asks you to do, even if it is difficult, He asks because He has something great in mind for you—
but in order to experience it, you will need to press through the
hard place.

Don't think or say, "This is just too hard" when you know you
need to do something. Be grateful that God never requires you to
handle more than you can bear. With every difficulty, He always
provides a way to overcome. You never have to say, "There is no
way," because He is the way (see John 14:6) and He makes a way
for you. You can do whatever God calls you to do in life! You have
what it takes!

Prayer of Thanks

I am grateful, Father, that You won't ask me to handle more
than I can bear. Today, as I press through the difficult areas in
my life, I thank You that I am not pressing through alone—You
are with me!

Thankful for Revelation from God

And they were completely astonished at His teaching, for He was teaching as One Who possessed authority, and not as the scribes.   MARK 1:22

It's sad to think that some people equate Christianity with just going to church and nothing more. In church, we are taught about God, but thankfully our life in Christ is more than just a weekly trip to church. Being a Christian is more than joining a church. It is a personal relationship with God through Jesus Christ.

To really know the Lord, we must be hungry for the type of knowledge that can only come from God Himself through revelation—this revelation is available through His Word and by His Holy Spirit in a personal and intimate way.

Revelation goes beyond what we think, see, or feel. It is an inner knowledge of God that cannot be taken from us. When we have this inner knowledge of God, we can be grateful and secure, knowing that nothing outward can sway us from our belief in God.

Prayer of Thanks

I am thankful, Father, that I can have a personal, intimate relationship with You. Today, I choose to listen for Your voice and follow Your leading. Thank You for Your revelation in my life.

Jesus Understands Your Weaknesses

For we do not have a High Priest Who is unable to understand and sympathize and have a shared feeling with our weaknesses and infirmities and liability to the assaults of temptation, but One Who has been tempted in every respect as we are, yet without sinning.   HEBREWS 4:15

The Word of God teaches that Jesus understands our weaknesses. He understands them because He took on human flesh in order to identify with us, and He was tempted in every respect as we are. And while He never sinned, He is not shocked when we fail.

It's okay to have weaknesses—it's only human. You are probably asking the same question I did when I dared to believe this freeing truth: "If I think I am free to have weakness, won't it just invite me to sin more?" The answer is no, it won't.

God's grace, and the freedom it offers, never entices us to sin more, but it does entice us to fall radically in love with Jesus. The more we realize that He loves us the way we are, the more grateful we become and the more we love Him. And that love for Him causes us to want to change for the right reason.

Prayer of Thanks
Father, thank You for the gift of grace. And thank You that You love me in spite of my failures and weaknesses. I know that You are strengthening me and making me more like Jesus. I am grateful for Your work, and I trust You every step of the way.

The Beauty of the New Covenant

For this is My blood of the new covenant, which [ratifies the agreement and] is being poured out for many for the forgiveness of sins.   MATTHEW 26:28

The new covenant is something to be forever grateful for. It is a better covenant that is far superior to the old. The old covenant was initiated with the blood of animals, but the new was initiated with the sinless blood of Jesus Christ. Under the new covenant, Jesus fulfilled or kept all of the Law of the old covenant and died in our place to pay for our sins and misdeeds.

Jesus took the punishment that we deserved and promised that if we would believe in Him and all that He did for us, He would forever stand in our place and our responsibility to keep the Law would be met in Him. The old covenant focused on what man could do, but the new covenant focuses on what God has done for us in Jesus Christ. (Read Hebrews 8 and 9 for more study in this area.)

Prayer of Thanks

I thank You, Father, that I can live in the powerful, freeing work of the new covenant. Thank You that You loved me enough to send Jesus to die for my sins. And thank You that I can live in an intimate, personal relationship with You.

When You Give God Your Best

*Do your best to present yourself to God as one approved, a worker
who does not need to be ashamed and who correctly handles the
word of truth.*   2 TIMOTHY 2:15 NIV

We can do our best for God, but we cannot offer Him perfection,
and we don't have to feel pressure to do so.

I heard a story about a student who turned a paper in to his
professor and the professor wrote on the bottom of it, "Is this the
best you can do?" Knowing it was not his best, the student did
the paper again, and once again the professor gave it back to him
with the same phrase at the bottom. This went on for about three
rounds and finally when the professor asked if it was the best he
could do, he thought for a moment and answered, "Yes, I believe
this is the best I can do." Then his professor said, "Good, now I
will accept it."

All God wants is our best—He can work with that. We can
be thankful that even though our best is not perfect, God can do
something perfectly amazing with it!

Prayer of Thanks
*Father, I am so thankful that You are pleased when I do my best
for You, even though my best is far from perfect. Thank You
that when I do my part, You are always faithful to do Your part
with my life.*

Are You Disappointed with God?

For as the heavens are higher than the earth, so are My
ways higher than your ways and My thoughts than your
thoughts.   ISAIAH 55:9

Perhaps you feel that God has let you down at some time in your life, or that one of His promises did not come true for you. If so, I urge you to realize that God doesn't always work within our time frame or in the ways that we would choose, but if you continue to trust Him, you will see the goodness of God in your life.

If you'll trust God each day, be thankful for the things He has done for you in the past, and decide to never give up, you will see Him doing amazing things in your life. God's faithfulness surrounds Him. It is part of His character, and we can count on Him to be with us and do all that He has promised to do. Don't let past disappointments hold you back—dare to trust God again today.

Prayer of Thanks

Father, help me to set aside my pain or disappointment and
learn to trust You again. I realize that even when I don't
understand Your plan, Your plan is still best. Thank You for
Your faithfulness and Your love for me.

Faithful to Forgive

. . . Their sins and their lawbreaking I will remember no more.

HEBREWS 10:17

God is always faithful to forgive our sins just as He promised He would. Sometimes people won't forgive us, but God always forgives sin and then forgets it. And we can be thankful to know that there is no limit to God's forgiveness.

People often have limits to what they are willing to forgive or how often they are willing to do it, but God's forgiveness never runs out. People may say they forgive us, and then remind us of what we did that hurt them, but God never reminds us of our past sins, because He has forgotten them (see Hebrews 10:17).

When we are reminded of past sins, it is not God bringing them to our remembrance; it is Satan, the accuser of God's people. Reject the lies of the enemy, and choose to receive the faithfulness of God to forgive.

Prayer of Thanks

I thank You today, Father, that You are always faithful to forgive. Regardless of how many times I mess up, I know that You love me and You are faithful to forgive my sins. I am grateful for Your forgiveness and I desire to live my best for You in response to Your goodness to me.

Your Unique Prayer

From His dwelling place He looks [intently] upon all the
inhabitants of the earth—He Who fashions the hearts of them all,
Who considers all their doings.   PSALM 33:14–15

Because God has fashioned our hearts individually, our prayers can flow naturally out of our hearts and be consistent with the way He has designed us. As we develop our individual styles of communication with God, we can learn from people who may be more experienced than we are, but we need to be careful not to make what others do our standard. Thankfully, Jesus is our standard, and He is the only standard we need.

Enjoy your time with the Lord. Don't try to force yourself to do what others do if you are not comfortable with that in your spirit. You don't have to keep up with others or copy their prayer styles. You can go before God with thanksgiving in your heart, knowing that He hears you and loves you just the way you are. You can pray as the "original" He has made you to be.

Prayer of Thanks

Father, I thank You that everything about me is unique—even the way I pray. Help me to shake off comparisons and just come to You with confidence as Your child. I love You, Father, and I love spending time with You.

Believing You Are a Disciplined Person

Rather, he must be hospitable, one who loves what is good, who is
self-controlled, upright, holy and disciplined.   TITUS 1:8 NIV

I frequently hear people say, "I am just not a disciplined person,"
or, "I just don't have any self-control," and they name a certain
area like eating, exercising, or keeping things organized. If you
are one of these people who believe you are not disciplined, then I
want to encourage you to change your thinking.

The apostle Paul stated that God hasn't given us a spirit of
fear, but of power, love, and a sound mind, and a spirit of discipline and self-control (see 2 Timothy 1:7). Be thankful—God has
already given you the discipline you need! It is time to start renewing your mind by meditating on this thought: *I am disciplined and
self-controlled.*

You will never rise above what you believe, and as long as you
believe you are not a disciplined person, then you won't be one.
Instead, believe God's Word and live in its truth. You have self-
control, and you are disciplined!

Prayer of Thanks
*Father, I thank You that You have provided all of the discipline
and self-control I need. Help me to renew my mind according to
the truth of Your Word. I thank You that, with Your help, I can
live a disciplined, overcoming life.*

When It's Time for Something New

To everything there is a season, and a time for every matter or
purpose under heaven.   ECCLESIASTES 3:1

When what you are doing no longer gives you joy—when there is
no life in it for you anymore—that is a strong indication that God
is finished with whatever He was doing through you. Prayer will
help you find out if God is leading you to make changes.

Some individuals don't have any joy because they are trying to
do things God is not calling them to do anymore. They are simply
trying to ride a dead horse, so to speak. My advice is this: When
the horse isn't moving, it is time to dismount!

Seek God's direction and have the boldness to say, "I did things
a certain way for a long time, and I was grateful to have the chance
to do it, but this isn't the way God is leading me now. I believe
God is leading me to do something new."

Prayer of Thanks

Father, thank You for showing me when it is time to do
something new. I trust You to lead and guide me, and I know
that joy always comes with Your plan. I thank You in advance
that You will make it abundantly clear which direction You
want me to take.

The Joy of Spiritual Growth

He is the one we proclaim, admonishing and teaching everyone
with all wisdom, so that we may present everyone fully mature
in Christ.   COLOSSIANS 1:28 NIV

As your relationship with God matures, you will find yourself living less by guidelines, rules, and regulations, and more by the desires of your heart. As you learn more of the Word, you will find His desires fill your heart with thanksgiving and joy. God wants you to know His heart well enough that you will want to follow the prompting, leading, and guidance of the Holy Spirit.

Once you are free in Christ, stand fast in that liberty and do not become ensnared with the joy stealer of legalism, which is the yoke of bondage that you have put off (see Galatians 5:1). God wants to bring you into a new place that is full of freedom, so follow your heart, because that is where His law abides.

Prayer of Thanks

Thank You, Father, that the more time I spend in Your Word,
the more I love it. I pray that Your Word would fill my heart so
that my desires will begin to line up with Your instruction and
direction for my life. Thank You that You are bringing me to
maturity in You.

Just Believe

But I fear, lest somehow, as the serpent deceived Eve by his craftiness, so your minds may be corrupted from the simplicity that is in Christ.   2 CORINTHIANS 11:3 NKJV

God's plan for us is actually so simple that many times we miss it. Jesus has told us what to do to begin to discover God's plan: Believe! (See John 1:12; 3:16.)

When God says something to you in your heart, or when you read something in the Bible, you should say: "Thank You, Lord. I believe it. If God says He will prosper me, I believe it (see Jeremiah 29:11). If God says I will reap what I sow, I believe it (see 2 Corinthians 9:6). If He says to pray for my enemies, I believe it, and I am going to do it (see Matthew 5:44). If He says to call things that are not as though they were, I believe it, and I am going to do it (see Romans 4:17 KJV)."

If you choose to start believing God's Word, even before you see your circumstances change, then you will have joy. Simply believe God!

Prayer of Thanks
Father, help me to simplify things today by simply believing Your Word. Thank You for the promises You have given me as Your child. Today, I choose to simply believe that what You have said is true in my life.

Say "Yes" to What Is Really Important

But seek (aim at and strive after) first of all His kingdom and His righteousness (His way of doing and being right), and then all these things taken together will be given you besides.

MATTHEW 6:33

If you want to live a less complicated life, you may have to simplify it by not doing so much. Most people who are stressed and frustrated have become burned out because they try to squeeze too much into their schedules.

So learn to say "no" to a few things. Practice saying it: "No!" It's a simple word that becomes easier to say with each use. And learn to say "yes" only to what is really important in life—the things you truly believe to be God's will for you.

Spend time with your family and your friends. Enjoy God. Don't get too busy to enjoy all God has given you. Take time to laugh and be thankful for life.

Prayer of Thanks

Father, I am so thankful for the things that are truly important in my life. Today, I choose to focus on those things and let go of some of the other things that are distracting me. Thank You that with Your help I can really enjoy my life.

Conflict-Free Relationships

*Remind [the people] of these facts and [solemnly] charge them in
the presence of the Lord to avoid petty controversy over words,
which does no good but upsets and undermines the faith of the
hearers.*   2 TIMOTHY 2:14

Peace is such an important ingredient to a happy life, but it is not
enough to simply desire peace. We must actually pursue peace in
our relationship with God and our relationships with others. Paul
understood how elusive peace can be unless we diligently seek
it, because in several of his letters, he urges believers to live in
harmony.

To live in harmony, we should be thankful for each other, make
allowances for each other, and overlook each other's mistakes and
faults. We should be humble, loving, compassionate, and courte-
ous. Always be willing to forgive quickly and frequently, and don't
be easily offended.

Unity, harmony, and agreement are all peaceful, and we will
experience them all if we seek them with our whole heart and are
willing to be peacemakers as we go through life.

Prayer of Thanks

*Father, when I am in a situation where I am tempted to bicker
or argue, help me to be a peacemaker instead. I thank You for
the fruit of self-control in my life. And thank You that I can live
in harmony with those around me.*

You Are Invited to a "Come as You Are" Party

It is through Him that we have received grace (God's unmerited favor)... and this includes you, called of Jesus Christ and invited [as you are] to belong to Him.

ROMANS 1:5–6 (EMPHASIS ADDED)

One of the first things we ask when we are invited to a party is, "How should I dress?" Most of us like it best when we feel that we can come as we are. We like it when we can relax and be ourselves. I love this Scripture because of the message of acceptance it brings.

God accepts us as we are and He works with us throughout our lives to help us become all that He wants us to be. Grace meets us where we are but, thankfully, it never leaves us where it found us.

God will work in you by His Holy Spirit and you will be changed! But you don't have to wait to come to Him. Thankfully, you can come right now just as you are. You don't have to stand off in the distance and only hear the music of the party; you are invited to attend.

Prayer of Thanks

I thank You, Father, that You love me just as I am. I know that You are working in my life to bring positive change, but I thank You that You still love me and accept me in the process. Thank You for Your grace that allows me to come to You just as I am.

Receiving an Inheritance

And if we are [His] children, then we are [His] heirs also: heirs
of God and fellow heirs with Christ [sharing His inheritance
with Him]; only we must share His suffering if we are to share
His glory.   ROMANS 8:17

Our view of God, ourselves, and His plan for us is too small. God
wants us to come out of smallness and see the greatness of His
calling and our inheritance in Him. When we inherit something,
it means that we get what someone else worked for. Jesus gained a
prize for us. He worked for what we inherit, and all we can do is be
grateful and receive it by faith. Nothing else is required.

One step of faith—simply believing and receiving God's
goodness—will put you in the middle of the greatest inheritance
ever passed from one person to another. That step of faith takes
the struggle and frustration out of life. As 1 John 4:17 says, even
"as He is, so are we in this world." That is good news to be thankful for!

Prayer of Thanks

Father, I am so thankful that I am Your child. Thank You for
every gift and every provision that You have promised. And
thank You that I have an inheritance of eternal life with You
because of the work of Jesus on my behalf.

Doing Something Great
with Your Life

I call heaven and earth to witness this day against you that
I have set before you life and death, the blessings and the
curses; therefore choose life, that you and your descendants
may live.   DEUTERONOMY 30:19

I have often pondered why some people do great things with their
lives while others do little or nothing at all. I know that the outcome of our lives is dependent not only upon God, but also upon
something in us. Each of us must decide whether or not we will
reach down deep inside and find the courage to press past fear,
mistakes, mistreatment at the hands of others, seeming injustices,
and all the challenges life presents. This is not something anyone
else can do for us; we must do it ourselves.

I encourage you to take responsibility for your life and its outcome. Be grateful for God's blessings of the past and believe for
even more in the future. What will you do with what God has
given you? God gives everyone equal opportunity—you can
choose life or death (see Deuteronomy 30:19). It is your choice,
and I believe you will make the right one!

Prayer of Thanks

Father, I am thankful for the opportunity to do great things for
You. I pray that You will help me make the most of each new
day. Thank You that I can dream big. And because You are with
me, nothing is impossible.

Becoming Good at Trusting God

The Lord is good, a stronghold in the day of trouble; and He
knows those who trust in Him.   NAHUM 1:7 NKJV

We can spend all our time thinking and talking about what is
wrong in the world or we can choose to concentrate on the good
things. We can focus on what is wrong with a family member,
friend, or coworker or we can purposely look for and highlight
what is right.

If nine things are wrong and we only see two we feel are right,
we can make the two seem larger than the nine—just by what we
choose to concentrate on. This is a good time to remind yourself
that you can choose your own thoughts. I have heard many people
say, "I just can't control my thought life." The truth is that they
chose to concentrate on the wrong thoughts.

Choose to concentrate on godly, faith-filled thoughts. Let your
first response in any situation be to see the good, not the bad.
Speak out loud and say, "I trust God completely. I know He has a
plan. He is going to do something good in my life!"

Prayer of Thanks
Father, thank You that there are good things all around me to
focus on. Help me see the best in people, not the worst. Thank
You that I can choose my thoughts and I can enjoy the life
You've given me.

What We Know (Part 1)

*[And I pray] that the participation in and sharing of your
faith may produce and promote full recognition and appreciation
and understanding and precise knowledge of every good [thing]
that is ours in [our identification with] Christ Jesus [and unto
His glory].*   PHILEMON 1:6

When you know the following scriptural truths, you can't help
being thankful...

We know that we *are* children of God, and that we *are* called,
anointed, and appointed by Him for greatness. We *are* destined to
bring glory to God and be molded into the image of Jesus Christ.
We *have* (not will have) righteousness, peace, and joy in the Holy
Spirit. We *are* forgiven for all of our sins—even ones we haven't
done yet—and our names are written in the Lamb's Book of Life.
Jesus *has* gone before us to prepare a place for us, so that where He
is, we may be also.

We know that until He returns for us, He *has* sent His Holy
Spirit as our guarantee of the even greater good things that *are* to
come. We *are* guaranteed an inheritance, for it *was* purchased with
the blood of Jesus. We *have* a new covenant and *are* offered a new
way of living!

Prayer of Thanks

*I thank You today, Father, for these promises that I can declare
with the authority of Scripture. I know that I am Yours and no
one and nothing can separate me from Your love. Thank You for
that assurance.*

What We Know (Part 2)

[And I pray] that the participation in and sharing of your
faith may produce and promote full recognition and appreciation
and understanding and precise knowledge of every good [thing]
that is ours in [our identification with] Christ Jesus [and unto
His glory].   PHILEMON 1:6

When you know the following scriptural truths, you can't help being thankful...

We *are* made new creatures in Christ, old things *have* passed away and all things *have* become brand-new. We *can* let go of past mistakes and press toward the mark of perfection. We know that *God loves us* with an everlasting, unconditional love, and that His mercy endures forever. We know that all things *are* possible with God and we *can* do all things through Christ who is our strength.

We know that God never allows more to come on us than we can bear, but He *always* provides a way out, a safe place to land. We know that *all* things work together for good to those who love God and *are* called according to His purpose, and that what our enemies meant for harm, God intends for good. We know that He *is* our Vindicator, our Redeemer, and Restorer. He makes all things new!

Prayer of Thanks

Father, I pray that those words won't just be something I read,
but they would take root deep in my heart. Thank You for Your
promises. I believe them and choose to live in them today and
from every day forward.

God Will Never Give Up on You

...Yes, I have loved you with an everlasting love; therefore with loving-kindness have I drawn you and continued My faithfulness to you.   JEREMIAH 31:3

What your life amounts to is directly connected to what you think of yourself. We need to learn to think like God thinks. We must learn to identify with Christ and the new person He has made us to be.

In Scripture, God uses words such as "beautiful," "honored," "valued," and "precious" when He is speaking of His children. There is no doubt that we are far less than perfect, that we have faults and weaknesses, but God is God and He views us the way He knows we can be.

He sees us as a finished project while we are making the journey. He sees the end from the beginning and is not worried about what takes place in between. He is not pleased with our sin and bad behavior, but He will never give up on us and He always encourages us to press on. God believes in you!

Prayer of Thanks

I am grateful, Father, that You are a good Father who loves me unconditionally. Help me to see myself as You see me. Thank You that even though I am a work in progress, You already have the finished result in mind.

Listening for His Voice

*Consequently, faith comes from hearing the message, and
the message is heard through the word about Christ.*

ROMANS 10:17 NIV

Learning to hear from God is very exciting. God wants to speak to
us about the plan He has for our lives. His plan is a good plan, but
we are in danger of missing it if we don't learn how to listen to and
obey God's voice.

God speaks to us in many ways. He speaks to us through His
Holy Spirit dwelling in us, through that "knowing" deep inside us,
and through peace. He may also speak through other people, circumstances, wisdom, nature, and even through dreams or visions.

However, the two most prevalent ways God speaks to us are
through His Word and the inward witness in our hearts. The Word
of God is a valuable gift that we should be thankful for because it
is God's direct message to us—it is unchanging and infallible. As
you are learning to hear from God, always make sure the inward
witness of your heart lines up with Scripture.

Prayer of Thanks

*Father, thank You that You still speak to Your children. I pray
that You will help me hear You and follow Your direction for my
life. Thank You that You are teaching me how to follow Your
leading in my life.*

You Are the Home of God

Anyone who confesses (acknowledges, owns) that Jesus is the
Son of God, God abides (lives, makes His home) in him and he
[abides, lives, makes his home] in God.   1 JOHN 4:15

As believers, we have the life of God inside of us. *We are the dwelling place or home of God.* This truth is necessary for each of us to understand in order to enjoy close fellowship and intimacy with God. God takes up residence within us when we give our lives to Jesus, believing in Him as the only Savior and Lord. From that position, He, by the power of the Holy Spirit, begins a wonderful work in us.

We can be thankful that God loves us and chooses to make His home in us. He has the ability to do what He wants, and He chooses to make His home in our hearts. This choice is based not on any good deeds we have done or ever could do, but solely on the grace, mercy, power, and love of God. As believers in Christ, we become God's dwelling place (see Ephesians 3:17; 2 Timothy 1:14).

Prayer of Thanks

Thank You, Father, for the way You take up residence in my
heart. You are not distant or out of reach. I thank You that You
dwell in me and are involved in every area of my life.

Anger vs. Love

Beloved, let us love one another, for love is (springs) from God;
and he who loves [his fellowmen] is begotten (born) of God
and is coming [progressively] to know and understand God [to
perceive and recognize and get a better and clearer knowledge of
Him].   1 JOHN 4:7

Anger is a powerful emotion, but love is much stronger. And love
is the model God has displayed for each of us.

- In anger we might criticize, but in love, we encourage.
- In anger we might turn away, but in love, we reach out.
- In anger we might withhold, but in love, we are
  generous.
- In anger we might glare, but in love, we smile.
- In anger we might blame, but in love, we forgive.

One of the best ways to show your gratitude for God's love is to
share that love with others. Don't just be a recipient of God's love;
be a dispenser of that love to all those you come in contact with.

Prayer of Thanks

Thank You, Father, for the display of love You have demonstrated
for me to follow. I am grateful that You love me, and with Your
help I am going to demonstrate that same love to others.

Honest and Heartfelt Prayers

The earnest (heartfelt, continued) prayer of a righteous man
makes tremendous power available [dynamic in its working].

JAMES 5:16

If I could only emphasize one thing about prayer, I would tell people that it is so much easier than we think. Thankfully, God has not made prayer complicated; it really is simple. Sometimes people make prayer dry and difficult; sometimes our religious mind-sets and "systems" present prayer in such a way that it seems out of reach for many of us.

I tell you the truth when I say that God desires our prayer lives to be natural and enjoyable. He wants our prayers to be honest and heartfelt, and He wants our communication with Him unencumbered by rules, regulations, obligations, and legalism. He intends for prayer to be an integral part of our everyday lives—the easiest thing we do each day.

Prayer of Thanks

Father, I thank You that I can speak to You naturally and honestly. Thank You that I can talk to You like a friend, and I can know that You are always there when I need You.

Thankful for the Power of Prayer

To whom God was pleased to make known how great for the
Gentiles are the riches of the glory of this mystery, which is
Christ within and among you, the Hope of [realizing the]
glory.   COLOSSIANS 1:27

Short, simple prayers can be mighty beyond description, but that
does not take away from the fact that prayer is also a grand mystery. Watchman Nee, a Chinese Christian who wrote many profound
books while imprisoned for his faith, writes, "Prayer is the most wonderful act in the spiritual realm, as well as a most mysterious affair."

I believe the greatest mystery of prayer is that it joins the hearts
of people on earth with God's heart in heaven. Prayer is spiritual
and it goes into the unseen realm; it brings things out of that
unseen realm into the realm we can see and into the world around
us, right where we live.

We can thank God that prayer ushers spiritual blessings into
our natural, everyday lives and brings spiritual power to bear on
our earthly circumstances. We human beings are the only creatures in our known universe who can stand in the natural realm
and touch the spiritual realm.

Prayer of Thanks

I thank You, Father, that You have entrusted to me the power
of prayer. Help me to know that when I pray to You, I am not
wasting words—I am connecting heaven to earth. Thank You,
Lord, for the mystery and power of prayer.

The Little Things Are Important Too

Keep on asking and it will be given you; keep on seeking and you
will find; keep on knocking [reverently] and [the door] will be
opened to you.   MATTHEW 7:7

It is difficult for our finite minds to grasp and believe that God
wants to be involved in even the smallest details of our lives. But
don't ever hesitate to take what you think are small things to God.
After all, *everything* is small to God.

I remember a woman who came to me for prayer and wanted to
know if it would be all right if she asked God for two things. If not,
she assured me that she would only ask for one. It makes me sad
when I hear people say things like that.

We can be thankful because God is generous and He wants to
give even more than we know how to ask for. You have not because
you ask not (see James 4:2), so go ahead and ask boldly, because it
is God's will that you do so.

Prayer of Thanks

Father, I am thankful that there is no prayer request too big
for You . . . and there is no prayer request too small for You.
Today, I choose to bring every prayer need and declaration of
thanksgiving to You, no matter how big or how small.

Following God's Direction

Direct me in the path of your commands, for there I find delight.
PSALM 119:35 NIV

It is vital to know what God's Word says about His role in your life, because it confirms His divine plan to be intimately involved with all that concerns you. God's Word says to acknowledge Him in all our ways and He will direct our paths (see Proverbs 3:6). To "acknowledge God" simply means to care what He thinks and to ask for His opinion.

Proverbs 3:7 says, "Be not wise in your own eyes." In other words, don't even think you can run your life and do a good job without God's help and direction. But, thank God, He *does* give us His direction so that we can discover all that He has for us as we follow Him! We can simply trust His leading and do what He tells us to do.

Prayer of Thanks

Father, when I am faced with a circumstance where I'm not sure what to do, I pray that You will give me clear direction. I thank You that I can acknowledge You and lean on Your Word to find guidance no matter what situation I am faced with.

Anytime, Anywhere Prayer

Bless (affectionately, gratefully praise) the Lord, O my soul; and all
that is [deepest] within me, bless His holy name!   PSALM 103:1

Praying our way through the day is equally as important as devoting set-apart time to prayer. I believe God wants us to offer up acknowledgments of Him, make requests, and offer thanksgivings throughout each day. Learn to let prayer be as comfortable as breathing.

Just think about how you would feel if your children said, "I love you, Mom!" or "I love you, Dad!" every time they walked by you. When one of my children stops by the house or my office and says, "Hey, Mom, you're awesome! Just came by to tell you that," it makes my day.

Just letting people know you think they're great is the kind of communication that develops relationships. When we treat the Lord that way, our relationship with Him goes deeper and grows stronger, and we stay connected to Him through "anytime, anywhere" prayer. And He loves it.

Prayer of Thanks

I love You, Father, and I am thankful that You love me too. I
want to take every opportunity to tell You how wonderful You
are and how blessed I am. Thank You that I can come to You in
prayer anytime, anywhere.

God Thinks You Are Amazing

I will praise You, for I am fearfully and wonderfully made;
marvelous are Your works, and that my soul knows very well.

PSALM 139:14 NKJV

You may not feel like you're amazing or awesome, but God says that you are. Psalm 139 says that we are "fearfully and wonderfully made." Studying how the human body functions reveals that we are truly amazing creations.

When you receive Jesus Christ as your Lord and Savior, something happens to you on the inside. Paul writes that "the old [previous moral and spiritual condition] has passed away. Behold, the fresh and new has come!" (2 Corinthians 5:17)

You may not notice any difference when you look in the mirror; your behavior may not change overnight; your struggles may not suddenly disappear, but when you are "in Christ," a gradual and patient work of transformation is under way in your life. God sees the end of things from the beginning, and He sees you complete in Him. He sees you, through Jesus Christ, as new and completely righteous.

Prayer of Thanks

Thank You, Father, that I am fearfully and wonderfully made. Help me to see myself as You see me—righteous, complete, and dearly loved—through Christ!

Every Day Is Thanksgiving

Let us come before His presence with thanksgiving; let us make a joyful noise to Him with songs of praise!   PSALM 95:2

Thanksgiving is not just a day to eat turkey and pumpkin pie, as we do in America. It was a day originally set aside to remember and give thanks to God for what He had done in protecting the first men and women who came to America, fleeing religious persecution in Europe. It was a type of harvest celebration like the one that the Jews celebrated; a day to give thanks for the crops they were able to harvest.

In addition to thanking God as we go through life, it is also a good idea to set aside special times of gratitude and giving thanks. Sometimes our family sits together and remembers where God has brought us from, and we thank Him for all He has done. Dave and I talk about our life when our children were all young and we lived in a tiny three-room apartment and had to cash in soda pop bottles to make it through until payday. I am sure you can recall times similar to those we had, and remembering them makes us thankful for how God brought us through them, and for all the progress we have made by His goodness.

Prayer of Thanks

Father, help me to realize that Thanksgiving is more than just a day on the calendar. I am grateful for all You have done in my life, not just today, but every day of the year.

Sometimes Love Is Just Being Friendly

This is My commandment: that you love one another [just]
as I have loved you.   JOHN 15:12

God has blessed us with many things, and when our heart is right, we are thankful for each blessing. But we can do more than just be thankful. We can demonstrate that gratitude by deciding to use the blessings in our lives to be a blessing to others everywhere we go.

You can do this in big ways or in small ways, but doing it always blesses someone else. You'll be amazed at the results. One way you can be a blessing is just by being friendly. Make a real effort to be friendly with people everywhere you go and show a genuine interest in them. Try to make shy people feel comfortable and confident. Try giving a kind word to encourage someone who seems to be down. There are countless ways we can be a blessing if we think about it creatively. Don't let the sun set on any day without reaching out in some way to someone else.

Prayer of Thanks

Father, I am so thankful, not just for the countless blessings You have given me, but for the chance to share those blessings with others. I pray that You will show me new and creative ways to be friendly and encouraging to someone today.

Respect and Value Yourself

For we know, brothers and sisters loved by God, that he has
chosen you.   1 THESSALONIANS 1:4 NIV

How we treat ourselves is often how we treat others. This is one
reason why we need to be good to ourselves, and yet not be self-
centered. We should respect and value ourselves.

Don't focus on your faults. We all have strengths and weaknesses. We should use our strengths and not stress out over our
weaknesses, realizing that God's strength shows itself strong in
them (see 2 Corinthians 12:9). After all, if we had no weaknesses,
we would not need Jesus. He came for those who are imperfect
and weak, and that is all of us.

You can enjoy peace with yourself, but you will have to pursue it. Make a decision that since you are with you all the time,
you should like yourself. God created you, and He does not make
junk, so start being grateful for your strengths and stop stressing
over your weaknesses.

Prayer of Thanks

I thank You today, Father, that You love me; You've chosen me
and created me as a beautiful, unique individual. Help me
see myself the same way You see me. Thank You that I can live
in peace, knowing that I have been fearfully and wonderfully
made by You.

Stress-Free Relationships

And become useful and helpful and kind to one another,
tenderhearted (compassionate, understanding, loving-hearted),
forgiving one another [readily and freely], as God in Christ
forgive you.   EPHESIANS 4:32

Do any totally stress-free relationships exist? I doubt it, but thankfully there are steps we can take to improve our relationships. Let me share four steps with you:

- Step 1: Develop and maintain peace with God and peace with yourself. Then and only then will you begin to develop a mind-set that allows you to live in peace with others.
- Step 2: Don't expect people to be perfect, because they won't be. This is an unrealistic expectation that will damage your relationships.
- Step 3: Don't expect everyone to be like you...because they aren't. Discovering that we are all uniquely different solves many relationship conflicts.
- Step 4: Be an encourager, not a discourager. Everyone loves to be with people who celebrate and notice strengths and choose to ignore weaknesses.

Prayer of Thanks

Father, I am grateful for the relationships I have with the
people in my life. Let Your love flow through me as I purpose
to strengthen these relationships. I thank You that I can do my
part to build healthy, life-giving, stress-free relationships.

Living in the Present... and Loving It

Forget the former things; do not dwell on the past.

ISAIAH 43:18 NIV

One of the beautiful things about life in Christ is that every day is a new beginning—a fresh start. We don't have to regret yesterday or dread tomorrow. We can celebrate today, thankful for God's presence in the moment.

There's a saying I love that goes like this: "Yesterday is history. Tomorrow is a mystery. Today is a gift; that's why it's called the present."

We can enjoy every moment of our lives and stay focused on the present. We shouldn't dwell on the past or look too far into the future, but we need to realize the present moment is God's gift to us *right now*. Let's make the decision to be grateful for today, live it to the full, and enjoy every part of it!

Prayer of Thanks

Father, thank You for the gift of today. Regardless of my past problems or my future challenges, I choose to celebrate my life with You in the present. Thank You that this is the day You have made; I will rejoice and be glad in it.

Boldly Facing Any New Challenge

*David said to the Philistine, "You come against me with sword
and spear and javelin, but I come against you in the name of the
Lord Almighty, the God of the armies of Israel, whom you have
defied."*   1 SAMUEL 17:45 NIV

Many times we are far too fearful of trials and trouble. At the first
sign of trouble, we begin to shrink back in fear. The believers who
lived in past centuries seemed to display a different strength than
most do today. We are rather accustomed to convenience and usually don't do well with suffering of any type; it frightens us.

Let's remember how David faced the giant Goliath and be
joyful and thankful that we can defeat our enemies too. We can
attack fear rather than letting it rule us. You are much more than
your feelings. You are a powerful, wise, beloved child of God, and
you can do whatever you need to do in life through Christ, who
is your strength (see Philippians 4:13).

Prayer of Thanks

*Thank You, Father, for the strength that I have because You
are with me. No matter how difficult a challenge may seem,
I will attack it with boldness because I know that nothing is
impossible for You.*

Are You Plugged In?

If you abide in Me, and My words abide in you, you will ask what
you desire, and it shall be done for you.   JOHN 15:7 NKJV

Faith is our plug into the grace and power of God. Think of a lamp.
The lamp can give light only if it is plugged into a power source.
If it is unplugged, it will not work, no matter how many times we
turn the switch on and off.

I was once in a hotel room trying to get a lamp to work, and
in frustration, thought, *Can't these hotels even provide a lamp that
works?!* Then someone from the maintenance department came to
my room, only to discover the lamp was unplugged.

Let me ask you, "Are you unplugged?" Have you let fear steal
your faith? If you have, don't worry about it. Just decide right now
that you are thankful for a new chance. Decide that you are going
to have a new attitude, one that is filled with boldness, courage,
and faith. "Plug in" and let your light shine.

Prayer of Thanks

Father, help me to plug into Your power today. I thank You
for the faith that You have given me that simply needs to be
activated. Today, I believe Your promises and I stand in faith
ready to see them come to pass in my life.

Praying, Saying, and Doing

Think of yourself with sober judgment, in accordance with the faith
God has distributed to each of you.   ROMANS 12:3 NIV

Faith is given to everyone, according to Romans 12:3, but that faith must be unleashed for it to do any practical good. It may sound spiritual to say, "I am full of faith," but are you using your faith? Faith is released by praying, saying, and doing whatever God asks us to do:

- Praying: We invite God to get involved in our situations through our prayers.
- Saying: It's important that we talk as if we truly believe God is working in our favor.
- Doing: The third ingredient in releasing your faith is to do whatever you believe God is asking you to do.

Be thankful for the faith God has given you and begin putting it to work in your life by praying, saying, and doing.

Prayer of Thanks

Father, I am thankful that I can release my faith by simply coming to You in prayer, speaking Your promises, and doing what You tell me to do. Help me to stand in faith when the circumstances are against me. I thank You that I can trust You completely.

Looking at the Whole Picture

If there is any virtue and excellence, if there is anything worthy of praise, think on and weigh and take account of these things [fix your minds on them].   PHILIPPIANS 4:8

When we focus on what has gone wrong in our lives, it can start to seem that nothing ever goes right, but that is simply not true. You may have had difficult things take place over the course of your life, but the mind-set of gratitude realizes that the good times have outnumbered the bad.

Look at your life as a whole rather than focusing on tragedies, trials, and disappointments. Looking at the good will give you courage to deal with the bad things and avoid living in fear. Realizing that God is with you, helping you along the way, provides the courage you need to face the future boldly, knowing that you truly can overcome any obstacle in the strength and power of the Lord.

Prayer of Thanks

Father, when I am feeling discouraged or overwhelmed by life, help me to see all the good things You have done. I thank You that the good outweighs the bad. And I thank You that there are many more good things to come.

Let God Help You

I am the Vine; you are the branches. Whoever lives in Me and I in him bears much (abundant) fruit. However, apart from Me [cut off from vital union with Me] you can do nothing.   JOHN 15:5

There have been times when we have all tried to handle our circumstances instead of trusting God to take care of them for us. It is not a sign of weakness to admit that we cannot help ourselves— it is the truth. You may be frustrated, struggling, and unhappy simply because you are trying to fix something you cannot do anything about. You may be trying to change something that only God can change.

While you are waiting for God to take care of the situation, I encourage you to be thankful that God is in control and to decide to enjoy the wait. That may be hard because it takes patience, but it pays marvelous dividends in the end. Waiting on God honors Him, and the Bible says that the person who honors God will be honored by Him (see 1 Samuel 2:30 NIV).

Prayer of Thanks

I thank You today, Father, that I don't have to handle my circumstances on my own, but that You are here to help me. While I wait on You, help me to enjoy the process, knowing that You have good things in store.

Changing the World Around You

And now these three remain: faith, hope and love. But the greatest of these is love. 1 CORINTHIANS 13:13 NIV

One of the best ways to get your mind off a problem or a troubling situation is to go help someone else. When you display love to others, it not only blesses you, but it changes the world around you. Those are two great reasons to start living in love.

We've all tried selfishness, discouragement, and self-pity—and we have seen the terrible fruit of that. The world has seen the results of those things too. But thankfully, genuine love is different!

Let's agree that we will live life God's way—in gratitude and love. Be mindful to be a blessing to others (see Galatians 6:10), put on love (see Colossians 3:14), and live like Jesus. Jesus got up daily and went about doing good (see Acts 10:38). If we will follow that example, we are sure to change the world.

Prayer of Thanks

I thank You, Father, that there is a better way to live my life than focusing on my problems. Today, I choose to go out and follow the example of Jesus by doing good to others. With Your help, I am going to be an agent of change in the world around me.

Joy Is a Decision

*This is the day which the Lord has brought about; we will rejoice
and be glad in it.*   PSALM 118:24

Enjoying the abundant life Jesus died to give you is based on a
decision you make, not on your circumstances. Thankfully, you
can decide to be happy right where you are and to enjoy the life
you have right now on the way to where you are going. You can
make a firm decision to enjoy your journey.

You can begin by saying out loud, "I am going to enjoy my life."
Until you get that thought established in your mind, every morning when you wake up, before you even get out of bed, I encourage
you to declare out loud, "I am going to enjoy this day! I am seizing
the day! I am taking authority over the devil—the joy thief—even
before he tries to come against me. I have made up my mind that
I am going to keep my joy today!" Having a right mind-set always
helps in every situation.

Prayer of Thanks

*I thank You today, Father, that I can choose to live in the
abundant life Jesus died to give me. I don't have to live a
miserable, unhappy life. I can choose to celebrate Your goodness
and enjoy the life You have given me.*

Choosing Positive Thinking

How precious and weighty also are Your thoughts to me, O God!
How vast is the sum of them!   PSALM 139:17

A confident person is a positive person. Confidence and negativity do not go together. They are like oil and water; they simply do not mix. I used to be a very negative person, but, thank God, He showed me that being positive is much more fun and fruitful.

When encouraged to think positively, people often retort, "That is not reality." But it has been said that 90 percent of what we worry about never happens. Why do people assume that being negative is more realistic than being positive?

Thinking positive thoughts is a simple matter of whether we want to look at things from God's perspective or Satan's. Are you doing your own thinking, choosing carefully to think thankful, positive thoughts—or are you passively thinking whatever kind of thoughts fill your mind? Thinking negatively makes you miserable. Why be miserable when you can be happy?

Prayer of Thanks

Father, I am so thankful that I can choose what thoughts to dwell on. With Your help, I can reject negative thinking, and I can focus on thoughts based on Your Word. Thank You that I can be a confident, positive person.

Discovering Your Destiny

The Lord will perfect that which concerns me; Your mercy and
loving-kindness, O Lord, endure forever—forsake not the works
of Your own hands.   PSALM 138:8

Many people are confused about what they are to do with their
lives. They don't know what God's will is for them; they are without direction. If you are doing nothing with your life because you
are not sure what to do, then I recommend that you pray, thank
God that He has a destiny for you, and begin trying some things. It
won't take long before you will feel comfortable with something. It
will be a perfect fit for you.

Think of it this way: When you go out to buy a new outfit, you
probably try on several things until you find what fits right, is comfortable, and looks good on you. Why not try the same thing with
discovering your destiny? As we take steps of faith, our destinies
unfold. A thankful person knows God is with him. He is not afraid
to make mistakes, and if he does, he recovers and presses on.

Prayer of Thanks

I thank You today, Father, that You have a divine destiny for
my life. As I step out in faith, help me discover Your good plan
for my future. I am grateful that You walk with me as I seek to
walk in Your path for my life.

New Beginnings

You were taught . . . to put off your old self, which is being corrupted
by its deceitful desires; to be made new in the attitude of your
minds; and to put on the new self, created to be like God in true
righteousness and holiness.   EPHESIANS 4:22–24 NIV

One of the great things about a relationship with God that we can
be grateful for is He always provides new beginnings. His Word
says that His mercy is new every day. Jesus chose disciples who
had weaknesses and made mistakes, but He continued working with them and helping them become all that they could be.
Thankfully, He will do the same thing for you, if you will let Him.

The apostle Paul emphatically said that it was important to let
go of what lies behind and press toward the things ahead (see Philippians 3:13). Don't be afraid of your past; it has no power over
you except what you give it. Be thankful for all you have learned in
the past, even from your mistakes, and also be thankful that today
is a new beginning and that something good is going to happen to
you today!

Prayer of Thanks

I am grateful, Father, that You have given me hope for the
future. Thank You that each day is a new beginning, and I don't
have to be controlled by my past any longer. I can receive Your
mercy and believe for good things each new day.

Recovering from Pain

To grant [consolation and joy] to those who mourn in Zion—to
give them an ornament (a garland or diadem) of beauty instead of
ashes, the oil of joy instead of mourning, the garment [expressive]
of praise instead of a heavy, burdened, and failing spirit—that
they may be called oaks of righteousness.   ISAIAH 61:3

Recovering from pain or disappointment of any kind is not something that just happens to some people and not to others. It is a
decision! You make a decision to let go and move on. You learn
from your mistakes. You gather up the fragments of your life and
give them to Jesus, and He will make sure that nothing is wasted
(see John 6:12). You refuse to think about what you have lost;
instead, you inventory what you have left and begin using it with
a thankful heart.

In Christ, not only can you recover, but you can also be used to
help other people recover. Be a living example of a thankful person
who always recovers from setbacks no matter how difficult or fre-
quent they are. Don't ever say, "I just cannot go on." Instead, say,
"I can do whatever I need to do through Christ. I will never quit,
because God is on my side."

Prayer of Thanks

Father, thank You that You bring healing in my life and You can
create beauty from ashes. I pray that You will help me press on,
refusing to quit. I want to use my experiences to help others
find the same healing that I have found.

The Power of Planting Seed

*Don't be misled—you cannot mock the justice of God. You will
always harvest what you plant.* GALATIANS 6:7 NLT

There is great joy and benefit in the principle of planting a seed.
When you give to others, the Lord blesses you in return—receive
His blessings with a grateful heart.

I have learned to enjoy a variety of seed planting. I love to give
to those in need and help bring them to a new level of joy, and I
also love to give to those who enjoy a level of life that I would like
to have.

If you want your ministry to grow, find a few larger ministries
you respect and sow into them. If you want your marriage healed,
sow into the life of someone who has a great marriage, releasing
your faith with your seed for a harvest in that area. If you want to
operate more fully in the fruit of the Spirit, find someone who is
more advanced in that area than you are and sow into their life.

Actually, the possibilities are endless. When you start using
what you have to be a blessing to others, your well will never
run dry.

Prayer of Thanks
*Father, I thank You that there is a harvest, or return, for every
seed I sow. I pray that as I bless others and invest in their lives,
You will do more with that seed than I ever could on my own.
Thank You that giving to others can be a blessing in my life.*

Choose Your Battles

Now may the Lord of peace Himself grant you His peace (the peace of His kingdom) at all times and in all ways [under all circumstances and conditions, whatever comes]. The Lord [be] with you all.   2 THESSALONIANS 3:16

I believe one of the best ways to enjoy the present moment and avoid undue stress is to refuse to let every little thing upset you. In other words, choose your battles, and don't make mountains out of molehills.

Before you devote time, energy, and emotion to an issue or a situation, ask yourself two questions. First, ask yourself how important it is; and second, ask yourself how much of your time, effort, and energy is really appropriate for you to put into it.

Know what really matters in life, be grateful for these things, and focus on them. Learn to discern the difference between major matters and minor matters. Life has plenty of strain without adding anything more. When you are tempted to take on a project, step back first and decide if it's worth what it will require of you.

***

Prayer of Thanks

Father, I am thankful that You give me the wisdom to discern between things that really matter and things that don't. I pray that You will help me learn to let unimportant things go. Thank You that I can save my time and energy for those things that are truly important.

Two Kinds of Love

For I am persuaded beyond doubt (am sure) that neither death nor life, nor angels nor principalities, nor things impending and threatening nor things to come, nor powers, nor height nor depth, nor anything else in all creation will be able to separate us from the love of God which is in Christ Jesus our Lord.   ROMANS 8:38–39

To fully understand all the different facets of love, we must understand there are two kinds of love: the God-kind of love and man's love.

- Man's love fails, it gives up; but God's love never fails.
- Man's love is finite, it comes to an end; but God's love is infinite and eternal.
- Man's love is dependent on favorable behavior and circumstances; God's love is not based on our performance.
- People place conditions on their love, but God's love is unconditional.

This unfailing, infinite, unconditional love is the love God has for you every day! Be grateful for His love; celebrate His love; and be secure in life because you know you have the unconditional love and acceptance of your heavenly Father.

Prayer of Thanks

Father, help me to celebrate Your perfect, unconditional love for me today. I thank You that Your love is a higher love than man's love, and I am grateful that You extend that love to me every single day.

The Importance of Faith

But without faith it is impossible to please and be satisfactory to Him. For whoever would come near to God must [necessarily] believe that God exists and that He is the rewarder of those who earnestly and diligently seek Him [out].   HEBREWS 11:6

Faith is a powerful force that we have access to and should be very thankful for. When we live by faith, we release God to do amazing things for us and through us. Faith is the leaning of the entire human personality on God in absolute confidence in His power, wisdom, and goodness (see Colossians 1:4). We can come to God in childlike faith, simply believing His Word and placing our faith in Him to do what He has promised.

Some people say that they have no faith, but that is not true. We all have faith, but we may not choose to put it in God. When you sit in a chair, you have faith that it will hold you up. When you deposit money in the bank, you have faith that you will be able to go back and get it when you need it. What, or whom, are you placing your faith in?

I urge you not to put your faith in something unstable and shaky, but put it in God Who is a solid Rock and never changes. He is faithful and will always do what He promises to do.

Prayer of Thanks

Father, I am thankful that You have given me a measure of faith. I release my faith in You and trust You to always meet my needs and take care of me. Thank You for Your goodness and Your love.

Ready for Battle

Do not be afraid of the enemy; [earnestly] remember the Lord and imprint Him [on your minds], great and terrible, and [take from Him courage to] fight for your brethren, your sons, your daughters, your wives, and your homes.   NEHEMIAH 4:14

The verse above (Nehemiah 4:14) shows us Nehemiah as a strong and wise leader. Not only did he seek and rely on God, he also knew that the people needed to be ready to fight in the strength of the Lord.

I want to echo Nehemiah's words to you today: Fight for your home! Fight for your children! Fight for your right to live free from guilt and condemnation! Fight for your right to live under the grace of God and not be bound to legalism! Fight for your right to be happy! Fight for the dreams God has put in your heart! Fight for what is important to you! As Paul told Timothy, we need to fight the good fight of faith. That means to hold on, don't give up, and above all that you do, trust God because He is fighting for and with you.

Refuse to settle for anything less than everything God has for you, and be thankful that with God on your side, there is no way you can lose the fight.

Prayer of Thanks

Father, I am thankful that You give me the strength and courage to fight for what is important in my life. No matter how big the opposition may seem, I thank You that You will give me the victory in Christ Jesus.

The Word of God Is a Powerful Weapon

*And take the helmet of salvation and the sword that the Spirit
wields, which is the Word of God.*   EPHESIANS 6:17

God gives us the weapons we need to win every battle we face.
God's Word is a sword for us, and we are able to wield it against
the enemy. Our swords will not do any good if we keep them in
their sheaths, just as a Bible won't help us if it just sits on a shelf
gathering dust. To use our swords is to know, believe, and speak
the Word of God.

If you wake up one morning and feel you want to give up, use
your sword by saying: "I will not give up! I am thankful that God
has plans to give me a future and a hope, and I am going to keep
pressing on in faith so I can experience those plans" (see Jeremiah
29:11). God gives us weapons of warfare so we can use them. If
you want to win, you will have to remain active. Passivity and
wishing never win the battle.

Prayer of Thanks

*I thank You, Father, that You have given me Your Word and
that I can use it to win the victory. Help me to remember to
lean on Your Word rather than my own strength. I am grateful
for Your promises that sustain me through every battle.*

Making a Thankful List

Enter into His gates with thanksgiving and a thank offering and into His courts with praise! Be thankful and say so to Him, bless and affectionately praise His name!   PSALM 100:4

To help you achieve and maintain a new level of contentment in your life, I encourage you to make a list of everything you have to be thankful for. Make it a long list, one that includes little things as well as big things. It should be long, because we all have *a lot* to be thankful for if we just look for it. I find new things daily to thank God for, and I am sure you will too.

Get out a piece of paper right now, or use your computer and start listing things you have to be thankful for. Keep the list and add to it frequently. Make it a point to think about the things that you're grateful for when you're driving the kids to an activity or waiting in line at the store. You can only learn the "power of thank you" by practicing it. The Bible says we are to be thankful and say so. Meditating on what you have to be thankful for every day and verbalizing it will be amazingly helpful to you.

Prayer of Thanks

Father, I thank You for the many provisions in my life You have blessed me with. I have so much to be grateful for because of Your overwhelming goodness. Help me never take any good thing—large or small—for granted.

Four Keys to Success

David acted wisely in all his ways and succeeded, and the Lord
was with him.   1 SAMUEL 18:14

There are four keys to success in any endeavor you undertake. If
these character traits and habits become part of the routine of your
life, they'll enable you to move toward the success you long for.

- Commitment: Without commitment, people give up
  easily; they have no staying power at all.
- Determination: Determination enables us to achieve
  goals and pursue dreams that seem impossible.
- Waiting on the Lord: When success does not come easily,
  we need to wait for the Lord and find our strength in Him.
- Be refreshed and renewed: We all need extended
  times of restoration and renewal to prepare us for new
  challenges ahead.

Examine your own life and ask yourself if you need to improve
in any of these areas and be thankful that you don't have to do
these things on your own. God is with you and, as you seek Him,
He will give you the commitment, determination, the ability to
wait on Him, and the renewal you need to succeed.

Prayer of Thanks

Father, when I am faced with a situation where success seems
impossible, help me to remember to look to You for strength. I
thank You that You will empower me to do what it takes to live
a life of excellence.

Don't Sell Yourself Short

He is a double-minded man, unstable in all his ways.

JAMES 1:8 NKJV

Self-doubt makes us double-minded, and James 1:8 teaches us that a double-minded man is unstable. He really cannot go forward until he decides to believe in God and trust God's plan for his life.

I encourage you to take a big step of faith and stop doubting yourself. As the old saying goes, "Don't sell yourself short." You have more capabilities than you think you do. You are able to do a lot more than you ever did in the past. God will help you if you will put your trust in Him and stop doubting yourself.

Like everyone else, you will make mistakes. But thankfully, God will allow you to learn from them and will actually work them out for your good if you will decide not to be defeated by them. When doubt begins to torment your mind, start speaking the Word of God out of your mouth—you will win the battle.

Prayer of Thanks

Father, I am so thankful that You can take even my mistakes and turn them into something good. I pray that You will help me put doubt aside and trust You completely. Thank You that in Christ I have everything I need; I never have to doubt again.

Dare to Dream Big Dreams for God

Jabez cried to the God of Israel, saying, Oh, that You would bless me and enlarge my border, and that Your hand might be with me, and You would keep me from evil so it might not hurt me! And God granted his request.   1 CHRONICLES 4:10

I hope you have a dream or a vision in your heart for something greater than what you have now. Ephesians 3:20 (KJV) tells us that God is able to do exceedingly abundantly above and beyond all that we can hope or ask or think. If we are not thinking, hoping, or asking for anything, we are cheating ourselves.

We need to be thankful for the things God has done in the past, but still have the faith to think big thoughts, hope for big things, and ask for big things for the future. I always say, "I would rather ask God for a lot and get half of it than ask Him for a little and get all of it."

Prayer of Thanks

I thank You today, Father, that You want me to dream big for You. Help me to refuse to place limits on my life. I believe You have great things for me, and I thank You that You do exceedingly abundantly above and beyond all I could hope or ask or think.

Investing in Your Dream

The appetite of the sluggard craves and gets nothing, but the appetite of the diligent is abundantly supplied.   PROVERBS 13:4

Dreams for the future are possibilities, but not what I call "positivelies." In other words, they are possible, but they will not positively occur unless we do our part.

Far too many people take the "quick fix" method for everything. They only want what makes them feel good right now. They are not willing to invest for the future. But you can be different! If you are willing to pursue what God has placed in your heart, He will bless your pursuit. You can be thankful, knowing that when you do what God asks you to do, He will always do what only He can do.

There is a gold mine hidden in every life, but we have to dig to get to it. Be willing to dig deeper and go beyond how you feel or what is convenient in order to see your dreams come true.

Prayer of Thanks

I am grateful, Father, that with diligence and You at my side, my possibilities can turn into "positivelies." No matter how much work it requires, I am going to go after what You have placed in my heart. Thank You that when I do my part, You promise to do Your part too.

Purity Leads to Power

Therefore, since we are surrounded by such a great cloud of witnesses, let us throw off everything that hinders and the sin that so easily entangles. And let us run with perseverance the race marked out for us.   HEBREWS 12:1 NIV

In order to live in victory, it's important that we make up our minds to live for God no matter what. Hebrews 12:1 tells us to throw off every sin that entangles us. It is virtually impossible to be a spiritual success with known, willful sin in our lives. I don't mean to say that we must be absolutely perfect in order for God to use us, but I am saying that we must have an aggressive attitude about keeping sin out of our lives.

When God says something is wrong, then it is wrong. We don't need to discuss, theorize, blame, make excuses, or feel sorry for ourselves—we need to agree with God, thank Him for showing us, ask for forgiveness, and work with the Holy Spirit to get whatever it is out of our lives forever. Purity leads to power, and with God's help, we can live abundant, powerful lives.

Prayer of Thanks

Father, I thank You that You point out sin in my life so that I can move past that sin and live in victory. Today, I want to set aside any sin that entangles me and live a pure and holy life for You. Thank You that You will help me every step of the way.

What Is Real Success?

For what will it profit a man if he gains the whole world and
forfeits his life [his blessed life in the kingdom of God]?

MATTHEW 16:26

Our real success and value in life is not found in climbing what
the world thinks to be the ladder of success. It is not in a job pro-
motion, a bigger house, a better-looking car, or being in the right
social circles. Thankfully, true success is more simple than that . . .
and more powerful.

True success is knowing God and the power of His resurrection. It is knowing that He loves you unconditionally and that you
are made acceptable in Jesus, the Beloved Son of God, who died
for you to pay for your sins. True success is found in living for God
and His glory. Be a good steward of the abilities and resources that
God has given you and you are sure to succeed, because He is with
you every step of the way.

You never have to compare yourself with anyone else to determine if you are successful. Be the best version of you that you can
be. You are a success!

Prayer of Thanks

Father, thank You that real success is found in You and not in
anything the world has to offer. I am grateful that I have the gift
of salvation and that You are with me always. As I do my best
for You, I know that I am destined to succeed.

The Best Deal Ever

For God so greatly loved and dearly prized the world that He [even] gave up His only begotten (unique) Son, so that whoever believes in (trusts in, clings to, relies on) Him shall not perish (come to destruction, be lost) but have eternal (everlasting) life.

JOHN 3:16

I have been offered once-in-a-lifetime deals from time to time, and I have found they are not always as good as they sound. They are usually intended to move us emotionally to make a quick decision so we don't miss this "marvelous, once-in-a-lifetime, never-to-be-repeated opportunity."

Thankfully, what God offers us in Christ is not a sales gimmick. It is available for anyone, any time they need it! Jesus, the substitutionary atonement, paid our penalty. He became guilty so that we could become innocent. He was guilty of no sin, yet He took on Himself the guilt of us all (see Isaiah 53:11). Live your life today thankful that your salvation is a free gift. There is no greater deal than that!

Prayer of Thanks

Father, I am thankful that I have the assurance of eternity in heaven with You. Thank You that Jesus took away my sins and gave me His righteousness. I will live every day grateful for my new life in Christ.

The Peace That Comes with Being Content

But if we have food and clothing, with these we shall be content
(satisfied).   1 TIMOTHY 6:8

Nobody has a perfect life, and it is entirely possible that if you want someone else's life, they are busy wanting someone else's too; perhaps they even want your life.

Unknown people want to be movie stars, but movie stars want privacy. The regular employee wants to be the boss, but the boss wishes he did not have so much responsibility. A single woman wants to be married, but quite often, a married woman wishes she were single.

Contentment with life is not a feeling—it is a decision. Contentment does not mean that we never want to see change or improvement, but it does mean that we will do the best we can with what we have. It means that we are thankful for what God has given us and we are determined to enjoy the gift of life.

Prayer of Thanks

When I am tempted to be jealous of someone else's life, Father,
I pray that You will help me to be content with who I am and
what You have given me. I thank You that I have a purpose and
destiny for my life. Today, I choose to be grateful and content.

Celebrating Life, Celebrating God

And they were continually in the temple celebrating with praises
and blessing and extolling God. Amen (so be it).   LUKE 24:53

Try beginning each day by saying, "I love my life!" Our own words
have an effect on our mood, so it is best to say something that will
help you feel good rather than something that will make you mad
or sad. You can let staying happy be a fun challenge. See how many
days you can go without getting into a bad mood or complaining.

Celebrating life is something we should do on purpose because
we understand what a gift life is. God is life (see John 1:4), so in
reality, when we celebrate life, we are celebrating God. Without
Him there would be no life at all. Go ahead and try to create a better mood by saying, "I am thankful and I love my life!" If you really
want to feel good, try this: "I love God, I love my life, I love myself,
and I love people."

Prayer of Thanks

Thank You, Father, that I am not a victim of my own moods. I
can speak positive, faith-filled words and improve my attitude
and my day. I am thankful for the life You have given me,
Father. I love my life!

Testimony Begins with T-E-S-T

Be assured and understand that the trial and proving of your
faith bring out endurance and steadfastness and patience.

JAMES 1:3

I always love to hear a great testimony, but I also know that behind every extraordinary account of someone's life lies some kind of challenge or difficulty. No one ever has a testimony without a test.

We can pass all kinds of tests as we go through our lives, and passing them is part of never giving up. It's vital for us to understand the important role that tests and trials play in our lives, because understanding them helps us endure them and actually be grateful for the strengthening effect they provide.

Everything God permits us to go through will ultimately be good for us—no matter how difficult it is. When we encounter tests and trials, if we will embrace them and refuse to run from them, we will learn some lessons that will help us in the future.

Prayer of Thanks

Father, help me to experience Your peace even in the midst of a
test I may be facing. I thank You that everything You permit me
to go through will work out for my good. And I thank You that
You give me the strength I need to overcome.

You Get to Decide

On the glorious splendor of Your majesty and on Your wondrous
works I will meditate.   PSALM 145:5

Much of our thinking is habitual. If we regularly think about God and good things, godly thoughts become natural. Thousands of thoughts flow through our minds every day. We may feel we have no control over them, but we do. Although we don't have to use any effort to think wrong thoughts, we have to use much effort to think good thoughts, especially while we are forming new habits and renewing our minds.

God has given us the power to decide—to choose right thinking over wrong. But once we make that choice, we must continue to choose right thoughts. It's not a once-and-for-all decision, but it does get easier. The more we fill our lives with reading the Bible, prayer, praise, and fellowship with other believers, the easier it is to continue choosing thankful, faith-filled, godly thoughts.

Prayer of Thanks

Father, I am so thankful that though many thoughts might flow through my mind each day, I get to decide which thoughts to dwell on. Today, with Your help, I make a decision to choose right thinking over wrong thinking. Thank You that the more I do so, the easier it will become.

What Does the Future Hold?

The Lord is my Light and my Salvation—whom shall I fear or dread? The Lord is the Refuge and Stronghold of my life—of whom shall I be afraid?   PSALM 27:1

The future holds a mixture of things we will enjoy and things we would rather do without, but both will come. In Philippians 4:11–12, Paul experienced times of being abased and times of abounding, but he also stated that he was able to be content in both, and we also have this option (and ability) as a gift from God. I am so thankful for the ability to be stable because I wasted many years being upset about things I could not control.

Jesus promised us that in the world we would have tribulation, but He told us to "cheer up" because He had overcome the world and deprived it of power to really harm us (see John 16:33). Make life as enjoyable as possible; be thankful for it, don't dread it. Face it with courage and say, "I will not fear, because greater is He that is in me than he that is in the world" (see 1 John 4:4).

Prayer of Thanks

I thank You today, Father, that I can have a positive, optimistic attitude about the future because I know I am not alone. No matter what obstacle I come up against, I can be of good cheer because You have overcome the world.

Choose to Bless the Lord at all Times

O give thanks to the Lord, call on His name; make known His
doings among the peoples!   1 CHRONICLES 16:8

Our son once went on an outreach with a team that visits the homeless each weekend. After helping in this ministry, he called me and said, "If I ever complain again, please knock me down for being so stupid!" He was appalled over the things he had murmured about in the past once he saw, by comparison, how some people were living.

Think about it: Those without a place to live would love to have a house to clean, while we complain about cleaning ours. They would delight in having a car to drive, while we complain about how old ours are. It is easy to lose sight of how blessed we are, but we should work at keeping it in the front of our thinking. Be thankful for what you have been blessed with!

Choose to bless God all the time, no matter what is going on, as David did: "I will bless the Lord at all times; His praise shall continually be in my mouth" (Psalm 34:1).

Prayer of Thanks
I am grateful, Father, for Your blessings in my life. Please
forgive me for the times I have taken Your goodness for granted.
Today I choose to have a heart of gratitude for every blessing,
no matter how small it may seem.

The Awesome Power of God Within You

And if the Spirit of Him Who raised up Jesus from the dead dwells in you, [then] He Who raised up Christ Jesus from the dead will also restore to life your mortal (short-lived, perishable) bodies through His Spirit Who dwells in you.   ROMANS 8:11

A group of pastors once asked me a question: Besides God Himself, what one thing helped me get from where I started in ministry to the level of success I currently enjoy? I immediately said, "I refused to give up!" There were thousands of times when I felt like giving up, thought about giving up, and was tempted to give up, but I always pressed on. I thank God for the determination He gives us.

Don't let life defeat you—face it with boldness and courage, and declare that you will enjoy every aspect of it. You can do that because you have the awesome power of God dwelling in you. God is never frustrated or discouraged. He always has peace and joy, and since He lives in us and we live in Him, we can enjoy the same thing. We are empowered by God for difficult things, and with His help, we never need to give up!

Prayer of Thanks

Father, thank You that with Your help, I can be determined never to give up. I pray that You will give me the boldness and courage I need to keep pressing on to do what You have called me to do. Thank You that Your awesome power resides in me.

Don't Be Afraid of What People Think

*The fear of man brings a snare, but whoever leans on, trusts
in, and puts his confidence in the Lord is safe and set on high.*

PROVERBS 29:25

We will never fulfill our destinies if we have undue concern over
what people think. Let them think what they want. What someone thinks of us doesn't need to affect us at all because the truth
is that their thoughts cannot hurt us if we don't worry about them.
The only thing that should be important to us is what God thinks
of us. It is not our reputation with people that is important, but it
is our reputation in heaven that is important.

Don't worry about what other people think, because it won't
change what they think anyway. Be thankful that God loves you
and thinks highly of you—that's the only thing that matters! If
you will break free from excessively caring about what other people think, you will instantly upgrade your level of living. You will
increase your joy and your peace one hundred–fold.

Prayer of Thanks

*Father, with Your help, I am going to stop worrying about what
other people think about me. I thank You that You love me and
You think good thoughts about me. Help me to realize that is all
that matters.*

You Can Be Confident

For in Him does our heart rejoice, because we have trusted (relied on and been confident) in His holy name. PSALM 33:21

God wants us to live with confidence and approach life boldly—and we can be thankful that He helps us do both. Make the choice today to start being more decisive. It may be a bold move for you if you have spent a lot of your life in fear and indecision, but it is necessary if you want to enjoy a life of peace. Indecision is not a peaceful place.

Put your confidence in Christ and who you are in Him, not in what people think of you. Know yourself! Know your heart, and don't wait for other people to dictate to you the truth about your value. Don't assume you are wrong every time someone does not agree with you. Believe that God's wisdom dwells inside of you. Believe you can make decisions. There is no point in believing something negative about yourself when it's just as easy to believe something positive—and it's certainly a lot more beneficial.

Prayer of Thanks

Father, I am thankful that my confidence is not in my own self or my abilities; my confidence is in Christ Jesus. I believe that I have Your wisdom and Your discernment. Today, I am going to live a bold, confident life.

Courageous People Wanted

Be strong (confident) and of good courage.   JOSHUA 1:6

Courage is a necessary quality if you intend to do great things for God. Leaders are not always the most gifted people, but they are people with courage. They are grateful for any new opportunity and they step out when others shrink back in fear. They take bold steps of faith. They may be wrong occasionally, but they are right enough of the time that it doesn't matter.

God expects us to increase, to be fruitful, and multiply (see Genesis 1:28). He admires courage; in fact, He demands it from those who work alongside of Him. The Lord told Joshua that he was to take Moses' place and lead the Israelites into the Promised Land, but there was one stipulation: He had to be strong and of good courage. The Lord was with Joshua to give him the courage he needed—and He is with you too.

Prayer of Thanks

Father, when I am in a situation that seems overwhelming, I thank you that You have already given me the courage I need. I thank You that You are with me and I have nothing to fear. Thank You that I can be strong and courageous.

Jesus' Prayer for You

*And now I am coming to You; I say these things while I am still
in the world, so that My joy may be made full and complete and
perfect in them [that they may experience My delight fulfilled
in them, that My enjoyment may be perfected in their own
souls, that they may have My gladness within them, filling their
hearts].*   JOHN 17:13

When Jesus prayed to the Father in John 17:13, He actually prayed
that we would have joy. He said, "I say these things...so that My
joy may be made full and complete and perfect in them..." With
Jesus Himself speaking and praying such powerful words about
His desire for us to have joy, how could we ever doubt that God
wants us to be happy and enjoy our lives?

If it is God's desire that we enjoy life, then why are so many
people miserable and unhappy? Perhaps it is because we fail to set
our minds to enjoy life. We can easily fall into a pattern of merely
surviving and enduring rather than enjoying. But a new mind-set
will release you to begin enjoying life like never before. The more
you enjoy life, the more enjoyable you will be to be around, so get
started today and don't delay.

Prayer of Thanks

*I thank You, Father, that it is Your will for me to have joy.
Regardless of what my circumstances look like around me, I will
choose to live the kind of life You have for me. Thank You that I
can have overwhelming, abundant joy every day of my life.*

Living a Balanced Life

Let your moderation be known unto all men. The Lord is at hand.
PHILIPPIANS 4:5 KJV

Maintaining a life of balance is possibly one of the biggest challenges we have. I encourage you to regularly examine your life and ask yourself honestly if you have allowed any area to get out of balance. A lack of balance could be the root cause of not enjoying life as well as many other problems.

For example: Work is good, and we are grateful for the opportunity to work, but too much of it causes stress. Food is good, and we are certainly thankful we have food to eat, but as most of us know, too much of it is not good. It is possible to spend too much money, but it is also possible to not spend enough. Any area that is out of balance causes confusion and distress in our lives and steals our joy.

Balance every area of your life and all your activities. Do all things in moderation. That way, you'll avoid burnout and be able to enjoy everything.

Prayer of Thanks

Father, I am thankful for the blessings of provision in my life: work, food, and finances. Help me to keep things in proper perspective and live in moderation. Thank You that, with Your help, I can live with balance.

Putting God First

*For from Him and through Him and to Him are all things.
[For all things originate with Him and come from Him; all
things live through Him, and all things center in and tend to
consummate and to end in Him.] To Him be glory forever! Amen
(so be it).* ROMANS 11:36

Everything God asks us to do is for our good. All of His instructions to us are intended to show us the way to righteousness, peace, and joy.

Jesus didn't die for us so we can have a religion, but so we can have a deep and intimate personal relationship with God through Him. He wants us to live with, through, and for Him. He created us for fellowship with Him—that is something to be thankful for!

The thing many people fail to realize is that they can never be fulfilled or have the satisfaction they desire apart from God. He created us for His pleasure and delight. He gives us life as a gift, and if we will freely offer it back to Him, then and only then can we live it fully and joyfully.

Prayer of Thanks

*I thank You today, Father, for the gift of relationship with You
through Christ Jesus. I am so grateful that everything You ask
of me is for my benefit and good. Thank You that You have a
wonderful plan for my life.*

Faith, Gratitude, and Rest

So that your faith might not rest in the wisdom of men (human philosophy), but in the power of God.   1 CORINTHIANS 2:5

Faith allows us to rest—both mentally and emotionally. Even our will gets a rest when we have faith in God. We don't worry or reason, we are not upset or downcast, and we are not trying to make something happen that is not God's will—we are thankful that God is in control so that we can rest!

Paul sang praises to God while he was in jail. Jesus prayed for others while He was being crucified. Joseph decided that if he was going to be a slave, he would be the best slave his owner ever had. All throughout Scripture, we see the connection between faith, gratitude, and rest.

We need to be honest about what the real cause of our stress is. Is it really our circumstances in life, or is it the way we respond to the circumstances? There is a rest that comes with gratitude and faith. This is a rest we can live in every day.

Prayer of Thanks

I thank You today, Father, that I can live in rest. I don't have to worry or be downcast when I face challenges. Thank You that I can have faith, knowing that You are the One in control.

The Waste of Worry

Cast your burden on the Lord [releasing the weight of it] and He will sustain you; He will never allow the [consistently] righteous to be moved (made to slip, fall, or fail).   PSALM 55:22

Worry is totally useless. As I often say, it is like rocking in a rocking chair all day—it keeps you busy, but gets you nowhere. When we begin to look at worry in a realistic manner, we see what a complete waste it is. Our minds revolve endlessly around and around a problem, searching for answers that only God has. Pondering something in God's grace is peaceful, but worry is tormenting.

We can pray and ask God to help us not to worry, but ultimately, we must choose to put our thoughts on something other than our problems. A refusal to worry is proof that we trust God—it releases Him to go to work on our behalf. If you are willing to give up worrying, then you will be able to enter into an attitude of celebration and thanksgiving. You can trust God and enjoy life while He solves your problems. Give yourself permission to stop worrying.

Prayer of Thanks

Father, thank You for the gift of peace. Help me to focus on You rather than focusing on my problems. I thank You that I don't have to let worry rule my life; I can choose to live with peace by trusting in You.

Do Yourself a Favor

Then Peter came up to Him and said, Lord, how many times may my brother sin against me and I forgive him and let it go? [As many as] up to seven times? Jesus answered him, I tell you, not up to seven times, but seventy times seven!   MATTHEW 18:21–22

As Christians, we should learn to be good at forgiving people, because we will be doing it all of our lives. The truth is, when we forgive, we are actually doing ourselves a favor. Thankfully, God has given us a way to free ourselves from the agony of anger and pain that come with unforgiveness—we can choose to forgive.

As long as we live, we will encounter people who hurt us, reject us, disappoint us, use the wrong tone of voice with us, fail to understand us, or let us down in times of need. Those experiences are part of human nature and they are part of the territory that comes with relationships. Why should we ruin our lives over other people's bad behavior? We can take the high road in Christ and forgive!

Prayer of Thanks

Father, I thank You that my peace and joy are not determined by the actions of others. With Your help, I can forgive those who offend or hurt me. Thank You, Father, that You have forgiven me and You give me the grace to forgive others.

About the Author

JOYCE MEYER is one of the world's leading practical Bible teachers. Her TV and radio broadcast, *Enjoying Everyday Life*, airs on hundreds of television networks and radio stations worldwide.

Joyce has written more than 100 inspirational books. Her bestsellers include *God Is Not Mad at You; Making Good Habits, Breaking Bad Habits; Do Yourself a Favor... Forgive; Living Beyond Your Feelings; Power Thoughts; Battlefield of the Mind; Look Great, Feel Great; The Confident Woman; I Dare You;* and *Never Give Up!*

Joyce travels extensively, holding conferences throughout the year, speaking to thousands around the world.

Joyce Meyer Ministries U.S.
& Foreign Office Addresses

Joyce Meyer Ministries

P.O. Box 655
Fenton, MO 63026
USA
(636) 349-0303

Joyce Meyer Ministries—Canada

P.O. Box 7700
Vancouver, BC V6B 4E2
Canada
(800) 868-1002

Joyce Meyer Ministries—Australia

Locked Bag 77
Mansfield Delivery Centre
Queensland 4122
Australia
(07) 3349 1200

Joyce Meyer Ministries—England

P.O. Box 1549
Windsor SL4 1GT
United Kingdom
01753 831102

Joyce Meyer Ministries—South Africa

P.O. Box 5
Cape Town 8000
South Africa
(27) 21-701-1056

Other Books by Joyce Meyer

100 Ways to Simplify Your Life
21 Ways to Finding Peace and Happiness
Any Minute
Approval Addiction
The Battle Belongs to the Lord
Battlefield of the Mind *
Battlefield of the Mind Devotional
Battlefield of the Mind for Kids
Battlefield of the Mind for Teens
Be Anxious for Nothing *
Beauty for Ashes
Being the Person God Made You to Be
Change Your Words, Change Your Life
The Confident Mom
The Confident Woman
The Confident Woman Devotional
Do Yourself a Favor...Forgive
Eat the Cookie...Buy the Shoes
Eight Ways to Keep the Devil Under Your Feet
Ending Your Day Right
Enjoying Where You Are on the Way to Where You Are Going
The Everyday Life Bible
Filled with the Spirit
Hearing from God Each Morning
How to Hear from God *
How to Succeed at Being Yourself
I Dare You
If Not for the Grace of God *

Starting Your Day Right
Straight Talk
Teenagers Are People Too!
Trusting God Day by Day
Woman to Woman
The Word, the Name, the Blood
You Can Begin Again

Joyce Meyer Spanish Titles

Belleza en Lugar de Cenizas (Beauty for Ashes)

Cambia Tus Palabras, Cambia Tu Vida (Change Your Words, Change Your Life)

Como Formar Buenos Habitos y Romper Malos Habitos (Making Good Habits, Breaking Bad Habits)

Dios No Está Enojado Contigo (God Is Not Mad at You)

El Campo de Batalla de la Mente (Battlefield of the Mind)

Empezando Tu Día Bien (Starting Your Day Right)

Hazte Un Favor a Ti Mismo…Perdona (Do Yourself a Favor…Forgive)

Madre Segura de sí Misma (The Confident Mom)

Pensamientos de Poder (Power Thoughts)

Termina Bien tu Día (Ending Your Day Right)

Usted Puede Comenzar de Nuevo (You Can Begin Again)

* Study Guide available for this title

Books By Dave Meyer

Life Lines